ACROSS FOUR CENTURIES

The Albin Family
in
England, Ireland
and America

Ray R. Albin

HERITAGE BOOKS
2018

HERITAGE BOOKS

AN IMPRINT OF HERITAGE BOOKS, INC.

Books, CDs, and more—Worldwide

For our listing of thousands of titles see our website
at
www.HeritageBooks.com

Published 2018 by
HERITAGE BOOKS, INC.
Publishing Division
5810 Ruatan Street
Berwyn Heights, Md. 20740

Heritage Books by the author:

Across Four Centuries: The Albin Family in England, Ireland and America

*Wealth Land and Slaveholding in Mississippi:
A Planter Family's Life of Privilege, 1818–1913*

International Standard Book Number
Paperbound: 978-0-7884-5854-5

DEDICATION

To William Albin Sr. (c1710-1765) who as a young orphan in Ireland probably never had a choice regarding his immigration to America.

To Dr. Catherine LaChapelle Albin, the twentieth century French connection in this line of Albins.

To Dr. Lauren Albin Roller and Ryan James Albin, descendants of William.

CONTENTS

vi

LIST OF ILLUSTRATIONS AND MAPS

ILLUSTRATIONS

MAPS

PREFACE

Through roughly four centuries, the Albins portrayed in the following narrative generally lacked fame and wealth. However, many were adventurous. Most were industrious as they sought to make a better life for themselves and their children. The unanticipated voyage of four young Albin orphans (one, William Albin, was the author's fifth great grandfather) from Ireland to America in the early 1720s altered the family chronicle forever. On a broader scale, once these four took their first uncertain steps on English colonial soil in southeastern Pennsylvania, they and their successors would play an unheralded, yet meaningful role in the development of a maturing colonial America and then later in the fabric of the expanding United States.

In England and Ireland in the seventeenth and early eighteenth centuries, at least two generations of Albins had maintained close ties to the land as yeoman farmers. William, one of the four Albin orphans, though barely twelve years old upon his arrival in America in 1722, conveyed (unwittingly) this particular Albin agricultural propensity across the Atlantic from Ireland to colonial Pennsylvania. As a result, subsequent Albin generations for more than two centuries lived on their farms and worked the soil, often on the fringes of civilization in wilderness Virginia, then western Pennsylvania and Kentucky.

Specifically, this chronicle traces the centuries-long saga, complete with struggle, triumph, and tragedy, of subsequent Albin generations, all descendants of William Albin. Their gradual, decades-long westward shift paralleled that of a young America as it expanded its own borders westward during the eighteenth and nineteenth centuries.

For the Albins and thousands of other pioneers during this challenging yet exciting phase of our country's development, a common denominator was landownership. Land acquisition made the difference between a chance for success or a life spent as a serf on the land. Land in America became available to newcomers regardless of one's previous social status. America thus presented William Albin with a unique opportunity for success as compared to the economically and socially stagnant life he would have likely endured had he remained in an increasingly land-starved Ireland. This history does not attempt to attain the broad scope of Ethel Winifred Albin's expansive *The Virginia Albins: The History of the Albin Family Out of Old Frederick County, Virginia* which traced multiple Albin generations with various family threads in dozens of states. Instead, it tracks specific Albin generations through four different centuries from approximately 1620-1990 in three different countries on two continents with very little deviation from its central focus, my nine Albin grandfathers.

References to the Albins in Ohio County, Kentucky, in the late 1800s found in two rare, wrinkled, and yellowed pages of a 1977 edition of the *Beaver Dam* (Kentucky) *Messenger* passed to the author by his aunt, Joann Albin Bombelis, in 1980 proved to be the stimulus for the research into the family's heretofore untold history. Using the information from reminiscences shared in the *Messenger* by a nineteenth century Albin descendant (the author's great aunt, Lola Albin Embry), combined with years of careful research — sifting through layers of Albin family-related references and documents all the while discovering, unraveling, and then piecing together the various threads — resulted in the completion of this Albin family story.

Two factors hindered the research in this project. Illiteracy was common in Ireland and within the isolated farming communities on the American frontier where the Albins lived from their arrival through the 1800s. As a result, successive early generations of Albins generally lacked education and remained illiterate resulting in an absence of written primary sources relating to the family's history. Likewise, Albin descendants spent their lives on small, rural farms and did not accumulate great wealth. Consequently, their names did not appear in as many documents over the years as compared to the more affluent planters, tradesmen, or professional people of their time.

Lastly, family trees and stories tend to generate interest primarily for descendants of the family members being researched and thus often lack a broader appeal. In accepting that reality, I retain the hope that this narrative provides a springboard for further family research by current and future Albin descendants or others while also serving to illuminate to an extent the broader scope of the unique American experience of which the Albins were a part. With that in mind, I felt compelled to include numerous source footnotes as reference guides aware that more of the Albin story awaits future discovery.

Ray Albin Jr.
San Jose, California

xii

ACKNOWLEDGEMENTS

Sincere thanks and appreciation to my two wonderful children, Lauren Simone Albin Roller and Ryan James Albin, for their willingness to offer suggestions regarding the manuscript and for carefully editing many of the chapters. Both jobs they happily accomplished pro bono!

The Characters in Ten Generations

Name	Born/Died	Spouse	Born/Died
Robert Albin ?	1620(?) - ?	Elizabeth ?	?
James Albin	1645?-1722	Ann	1646(?)-1722?
James Albin Jr.	1676(?)-1720?	Sarah Cansey	1680?-1720?
William Albin	1710?-1765	Mary Bruce	1715-1772?
William Albin Jr.	1748-1796	"Liney" Shepler	1752-1813?
Absalom Albin	1778-1850?	Piety Bruce	1784-1850?
Benjamin Tolbert Albin	1818-1889	[1]Cynthia Faught	1822-1849
		[2]Clarissa Watson	1822-1899
James B. Albin	1843-1927	[1]Elizabeth Baize	1847-1926
		[2]Lenileoti James	1858-1928
James O. Albin	1883-1931	Anna Cook	1888-1971
James Glendon (Ray) Albin Sr.	1922-1996	[1]Geraldine Abt	1917-1971
		[2]Jean Warren	1932- ?
		[3]Dorothy Davenport	? -2013

CHAPTER I

The Early Albins

England and Ireland

The *early* history of these ten generations of Albins is difficult to document. During the seventeenth century and before in both England and Ireland, records noting significant Albin family events such as births, marriages, deaths, and migrations are for the most part non existent. Internet references to this line of Albins often lack any credible historical references or validation. Early Albin family trees posted by "contributors" on the Mormon Family History Library site also demand serious scrutiny. *Only when the Albin story moves into the early 1700s do several book sources and more reliable documentation appear.* With that said, I cautiously begin piecing together in this chapter snippets of these early Albins in seventeenth century England and later in Ireland.

ROBERT(?) ALBIN 1620 (?) - ?

The sketchy, and as of now, unverifiable roots of the earliest traceable ancestor in this line of the Albin family seem to point to a Robert Albin, born in approximately 1620 in the reign of King James I of England around the time the Pilgrims were struggling to survive in Massachusetts. More certain is the notion that both the elusive Robert and his progeny initially resided in the green, lush East Midlands of northern England in the county of Derbyshire (Dar bee sher) (Map 1). Eventually, future generations followed, producing a complicated family tree spanning hundreds of years in three countries and on two continents.

Long before Robert Albin, variations of the Albin name appeared in the ancient history of Great Britain. Early Scottish Highlanders, in an effort to distinguish themselves from the Irish, called themselves Gael Albinnich, or Gael of Albin. Also, the entire island of Great Britain in ancient times was known as Albin, or Albion. In France the Gauls referred to Great Britain as Albinn, meaning "Fair or White Island", based on the chalk white appearance of England's southern coastline (White Cliffs of Dover) as viewed from the opposite side (the French side) of the English Channel.[1]

Later, in early Derbyshire and its environs, several variations of the Albin name appear. The first Abbott of Darley (Derby) was Albinus, mentioned in approximately1160. In 1175, in what seems to be another reference to Albinus, "Hubert Fitz Ralph granted to Albin, abbot of Derley (Darby), and the canons there, the church of Criche, which his [Hubert's] father before ... had granted them...."[2] Likewise, in the same area, this time in Wakefield, West Yorkshire, north of Derbyshire, a Robert Albin appeared as a witness to a land transaction circa 1265.[3] However, there is no documentation linking Albinus or Robert Albin to this family tree.

In the seventeenth century, between 1601-1635, several Albins continued to maintain a presence in Derbyshire. Mentioned in the Chesterfield Parish Register are: "Ann, spurious daughter of Ann Albin bapt[ized] 09 Oct 1619, Elizabeth dau of William Albin bur[ied] 12 Feb 1621, John son of William Albin bapt[ized] 15 Dec 1625 [buried 24 Dec 1625], Robert son of Thomas, bur 08 Feb 1618, [and] Samuell son of William Albin bapt. 06 Jun[e] 1622."[4] Again, there is no evidence that any of these Albins were related to the later Albins mentioned in this history.

Thus, attempts to link Robert Albin of Derbyshire (1620) to specific future generations of Albins proved difficult. However, the prevailing tendency of some seventeenth and eighteenth century English families to follow particular familial naming patterns offered hope. Though sometimes inexact, these naming patterns emerge as the only means available to potentially link Robert to his next generation. In the case of James Albin, the suspected son

---

[1]George Craik, *The Pictorial History of England*, (New York: Harper & Bros., 1846-48), Volume 1, 21. Coincidentally, the Roman governor of Great Britain from 192 to 197 A.D. was Decimus Clodius Albinus.

[2]Stephen Glover, *The History of the County of Derby, Part II,* (Derbyshire, England: H. Mozley and Son, 1829), 320.

[3]UK National Archives, accessed April 6, 2013, http://www.nationalarchives.gov.uk/a2a/records.aspx?cat=202-spst_1&cid=4-11-127-2#4-11-127-2.

[4]"Derbyshire, England Parish and Probate Records", Chesterfield Parish Register 1601-1635, sv Albin, *Ancestry.com*.

of Robert, the names of both James' parents may be inferred by
examining the names of James' children.

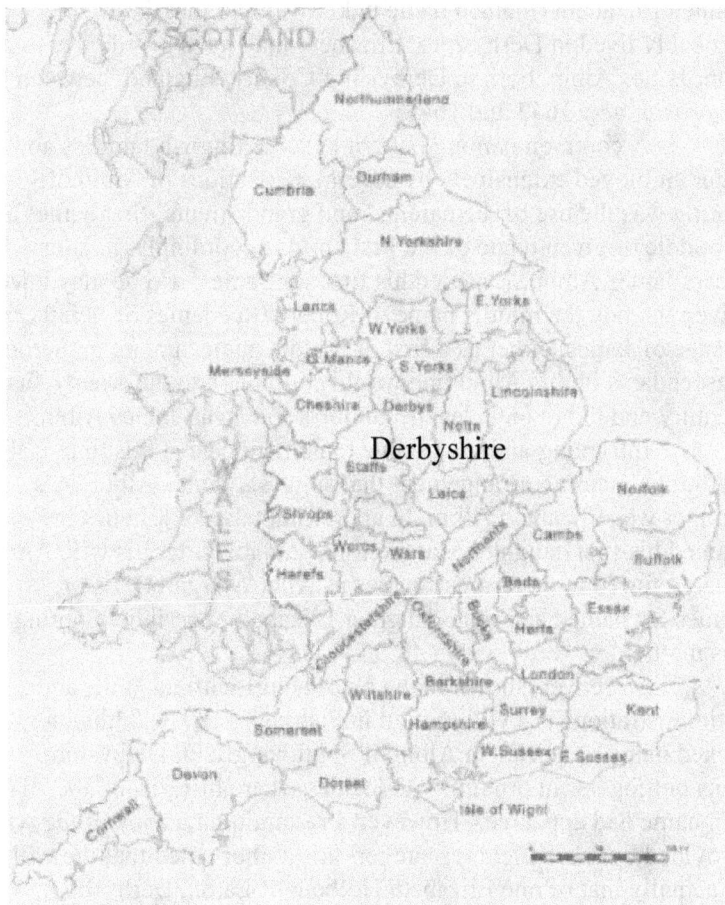

Map 1
County Map of England
(Derbys = Derbyshire)

JAMES ALBIN SR. 1642-45 (?) - 1722

Vague evidence indicates Robert Albin married a woman named Elizabeth (maiden name unknown) and that the couple probably lived in Derbyshire. Elizabeth may have given birth to a son, James Albin, born in Derbyshire County, England, between *approximately* 1642 and 1645.

A common naming pattern in some English families and later employed extensively by several generations of Albin offspring was the use of the parents' and grandparents' first names as a middle or given name of the first child. Accordingly, in later years James Albin Sr. named his first son James, and he may have given the boy the middle name of Robert after James Sr.'s father. Usage of James, either as a first or middle name, among numerous descendants in this Albin line would continue into the twenty-first century and today includes the author's son Ryan James Albin.

Intriguing and impossible to authenticate at this time is the additional naming arrangement that suggests James Albin Sr.'s mother was Elizabeth Albin. In approximately 1668 James Sr. named his first daughter Margaret, presumably after his wife Anne (also referred to in various sources as Anne Margaret). Later, James Sr. named a second daughter Elizabeth, possibly honoring his mother.[5]

Moreover, shown in the records of Lichfield Wills and Administrations is a will written in February 1641 with the indexed name of Elizabeth Albin of Southwingfield, Derbyshire, thus putting her in proximity to locales where historically the Albin name had appeared.[6] However, in examining a copy of the will provided by a Lichfield researcher, this author noted that the will is actually that of one Elizabeth Holbein of Eaton, Derbyshire.

---

[5]Ethel Winifred Albin, *The Virginia Albins: The History of the Albin Family Out of Old Frederick County Virginia,* (Decorah, Iowa: Anundsen Pub. Co., 1989), 11. Albin's source for this information regarding James Albin Sr.'s children is a reliable microfilm copy of *Betham's Genealogical Abstracts, Prerogative Wills of Ireland.* In it are listed the six children of James Albin Sr. and his wife Anne (Margaret). The will also provides the names of their grandchildren.
[6]W.P. Phillimore, (ed.) *Calendars of Wills & Administrations in the Consistory Court of the Bishop of Lichfield and Conventry, 1516 to 1652,* London, England: Litchfield, Birmingham, and Derby, England, British Record Society Limited, 1892), 402.

Though the handwriting in most parts of the will is illegible, the name Holbein appears often. However, despite the fact that Phillimore's *Calendar of Wills* clearly mentions Elizabeth Albin in its index, it is the author's contention that this will is *not* that of Elizabeth *Albin* because of the different surname shown and because Eaton is a separate village more than twenty miles from Southwingfield. Further research in the Lichfield records may actually produce the will of Elizabeth Albin.

On the other hand, evidence of another Albin in South Wingfield does exist in the form of a burial notice. A female, Vidna Albin, age unknown, was buried December 13, 1642, in South Wingfield, Derbyshire, England.[7]

While in his twenties, James Sr. left England. In the mid 1660s, uprooting himself from the pastoral English countryside in Derbyshire, he settled north of Dublin, in County Meath, Ireland. Albin must have been possessed of a certain amount of courage and self-confidence to abandon his ancestral homeland while simultaneously parting with friends and whatever remaining family he had. At that time in English history, generations of villagers showed little mobility, as they tended to reside in the same area and in the same village for decades or longer. Thus, James Albin's decision to relocate (to a new country!) raises the fundamental question as to his motive(s).

One possible push factor in James' relocation to Ireland might be linked to England's growing population and perhaps rent increases James and others faced in Derbyshire. On the other end, a pull factor may have had to do with land ownership and James' hope of acquiring property in the sparsely populated, but land-rich, Irish countryside.

In short, people tended to move to places where opportunity existed. At that time many Irish Catholics had been forcefully subordinated to English Protestant rule. As a result of a Parliamentary edict, Catholics had been compelled to forfeit their lands. Eager Englishmen soon acquired ownership of these tracts

---

[7]"England, Derbyshire, Church of England Parish Registers, 1538-1910," index, *Family Search* accessed August 6, 2015, (https://familysearch.org/pal:/MM9.1.1/KBDB-DMV: citing Burial, South Wingfield, Derbyshire, England, Record Office, Matlock; FHL microfilm 1041630, image 13.

from their dispossessed Catholic owners. Though James Albin appeared in Ireland almost a decade and a half after the onset of the English confiscation, he may have hoped that he could somehow acquire acreage in the Irish countryside either through forfeiture or purchase.

Another possible reason for James Albin's migration, though *highly speculative*, concerns the Black Death. *If* James had removed from England in 1665 or even 1666, his departure would have coincided with the onset of the deadly plague of 1665 then sweeping through London and eventually emerging in James' home county of Derbyshire. In the *History, Gazetteer and Directory of Derbyshire* published in 1846 an entry for 1665 reads: "Derby was again visited by the plague: the town was forsaken; the farmers declined the market place and grass grew on the spot on which the necessaries of life had been sold."[8] Perhaps, then, James had sought refuge from this potentially fatal outbreak by fleeing across the sea to a then plague-free Ireland. Whatever Albin's motive(s) for leaving his ancestral English homeland may have been, his was a bold decision.

James' passage to Ireland from Derbyshire would have required that he first secure a wagon or horse for the initial leg of his journey. He would then have proceeded to Liverpool, the nearest large port on England's west coast. Arriving there James would likely have boarded a sailing vessel for his passage across the Irish Sea between England and Ireland, a voyage that would have taken no more than two days depending on the quality of sea transportation and weather. Based on the location of his subsequent resettlement in County Meath, Ireland, Albin may have landed in nearby Dublin.

At some point either prior to or after his voyage to Ireland, James married Anne (sometimes shown with the middle name of Margaret), maiden name unknown.[9] The location of their marriage

---

[8]Samuel Bagshaw, *History, Gazetteer and Directory of Derbyshire*, (Sheffield: William Saxton, 1846), 87.

[9]Many online references mistakenly refer to Anne's last name as Yeoman. This is a misinterpretation in reading the source. Instead the term 'yeoman' refers to her husband James's occupation - yeoman, as in yeoman farmer, and not her last name. The reference to James Albin's will in Bethem's *Genealogical Abstracts, Wills of Ireland* reads as follows: "James Albin (wife Anne) Yeoman." Note how

is unclear, with some unverified sources stating that their marriage occurred in County Wicklow, Ireland, in 1665, while other references suggest it occurred in Derbyshire at about the same time. In addition to these conflicting versions as to where the couple may have wed, Anne's birth year and birthplace are indeterminate. Certain sources indicate she may have been born in Derbyshire County, England, perhaps around 1646, making her nearly the same age as her husband. Despite their English birth and upbringing, the married couple began a lifelong residence in Ireland. Though both James and probably Anne were of English background, it seems that here the *imaginary* Albin Irish heritage connection passed down through generations and extending to the twenty-first century began. As of this writing there appears to be no substantiated evidence that any member of the Albin family was actually Irish, contrary to some family lore. Living in Ireland seems to have been confused with being of Irish blood. (Appendix IV) However, a slight possibility does exist that one of James' and Anne's children may have married a woman of Irish extraction. (See below)

After arriving in Ireland, James eventually made his way to County Meath, in Leinster Province. County Meath possessed an abundance of green farmland undoubtedly triggering in James' mind images of his native Derbyshire countryside. One writer later described County Meath as

> the great grazing ground of Ireland, and consists almost entirely of pastureland, vying in its external aspect with the richest of all English counties . . . the fields have, at all times and seasons, that brilliant green so refreshing to the eye.... There is indeed, no part of Ireland where the Englishman will find himself so completely at home.[10]

Anne's name is within the parentheses, yet the term Yeoman remains outside, indicating a reference to James' occupation. Ann Albin's middle name may have been Margaret based on the fact that the Albins later named their first daughter Margaret.

[10]Mr. and Mrs. S. C. Hall in Thomas Walter Freeman, *Pre-Famine Ireland: A Study in Historical Geography*, (Manchester: Manchester University Press, 1957), 168.

Near a small farming village, Rogerstown(e), in the lush Meath countryside, the Albins began their new life. Rogerstown, described as just inland from "ye [Irish] Sea" in the Parish of Julianstown, is located approximately twenty-eight miles north of Dublin and just over five miles southeast of Drogheda. It is not to be confused with villages of the same name found in Counties Dublin, Louth, and West Meath. Rogerstown is recorded in *The Civil Survey AD 1654-1656 County of Meath* as being near Julianstowne, Smithtowne, and Ministowne and "bounded on the east with the lands of Smithstowne one [sic] the South with the River Nanny on the West with the lands of Ballaghn & on the North [actually West] with the lands of Callightown (Map 2)."[11]

Along with Rogerstown these villages and others were all situated in the northeast corner of the Barony of Duleek.[12] Of the three baronies in Meath, Duleek claimed the largest population in 1659, prior to the Albins' arrival, with 3,919 people - 616 English and 3,303 Irish.[13] Rogerstown, however, counted just thirty-nine people, nine English and thirty Irish.[14] (Note the large discrepancy between the numbers of English and Irish.)

According to the Down Survey, in 1641 Irish Catholics owned 42.2% of Ireland's land while the Protestant minority claimed nearly the same amount at 42.1%.[15] Eight years later, as a result of the Cromwellian conquest of Ireland in 1649 and the ensuing punitive measures Cromwell instituted, almost all lands owned by Catholics were confiscated and turned over to British settlers. By 1670 Protestants owned 69.8% of Ireland's land, while Catholics claimed only 16.6%, a dramatic turnabout in just under three decades.

In County Meath by 1670, a similar disparity existed between Catholics and Protestants. Protestants owned 73.9% of the

---

[11]Robert C. Simington, *The Civil Survey AD 1654-1656 County of Meath*, (Dublin: The Stationery Office, 1940), volume 5, 6.

[12]A barony was a subdivision of a county.

[13]Seamus Pender (ed.), *A Census of Ireland Circa 1659*, (Dublin: Stationery Office, 1939), xvi.

[14]Ibid., 482.

[15]Carried out between 1656-1658, the Down Survey of Ireland was the world's first detailed land survey achieved on a national scale. *The Down Survey of Ireland,* accessed January 24, 2014, http://downsurvey.tcd.ie/religion.php.

land, whereas in 1641 they had claimed just 30%.[16] Therefore, in the 1670s, James Albin in County Meath resided where minority Protestants like himself, who shared common core religious beliefs and an English heritage, owned nearly three-fourths of the land, much of it gained through expropriation.

Near Rogerstown James, according to his will, worked as a yeoman farmer, a free man owning land. We have no way of knowing the number of acres James Albin claimed, but the freedom he enjoyed allowed him to grow and sell his crops for profit. Furthermore, the fact that James owned the land he farmed and that he possessed enough money to have a will written in his later years indicated he might have been a man of some means.

The proximity of James' land to the nearby port of Drogheda, situated at the mouth of the Boyne River on the Irish Sea, may have proven very advantageous. In the near absence of any roads traversing the Irish countryside, access to a port would have allowed James to more easily transport the crop(s) he didn't sell locally to other markets in Ireland (Dublin?) and perhaps England. Of course, James would have had to first convey his goods to Drogheda, some five miles from his farm, for shipment. In addition, even closer to James' Rogerstown property was the Nanny River that also flowed eastward to the Irish Sea. The Nanny would have offered Albin a second potential choice for transporting his harvests to more distant buyers.

Beginning in Ireland in the late 1660s, an era of kings, queens, lords, and dukes, James Albin had undertaken an occupation that would be followed by at least one of his male descendants in each of nine subsequent generations all the way into the twenty-first century.[17] Linking the past with the present, as late as 2016, a ninth generation grandson of James Albin Sr., also James Albin, maintained a forty-acre farm in Kentucky.

The Albins raised six children, their births probably spanning the years 1668-1676. Unreliable internet sources list varying birth dates and Irish birth locations for each child. The most relia-

---

[16]*Ibid.,* "Ownership by Religion," accessed January 27, 2014, http://downsurvey.tcd.ie/religion.php#c=Meath&indexOfObjectValue=-1&indexOfObjectValueSubstring=-1&p=Leinster.

[17]It is possible that James Albin Sr.'s ancestors also had farmed the English countryside near Derbyshire.

ble basis for ascertaining the names and possibly the birth order of the six Albin children is the will of James Albin Sr., though it included neither birth locations nor birth years for any of his offspring. With the possible exception of a daughter, Margaret, however, all were probably born in County Meath, Ireland. In his will James seems to have listed the children in the order of their birth with the oldest child likely appearing first. According to James' will dated December 29, 1720, his and Anne's children were:

James Albin Sr. family[18]

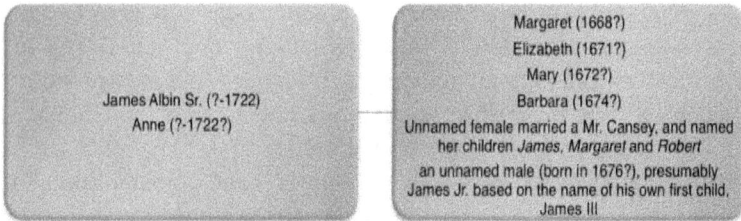

James Albin Sr. (?-1722)
Anne (?-1722?)

Margaret (1668?)
Elizabeth (1671?)
Mary (1672?)
Barbara (1674?)
Unnamed female married a Mr. Cansey, and named her children *James, Margaret* and *Robert*
an unnamed male (born in 1676?), presumably James Jr. based on the name of his own first child, James III

     As time passed, Anne and James' children married. Margaret (naming pattern identification suggests that as the first born daughter, her mother's name may indeed have been Anne Margaret) married John Hunter, while her sister Elizabeth married a Mr. Evans. Mary wed a Mr. Guest and Barbara married Martin Delaney.[19] The Albin's fifth daughter wed a Mr. Cansey, while the only son James Albin Jr. possibly married Sarah Cansey. More than likely Sarah and the Mr. Cansey were related, perhaps as sister and brother.

---

[18]Albin, *Virginia Albins*, 11. Based on a variety of sources, the *possible* birth years of James and Anne Albin's children were added by the author and are shown in parentheses. Some sources state that Margaret was born in Derbyshire, England, while others mention her birth occurred in County Meath, Ireland.

[19]Albin, *Virginia Albins*, 11,12. See also, No author, "Hearth Money Rolls for the Barony of Orior,"*Journal of the County of Louth Archaeological Society*, Vol. 7, No. 3, (December 1931), 421. In Ballymore, West Meath, a Thomas Guest is shown. Perhaps he is a Guest family member or even Mary Albin's husband.

It appears that at least two of these Albin children married into families with means. Margaret's husband, John Hunter, held the rank of captain in the army of King William III and later became a substantial landowner. Barbara Albin Delaney's husband, Martin, claimed the title of 'gentleman', an independently wealthy person who gained income from property or inheritance. That two of the female Albin children were able to associate with then marry men of such respectable social standing may lend further credence to the notion that their father James Albin Sr. was a successful yeoman.

Map 2
An early land ownership map, c1659, showing a part of the Barony of Duleek, County Meath, Rogerstown[e], where James Albin Sr. settled, and neighboring villages. The River Nanny can be seen in the lower left.[20] Dublin lies to the south, Drogheda to the northwest.

With the births of most of James and Anne's six children in Ireland (Margaret's birthplace remain in question) in the 1660s - 1670s and continuing with their Ireland-born grandchildren, a fun-

---

[20]*Ibid.*, http://downsurvey.tcd.ie/down-survey-maps.php#bm=Duleek&c=Meath&indexOfObjectValue=-q1&indexOfObjectValueSubstring=-1&p=Killcarvan, accessed April 11, 2016.

damental question arises as to the Albin family's cultural identity.
Were James II and his five siblings, English or Irish? The bloodline of course points to English. But, as one writer noted, by the
late seventeenth century the so-called New English in Ireland
dominated Irish society, ". . . and the Protestants in Ireland,
though undoubtedly a minority [comprising just 30% of Ireland's
population by 1700] and in control of the majority Catholic population, thought of themselves as Irish. . . ."[21] (See the next chapter
for reference to the Protestant Ascendancy in Ireland.) According
to Kumar,

> it is impossible for such a large section of the population
> [English Protestants] to regard themselves as an embattled
> minority for any length of time. *Adaptation and acclimati-
> zation* [italics mine] are the inevitable results of such a
> prolonged presence in a new land. . . . [22]

Thus, the birth and residence in Ireland of James and
Anne's children and grandchildren most likely caused these subsequent generations to adopt Irish manners and customs. The Albins in Ireland not only experienced a gradual assimilation into
Irish culture, but at the same time they were emerging in the late
seventeenth century and into the eighteenth as a group distinct
from the Protestants in their English homeland. James and Anne
likely grew uneasy while witnessing this ethnic transformation in
their offspring, and in turn perhaps feared that over time this Irish
influence would smother the family's English heritage. They may
have realized that immigrants like themselves were only 'immigrants' for a generation at most.

---

[21]Krishawn Kumar, *The Making of English National Identity*, (New York: Cambridge University Press, 2003), 141-142.

[22]Ibid., 142. Most immigrants arriving America eventually fell into this same
pattern of adaptation and acclimatization.

CHAPTER II

James Robert(?) Albin Jr. (1676?-1720)
and
Captain John Hunter and Margaret Albin Hunter

Ireland

As with many of the early Albins, not much is known of the life of James and Anne's only son, James Albin II. Alternately shown as James or Robert Albin depending on the source consulted, he was born perhaps in 1676, most likely in Rogerstown. He may have been the youngest of the six children. It is assumed that he married a Sarah Cansey sometime before 1708.

Sarah may have been of English extraction, like her husband, but she may have been born in Ireland. In the Hearth Money Roll for County Wicklow, Ireland, where assessors counted hearths and then levied a tax, occasionally heads of household also were named. In the Wicklow hearth records, a Richard Cansey appears in 1668, the only Cansey shown in the county.[1] The Cansey surname appears infrequently in Irish records, and thus it is possible that Sarah Cansey hailed from the Wicklow Canseys. If so, was she a member of a transplanted English family, or was she of Irish blood? If the latter is true, then she may be an Irish link and thereby a contributor of any, as of yet indeterminate, Irish blood in this Albin line.

Rogerstown appears to have been the birthplace of James and Sarah's four children, the second Irish-born Albin generation. Based on the order that *James Sr.* listed his four grandchildren in his will of 1720, their names and approximate birthdates with their more definite death years are:[2]

---

[1]Liam Price, "Hearth Money Roll for County Wicklow," *Journal of the Royal Society of Antiquaries of Ireland*, Seventh Series, Vol. 1, No. 2, (December 31, 1931), 177. Wicklow, it will be remembered, was a supposed site of James Albin Sr. and Anne Albin's marriage, so perhaps a link was forged between the Canseys of Wicklow and the Albin family during that time. Unlike most of their neighbors, the Canseys counted not one, but two hearths indicating some affluence.

[2]Albin, *Virginia Albins*, 11, 13, 14 and notes to Chapter Two, p. ii, fn 7, for the 1708-9 birth of James III in Ireland.

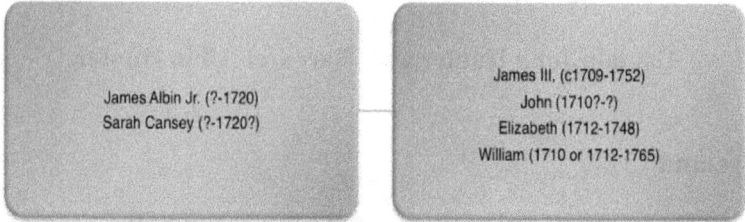

James Albin Jr. (?-1720)
Sarah Cansey (?-1720?)

James III, (c1709-1752)
John (1710?-?)
Elizabeth (1712-1748)
William (1710 or 1712-1765)

(Note the name of James and Sarah's daughter, Elizabeth, which again seems to perpetuate via the often-used naming pattern the inferred name of James Sr.'s mother.)

Tragically, it seems by 1720, James Jr. and Sarah Albin had passed away. While the exact date of Sarah's death is un-known, circumstantial evidence seems to indicate that James Jr. died in or about 1720. His father's will was written that year and he (Jr.) was not named an executor as would be expected of an only son.

James Jr. apparently left a will of his own (not found by the author) that probated in 1720.[3] If indeed the will did belong to our James Albin Jr. (the year of probate corresponds to the possi-ble year of his death), it provides additional confirmation of the date of his passing. James Jr.'s will probated in the Diocese of Kildare, in County Kildare bordering County Meath, just twenty-seven miles from Rogerstown. The record mentions *James Albin of Kilcock.*

Thus, James and Sarah it appears had moved their family from Rogerstown at some point to County Kildare settling in or near Kilcock. Originally a small, medieval settlement dating from 550, it had become by 1720 a vibrant trade center (Map 3).

Following the death of both their parents, it is likely, but not proven, that the four young Albin children, ranging in age from approximately eight to eleven years, would have resided with their elderly grandparents back in Rogerstown, County Meath.

---

[3]Sydney Cary (ed.), "Index to the Wills of the Diocese of Kildare," *Journal of the County Kildare Archeological Society,* Vol. IV, (July 1903-1905), 1905, 473. See also, *Ancestry.com, Index to Irish Wills 1909,* Volume 1, "A Calendar of Wills in the Diocese of Kildare," accessed August 5, 2013, sv. James Robert Albin.

However, any time spent under their care would have been very brief. Two years later in September 1722, at approximately seventy-seven years of age, James Albin Sr. died in Rogerstown. Anne Albin also died at nearly the same time.[4] The untimely deaths of their grandparents meant their four underage grandchildren, James, Elizabeth, William, and John, were again left as orphans. However, James Sr.'s foresight in naming *two* executors in his will proved to be both fortunate and wise.

Captain John Hunter and Margaret Albin Hunter

On December 29, 1720, two years prior to his death, James Albin Sr. completed a will that later probated in approximately 1722.[5] James designated his wife Anne *and* his son in law John Hunter (his daughter Margaret's husband) as executors of his estate.[6] James' selection of Hunter as a co-executor soon proved to be a key factor in the lives of Albin Sr.'s four grandchildren impacting not only them, but also generations of future Albin descendants.

With the ill-timed and nearly simultaneous deaths of James Sr. and Ann, Captain John Hunter, a career soldier in the English Army, emerged as the Albin children's benefactor and the sole executor of Albin Sr.'s will. With his wife, Margaret Albin Hunter (the children's aunt), John Hunter would have logically taken responsibility for their four nieces and nephews. Because of the exceptionally significant and timely role the Hunters would play in the lives of the Albin children, their brief biography merits

---

[4]Some internet postings state Anne died in 1693, but with Ann named as a co-executor of her husband James' will in 1720, it is improbable James Sr. would have done so had Anne been deceased for twenty-seven years.

[5]Albin, *Virginia Albins*, 11. Sir Arthur Vicars, *Index to the Prerogative Wills of Ireland 1536-1810*, (Baltimore: Genealogical Publishing Company, 1897), 4. Worth noting is that James Sr. made this will in 1720, not long after the death of his son James Jr. who had died in that same year. Fire later destroyed the original will in Dublin in 1922. Prior to the Dublin fire, Sir William Betham, Ulster King of Arms, had taken genealogical notes, indexed each will, and then deposited them in the Office of Arms, Dublin. Vicars based his publication on Betham's transcripts, abstracts, and notes painstakingly taken from the original wills.

[6]Ibid., *Virginia Albins*, 11.

mention. In presenting the Hunter's story, we must return to the decades before the deaths of both James Albin Senior and Junior.

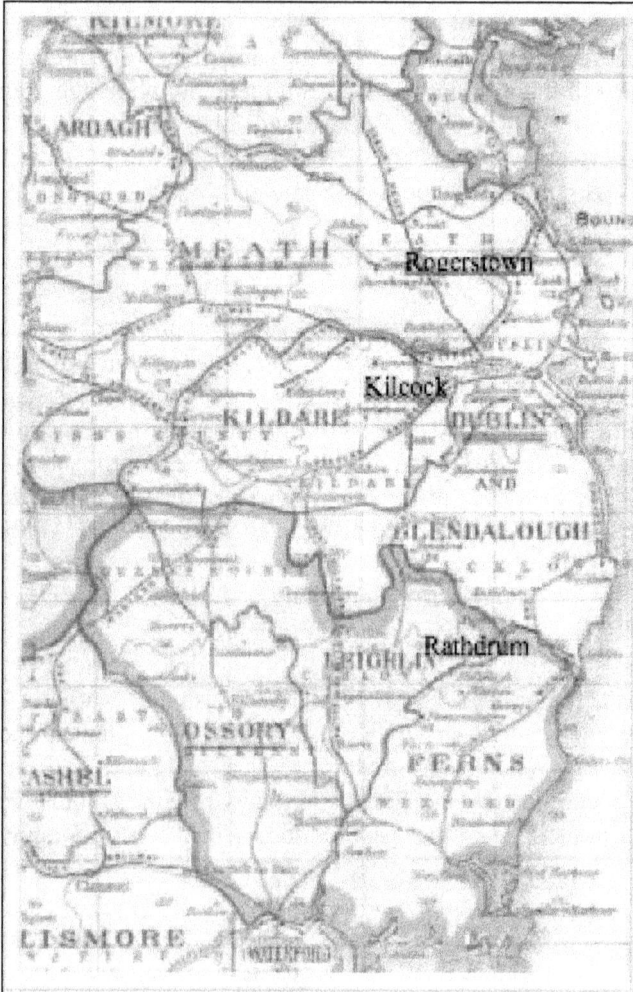

Map 3
Rogerstown, County Meath, home of James Albin Sr. Kilcock, County
Kildare, home of James Albin Jr., and Rathdrum, County Wicklow, home of John
and Margaret Albin Hunter

John Hunter's early life spans both England and neighboring Ireland. His birth in the north of England supposedly in the Derbyshire town of East Cottingwith in 1667 meant he shared a common geographic link to the Derbyshire Albins.[7] A Protestant, Hunter may have fled England upon the accession of the Catholic monarch James II in 1685. Hunter subsequently settled in Rathdrum, County Wicklow, Ireland, perhaps after 1690 (Map 3). While the date of John Hunter's arrival in Wicklow remains uncertain, it seems that one of Hunter's brothers may have settled there by at least 1685.[8] John Hunter and Margaret Albin married, most likely in 1689, perhaps in Derbyshire, England, while John was on his way to Londonderry (Derry) to join his military unit.[9]

---

[7]*Edward Hunter Family History Collection* – Documents, Section 12, Pedigree Chart of John Hunter, found about half way through the document: http://www.georgeqcannon.com/edward_hunter_docs.htm, accessed April 17, 2013. The source for Hunter's birth in East Cottingwith is not provided on the chart. Many unsubstantiated sources declare that Hunter was born in Medomsley, in Durham County, England, far north of Derbyshire. I have found no record of this John Hunter in the Hunters of Medomsley pedigree chart or anywhere else.

[8]Ibid., Pedigree Chart of Peter Hunter (John's brother) showing the birth of a daughter on May 6, 1685, at Rathdrum, Ireland. Several of the documents regarding the Hunter family were compiled using the records found in the Latter Day Saints (LDS) Library in Salt Lake City. Some inconsistencies appear throughout the Hunter-Albin family accounts in this group. Efforts at cross-referencing the information included therein were not always successful and will be so noted. This material for Peter Hunter's family stands unsubstantiated in the historical record at this time.

[9]The reference to the Hunter's marriage occurring in Derbyshire is derived from an anonymous two and one-half page typewritten source in the (Bishop) *Edward Hunter Family History Collection*, Section 12, titled, "Notes About Our Immigrant Ancestor, Captain John Hunter." While the author is extremely reluctant to use anonymous sources, especially those found online, I have located supporting documentation for other references in the article regarding Hunter. I offer the Derbyshire reference then with some hesitancy having been unable to locate another reliable source that supports it. But, mindful of the fact that both Margaret Albin and John Hunter are reportedly known to have been born in Derbyshire, it would seem likely they could have been married there though Margaret's parents, John and Anne Albin, resided in Rogerstown, Ireland, at that time. This reference sheet also shows a date of 1689 for the Hunters' marriage. Furthermore, the LDS Library seems to have taken a strong interest in compiling as much information as possible on John Hunter and his family because John and Margaret's great grandson Edward Hunter (1793-1883) was the longest tenured Presiding Bishop in the history of the LDS Church having converted to Mormonism in 1840. As

The Hunters' presence in Derry in 1689 thus supports the belief they were married sometime during that year. In the aftermath of the unsuccessful 105-day siege of that city from April to August 1689 by supporters of the Catholic King James II during the Williamite War (see below), the Protestant Hunters had joined Captain Henry Hunter there. Hunter, an apparent relative of John Hunter, is mentioned along with "Two members of the [his] family," John and Margaret Hunter, in Derry records.[10] Their signatures as husband and wife appear on a document titled *Derry Corporation's 1690 Commission*, a petition to the government in London.

In the English Army, the twenty-four year old Hunter served as a cornet in the Protestant William of Orange's cavalry (dragoons) and apparently fought at the decisive Battle of the Boyne (River) in County Meath.[11] Fought on July 1, 1690, (approximately one year after the siege at Derry had ended) near Drogheda, not far from Rogerstown, this engagement resulted in a historically significant Protestant victory. It allowed William of Orange to emerge triumphant over the defeated French and Irish Catholic allies of the English Catholic King James II, his father-in-law. Furthermore, William's victory compelled James II, the last Catholic King of England, to flee to the continent. At the same time, it assured the triumph of the Glorious Revolution (the overthrow of King James), and allowed William III and his wife Mary

---

would be expected, Bishop Hunter and his contemporary Brigham Young, a key figure in the history of the Mormon religion, maintained a close relationship.

[10]William R. Young, *Fighters of Derry, Their Deeds and Descendants*, (London: Eyre and Spottiswoode, 1932), 183. Nearly every reference to the marriage of Hunter and Margaret Albin indicates they were married in 1693. This inference seems to be based on an often-mentioned ring that Margaret apparently gave to John, inscribed "keep this in remembrance of me, 1693." Researchers have erroneously, in my opinion, labeled this the Hunter "wedding ring."

[11]Andrew Jenson, *Latter-Day Saint Biographical Encyclopedia: A Compilation of Biographical Sketches of Prominent Men and Women in the Church of Jesus Christ of Latter-day Saints Volume 1*, (Salt Lake City: Jenson History Company, 1901), 227. This source indicates that Hunter served as a lieutenant at the Battle of the Boyne. Other sources mention Hunter's service at the Boyne without indicating his rank. However, this author could locate no specific statement of Hunter's presence there in any *military* history of the time. Later records of Hunter's military service (when he held an officer's rank) over the next two decades in the English Army confirm his rank, location of service, and dates.

to assume the throne of England thus affirming the Protestant ascendancy in Ireland.

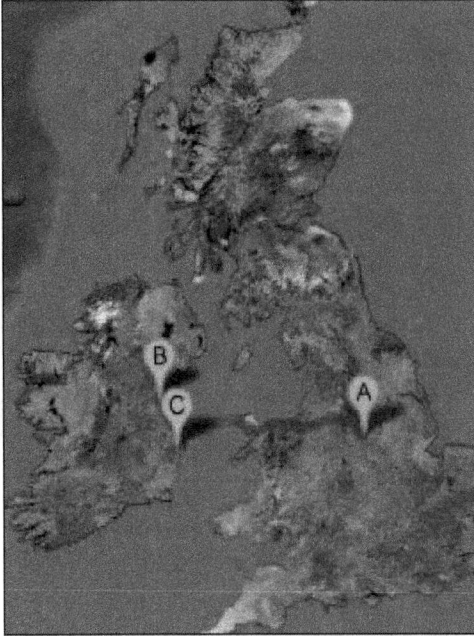

Map 4
The Albins in England and Ireland

A - Derbyshire, England
B - Rogerstown, County Meath, Ireland
C - Rathdrum, County Wicklow - John and Margaret Albin Hunter's home
(The dark line represents the likely route James Albin Sr. would have followed
on his journey from Derbyshire to County Meath.)

Whether the English Protestant family of James Albin Sr. had remained in the remote Rogerstown area before or during the engagement between William and James II's forces at the nearby Boyne River is unknown. If so, they could well have suffered hardships at the hands of either the civilian Catholic majority residing in the area or from James II's Catholic forces who encamped nearby, just south of the Boyne (Map 5). Indeed, English Protestant settlers in Wicklow during the year immediately preceding the Battle of the Boyne left the area entirely fearing retribution

by Catholics.[12] In addition to potential threats because of their
Protestant affiliation, the Albins in Rogerstown may well have had
another reason to fear for their safety. If the assembling Catholic
forces under King James learned that the Albins' son in law John
Hunter was serving in William's opposition army, they might have
taken immediate punitive action against the entire Albin family. In
the interest of safety, the Albins including fourteen-year old James
Jr. may have wisely abandoned their Rogerstown farm at this critical time, only to return later after the defeated forces of James II
had retreated and when William's forces had restored order.

In both the larger historical perspective and of immediate
significance for Protestants like the Albin and Hunter families, the
Protestant King William's landmark victory (or James II's defeat)
virtually eliminated Old English and Old Irish political cultures.
From then (1690) on, "there were only two cultures in Ireland:
New English - the culture of the dominant Protestant power holders - and New Irish – the culture of the disenfranchised and embit-
tered Catholic population."[13]

Thus, it was in this Protestant-dominated Irish setting that
James Albin Sr. raised his family. What Protestant rule under King
William of Orange meant in specific terms for the Albins in County Meath and later James Jr. in County Kildare is unknown. Not
part of the elite class of wealthy Protestants who were the main
beneficiaries of the Ascendancy, the Albins, in comparison, may
not have profited as much from the Protestant domination other
than attaining an elevated social rank above the native-born Catholic Irish.

Following the Williamite war, John and Margaret Albin
Hunter resided south of Dublin in Rathdrum, County Wicklow, in
close proximity to Hunter's brother (Map 3). In lieu of pay, the
victorious King William had granted to some of his soldiers Irish
land confiscated from the rebellious Irish Catholics who had supported James II.[14] This so-called bounty land that King William
awarded his officers of merit may have allowed Hunter to establish a farm and to begin raising livestock and crops.

---

[12]Thomas Allan Glenn, *Some Colonial Mansions and Those Who Lived in Them,
Vol. 2,* (Philadelphia: H.T. Coates & Co., 1900), 284.
[13]Kumar, *The Making of English National Identity,* 141.
[14]Glenn, *Some Colonial Mansions Vol. 2,* 284-285.

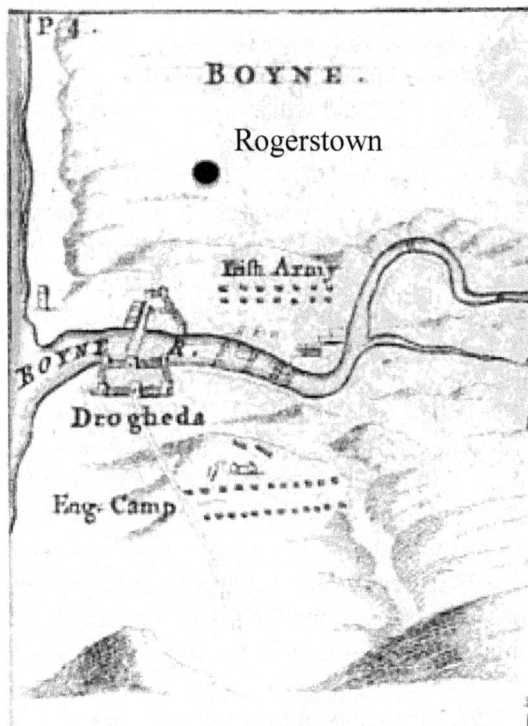

Map 5
The English and Irish encampments at the Battle of the Boyne (looking south).
Rogerstown, where the James Albin Sr. family lived, lies approximately four
miles behind the Irish Army encampment shown on the map.[15]

With peace restored and while residing at Rathdrum, Margaret and John Hunter began raising a family. From 1694 to 1716 records in the LDS Library show the births of eleven Hunter children.[16] Hunter's frequent military deployments meant that Margaret might have assumed the primary responsibility of caring for the growing family.

---

[15]John Tincey, *The British Army 1660-1704,* (Oxford, England: Osprey Publishing Co., 1994), 9.
[16]*Edward Hunter Family History Collection,* Section 12, Family Record Group of John Hunter.

After the Battle at the Boyne River, Hunter remained in the army of King William. He rose through the officer ranks, first as a cornet, then a lieutenant in the Royal Regiment of the Dragoons of Ireland, and finally achieving the rank of captain in 1713. Hunter's military records show that he participated in campaigns on the European continent: at Flanders from 1694-1697, in the bloody Battles at Blenheim (1704)[17], Ramillies (1706), Oudenarde (1708), and Malplaquet (1709) during the War of Spanish Succession (1702-1713) where his unit, the Fifth Dragoons, distinguished itself on at least two occasions.[18] In some of these engagements Hunter served under the command of the Duke of Marlborough, John Churchill, the ancestor of Sir Winston Churchill, the World War II British Prime Minister.

By 1713 years before the death of his brother-in-law James Albin Jr., the forty-six year old Hunter probably had seen enough fighting. Following his promotion to Captain of the Foot on June 9, 1713, Hunter is not mentioned again in any military records found by the author. Thus, it appears that either in 1713, or some time shortly thereafter, he may have retired from military service. Hunter soon settled into the life of a civilian at Rathdrum, exchanging his pistol and sword for the more peaceful life a full-time farmer.

Following the deaths of his brother-in-law and father-in-law (James Albin Jr. and Sr.) and their wives, the Hunters, probably by 1722, had incorporated the four young Albin children into their family at least temporarily. Significantly, in that same year, the Hunter clan, along *with the Albin children*, sailed across the Atlantic and settled in Pennsylvania.

Ethel Albin in her *Virginia Albins* maintains that the Hunters moved to America in 1711.[19] This is incorrect. John Hunter's great grandson, Edward Hunter II, years later recalled

---

[17]Charles Dalton, *English Army Lists and Commission Registers, 1661-1714, Volume 6* (Great Britain: Eyre and Spottiswoode, 1904), 39, 199, 316 and Volume 4, 60. At Blenheim Hunter sustained a wound to his left hip resulting in a slight lameness he endured for the remainder of his life. Volume 4, 52.

[18]Walter T. Willcox, *The Historical Records of the Fifth (Royal Irish) Lancers: From Their Foundation as Wynne's Dragoons (in 1689) to the Present Day,* (London: Arthur Doubleday and Company, 1908), xli. See also 96.

[19]Albin, *Virginia Albins*, 12.

hearing his father (Edward Hunter I) state that his grandfather, John Hunter, had left for America in 1722.[20] It is also highly unlikely that James Albin Sr. would have named John Hunter an executor of his will in 1720 if Hunter lived 3,000 miles away in Pennsylvania in 1711.[21]

As the lone executor of James Albin Sr.'s will, John Hunter, along with his wife Margaret, may have delayed their departure for Pennsylvania until the Albin will had probated in 1722. Residing in America by this time were three of the Hunters' daughters. Mary Hunter had arrived from Ireland with her husband William Hill in approximately 1720. Another daughter, Ann Hunter, married Samuel Baker in Philadelphia's Christ Church on May 29, 1720.[22] A third daughter, Elizabeth Hunter, married Robert Steel, also in Pennsylvania, on May 15, 1722.

In addition to the Hunter's three married daughters, Hunter's niece and his brother had also moved earlier from Rathdrum to Penn's colony. Upon their arrival, John and Margaret Hunter joined their married niece, Elizabeth Hunter Aston the daughter of John's brother Peter, near Downington in Chester County. Moreover, since about 1709, Peter Hunter had lived in nearby Middletown with his son Jonathan and daughter in law Margery. Therefore, when they arrived, John and Margaret Hunter and their younger children were able to reconnect with several other family members already living in Pennsylvania. Consequently, their move to Pennsylvania in 1722 was anything but an ill-conceived plunge into a land void of friends and relatives. In fact, it seems that John and Margaret were the last of their family to arrive in America.

Over the years John Hunter had formed a strong friendship with his army comrade and Rathdrum neighbor Captain An-

---

[20]*Diary of Bishop Edward Hunter*, http://www.georgeqcannon.com/edward_hunter_docs.htm, accessed April 11, 2013.

[21]Hunter Family records in the LDS Library in Salt Lake City show the last child of John and Margaret Hunter was born in Rathdrum in 1716.

[22]Clarence M. Busch, *Record of Pennsylvania Marriages Prior to 1810*, Pennsylvania Archives, Second Series, Volume 8, Marriage Record of Christ Church Philadelphia, 1709 -1806 (Philadelphia: State Printer of Pennsylvania, 1895), 113, accessed April 22, 2009, http://www.usgwarchives.net/pa/1pa/paarchivesseries/series2/vol8/pass84.html.

thony Wayne (grandfather of the famous American Revolutionary War general of the same name). Hunter and Wayne are said to have served together at the Boyne Battle and under the Duke of Marlborough. Like the Albins and perhaps John Hunter, the Wayne family claimed a Derbyshire origin.[23] Together, both men may have developed the idea of moving their families to Pennsylvania. The Hunter-Wayne friendship, fostered by their Northern England heritage, shared Army service, and their common residence in Wicklow, made their collaboration and decision to relocate much easier. As a result, the Wayne family may have sailed with the Hunters. According to Albin family historian Ethel Albin, the Albin children's aunt, Mrs. Cansey, and her three children may have also joined the group. Departing perhaps from Londonderry, the Hunters (and Waynes?) made the 3,000-mile transatlantic voyage probably in six to eight weeks.[24] Sometime prior to March 16, 1722 (the date of Hunter's initial land purchase in Pennsylvania) they arrived, sailed up the Delaware River and disembarked most likely at Philadelphia, the foremost city in William Penn's thriving Pennsylvania colony.[25] *Thus, the arrival of this line of Albins in America can be traced to the weeks or months prior to March 1722.*

---

[23]Wayne was born in Chesterfield. The Wayne family had lived in Derbyshire or southern Yorkshire for centuries. Captain Wayne had moved to County Wicklow, Ireland, probably during the rift then developing between James II and William of Orange. Wayne commanded a company of dragoons in King William's campaign in Ireland against James II that had culminated in the Battle of the Boyne. Wayne, too, was awarded confiscated land near Rathdrum. He had married in Rathdrum in 1687 or 1690.

[24]Ethel Albin is the only source found by the author who mentions the Albin children making the voyage with the Hunter family. However, Chester County records show three of the four Albin children, John, James, and Elizabeth, residing there as adults. The latter two appear to have lived out their lives in Chester County dying there in 1752 and 1748 respectively.

[25]Edwin Sellers, *English Ancestry of the Wayne Family of Pennsylvania*, (Philadelphia: Press of Allen, Lane & Scott, 1927), 25. See also, Samuel Hazzard, *The Register of Pennsylvania*, (Philadelphia: W. F. Geddes, 1829), 369. Neither Sellers nor Hazzard mentions the Hunter family making the voyage with the Waynes. However, if both traveled to America in 1722, the strong likelihood is the families traveled together. Another source indicates Wayne and his family arrived in Boston in 1723 after the Hunters' arrival in 1722: Glenn, *Some Colonial Mansions, Volume 2*, 287-288.

Near the time of the Hunters' arrival, Chester County's population numbered approximately 10,000 with most people residing along the Delaware River.[26] However, Downingtown, where the Hunters first settled, was very remote, situated some twenty-five miles from Philadelphia. This isolation so troubled Margaret Hunter that the Hunters abruptly moved to Newtown Township, a more populated setting and the home to many Quakers.[27]

Hunter, described in Chester County records as "late of Ireland", purchased a 350-acre tract in Newtown Township, Chester County, on March 16, 1722, from local Quaker Daniel Williamson.[28] (Wayne also purchased land in Chester County at approximately the same time.) This prime location eventually would become the most densely populated area of the colony. Soon, Hunter constructed a "pretentious" mansion house situated near the Delaware River, only fifteen miles below Philadelphia and fourteen miles from Wilmington (photo below). It would remain the Hunter family residence for generations.

---

[26]Kerby Miller, *Irish Immigrants in the Land of Canaan: Letters and Memoirs from Colonial and Revolutionary America, 1675-1815,* (New York: Oxford University Press, 2004), 74.

[27]Wilmot J. Hunter, *A Brief History of the Hunter Family,* (Vineland, Ontario, Canada: Glenaden Press, 2002), 16.

[28]Ibid. See also, "Deed Books, Grantee (Buyer) Index. H, 1688-1820" *Chester County, Pennsylvania, Archives and Records Services,* accessed February 11, 2014, http://pa-chestercounty.civicplus.com/DocumentCenter/View/3896. This document shows the 1723 release date of Hunter's deed. Scroll to find John Hunter. Hunter at Newtown and Wayne at Easttown. Both appear in the *Chester County Archives 1720-1729,* "Tax Index H and W" online. For Hunter see, http://www.chesco.org/DocumentCenter/View/5396 in 1724. For Wayne, also in 1724, see http://www.chesco.org/DocumentCenter/View/5390, accessed February 10, 2014. See also, No author, "The Hunter Family of Chester and Delaware Counties," *The Literary Era,* vol. 4, no. 8, (August 1897), 276, *Google Books,* accessed February 10, 2014, https://books.google.com/books?id=v-s5AQAAMAAJ&pg=PA275&lpg=PA275&dq=The+Hunter+Family+of+Chester+and+Delaware+Counties&source=bl&ots=eeGdezYOkQ&sig=-P7000WUF_kIGgl9fAZbUo5jerE&hl=en&sa=X&ved=0ahUKEwj_n5nl8qzOAh URy2MKHY4bAlAQ6AEILzAE#v=onepage&q=The%20Hunter%20Family%20of%20Chester%20and%20Delaware%20Counties&f=false, where a Chester County deed dated March 16, 1722, shows that Hunter purchased land on that date and obtained the above-referenced release one year later in 1723.

A contemporary of John Hunter, the Irish Quaker Robert Parke, described this same Chester County in a letter to his sister in 1725: "There is not one of the family what likes the country very well and wod [sic] If we were in Ireland again come here [Chester County] Directly it being the best country for working folk and Tradesmen of any in the world."[29]

The exact reasons for Hunter and Wayne's departure from Ireland have never been firmly established by historians. Some have speculated about Wayne's dissatisfaction with perceived slights regarding his status as an army veteran as a possible cause. Hunter's motives are similarly unknown and would involve additional speculation. However, in a copy of Bishop Hunter's Diary, the Bishop indicates his ancestor John Hunter may have left Ireland due to his dissatisfaction with the manner in which the Protestants in Ireland were treating the Catholics.[30] But, the fact that Hunter already had extensive family ties in Pennsylvania may have been the most compelling factor in his decision to relocate. Regardless of their reasons for migrating, Hunter and Wayne both had given up their estates in Wicklow as a part of their relocation to America. It would seem that Hunter at age fifty-four and Wayne at fifty-six were well past the period in their lives when they would want to undertake such a dramatic, risky, and expensive move - essentially starting over in a new land thousands of miles away. But, the unique combination of factors drawing them to America evidently suited their strong characters that were perhaps bolstered by their years in the military when they had grown accustomed to risk-taking.

For the young Albin orphans, now under the guardianship of their aunt and uncle, it must have been an unnerving chain of events that resulted in their arrival in America: the passing of their parents, then two years later suffering the deaths of their grandparents. Compounding their mental burden was the prospect of a

---

[29]Robert Parke in John Sandifer, *Tracking TJ*, (Xlibris Corporation), 2010, 23.
[30]Bishop Edward Hunter's son related this anecdote, as the original sheet to his father's diary was lost. The younger Hunter mistakenly attributed the motive for John Hunter's move from Ireland in 1722 to a 'William' Hunter who was John Hunter's sixteen year old son at that time.

long, arduous, and dangerous sea voyage from their traditional
Irish homeland to a new, unfamiliar, and distant country.

Hunter, in addition to paying for his own family's passage
along with that of the four Albin children, might have also paid the
way for several families of redemptionists (an individual who
traveled from Europe to America without paying a fare and upon
arrival in the New World was required to "redeem" himself by
collecting funds from relatives or friends; if the funds could not be
obtained, the person was sold into indentured servitude). Consequently, upon his arrival in Newtown, Hunter may have used these
indebted redemptionists to help construct his Chester County
home.

Because the Albin children in 1722 would have been unable to pay for their passage, upon their arrival in America they
may have been indentured to someone, perhaps even their Uncle
John, to learn a trade. Yet, Newton Township/Chester County records dating from 1700 make no *specific* reference to Albins as indentured servants.

An indenture, even between relatives would not have been
uncommon in colonial times. According to one historian, "many
of the [indentured] servants were actually nephews, nieces, cousins, and children of friends of emigrating Englishmen, who paid
their passage in return for their labor and service once in America."[31] While the exact amount of the Albin children's indebtedness
to Hunter is unknown, their passage in the 1720s would have cost
about £8 in Pennsylvania currency. In turn, if Hunter indentured
any or all of the Albin children to another they would have
brought between £12-35 depending on such factors as "age, sex,
skills and length of service."[32]

---

[31]Gary Nash, *The Urban Crucible: Social Change, Political Consciousness, and
the Origins of the American Revolution*, (Harvard University Press: Cambridge,
Mass., 1979), 15.

[32]Don Corbly, Letters, Journals, & Diaries of ye Colonial America, (Lulu.com,
2009), 104, accessed August 1, 2016,
https://books.google.com/books?id=BIaVAgAAQBAJ&q=12-
35#v=onepage&q=12-
35&f=false%2C%20%26%20Diaries%20of%20ye%20Colonial%20America&f=
false.

In colonial Chester County records, a reference to one of the four Albins may indicate just such an indenture. Several decades after coming to America, John Albin (also spelled Alban), William Albin's older brother, appears in the 1758, 1763, and 1765 tax records for Charlestown Township (sixteen miles from the Hunters' Newtown Township residence - Map 6). Of particular interest are the tax records for 1758 and 1763. Located in the *Category* column following John Albin's name in each of these two archives is the designation "Freeman". From this notation it may be inferred that upon his arrival John had been indentured for an unspecified time, and at his release he had attained a freeman's status.[33] The records make no mention of John's master.

Noteworthy is that John Albin's position as an indentured servant strongly suggests a similar indenture for one or more of his three siblings, although no records were found to support such a conclusion. William Albin's name does not appear in any local tax records, but his brother James is shown as a *landowner* in the Newtown Township records (minus any freeman designation) as early as 1736.

James Albin appears to have prospered in Pennsylvania having left a "considerable estate" at the time of his death in 1752. It is therefore possible that James had not been indentured at all, but instead was apprenticed, eventually working as a tailor from approximately 1736 until his death. As the oldest son, he may have inherited any wealth left by his father and grandfather according to eighteenth century custom thus eliminating any need for him to serve an indenture.[34]

Any contract for an indenture normally would have lasted for perhaps four or five years. However, as minors upon their arrival, the Albin children customarily would have served until they reached the age of maturity, twenty-one or twenty-two for males (until approximately 1733 for William) and eighteen for females.

---

[33]"Tax Indexes, 18th Century Tax Records 1747-1764, A-B", *Chester County, Pennsylvania, Archives and Records Services,* accessed February 28, 2014, http://www.chesco.org/DocumentCenter/View/5405. See also 1765-1766, John "Alban". Freemen in Chester County were an important part of the free labor force of non landholders. On the social ladder, they were above slaves and indentured servants.

[34]See James Albin in Appendix I for a description of his holdings.

Based on the author's examination of indentures in the Early Court
Records of Chester County in 1697, most males indentured at an
early age served until they reached twenty-one. It should be noted
that indentured servitude carried no dishonor as evidenced by the
fact that following their indenture, servants (like John) were welcomed into society as freemen.

William Albin remained illiterate for the rest of his life,
and because he later farmed, a local landowner or possibly his Uncle John may have held any supposed indenture for the boy.[35]
("John Hunter - yeoman farmer" according to Chester County records.) Thus, it appears that William was either not suited to school
or that Hunter or any supposed master neglected the boy's education altogether.

Over the years the Albins in Chester County maintained
their relationship with their Hunter cousins and even the Waynes.
In the will of James Albin dated 1750, the names of Francis
Wayne (son of Anthony Sr.) and James Hunter (son of John) appear.[36] In later years, Albin and Wayne descendants continued
their association. Sharp Delaney (1739-1799), a colonel in the colonial army during the Revolutionary War and the grandson of
Martin and Barbara Albin Delaney of Ireland (William Albin's
other aunt), became a trusted and close assistant to General Mad
Anthony Wayne (grandson of Anthony Wayne Sr., John Hunter's
army comrade). Delaney later became a personal friend to George
Washington and later the executor of General Anthony Wayne's

---

[35]Albin, *Virginia Albins*, 12, 15. The signature is written by another, but the small
circle inside the larger circle with the X is in William's hand:

In the Albin family oral history, one of the few stories passed to me
from both an aunt and my father was that either two or three Albin brothers migrated from Ireland and settled in Virginia. In reality it was three brothers and a
sister who arrived in Pennsylvania, and only one would later settle in Virginia.
[36]"Pennsylvania, Probate Records, 1683-1994," Family Search
https://familysearch.org/pal:/MM9.3.1/TH-1971-28767-13044-
5?cc=1999196&wc=9PM6-92D:268496301,268575301, accessed February 11,
2015, Chester Decedents records 1741-1810 A, images 39 and 46.

will in which Wayne referred to him "my much Esteemed friend."[37]

    In April 1734 twelve years after arriving in Pennsylvania, John Hunter, age sixty-eight, died. Dated January 30, 1734, his will probated on May 19, 1736. Hunter's grave in the churchyard at St. David's Episcopal Church, Radnor is near that of his friend Anthony Wayne.

    Hunter's children, the Albin's cousins, were John, William (whose son was named *Albin* Hunter), Mary, Margaret, George, Peter, Martha, Ann, Elizabeth, and James.[38] Many Hunters continued to reside in Chester County for generations. His wife Margaret Albin Hunter apparently died in Chester County, but no record of her death could be located.

    Of utmost importance to this Albin story is the arrival of young William Albin with the Hunters in 1722. The youthful William, of English heritage but born in Ireland, who grew up absorbing both Irish and English culture and customs, would become the progenitor of this Albin family line in America. Subsequent generations of William's descendants would eventually settle and become landowners in the fertile wilderness of western Virginia, then western Pennsylvania, and eventually Kentucky. Had William for whatever reason remained in a socially immobile Ireland, he likely could not have experienced the same chances for success and land acquisition then available to many of the thousands of other immigrants like himself who would eventually colonize an expanding American landscape. While William emerged to a degree as a self-made man through hard work and drive, his opportunities in America were set in motion because of John and Margaret Hunter's correct choice to include William and his siblings in the Hunter family's planned relocation to America. That pro-

---

[37]In the 1740s-1750s, a youthful George Washington more than likely knew or knew of William Albin and his sons in Frederick County, Virginia, where the Albins then lived. Washington had a lengthy and strong connection to Frederick County where he made land surveys and later maintained his military headquarters in Winchester during the French and Indian War in the late 1750s.

[38]William W. H. Davis, *History of Bucks County, Pennsylvania*, (New York-Chicago: The Lewis Publishing Company, 1905), III, 199-200, 469.

found decision affected the Albin generations described in the following chapters.[39]

The John Hunter House today
405 College Avenue, Newtown Township

Built in 1722 by John Hunter, it may have been the home of the four Albin children for a brief time. Subsequent owners changed parts of the stucco over stone
house, but it has retained numerous old features, eighteen-inch stone walls, original flooring in many rooms, five fireplaces, and hand carved mantels and window
sills. A large addition was added to the house in 1820.

---

[39]See Appendix I for brief accounts of the lives of the other Albin children who
made the voyage with the Hunters.

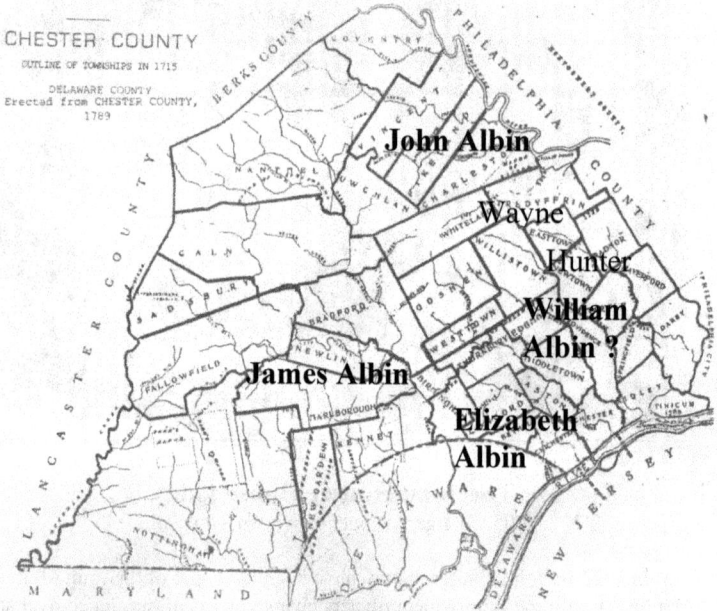

Map 6
Chester County, Pennsylvania, Townships 1715

Between 1722 and 1765, Chester County records reference the location of James Albin in Marlborough Township, John Albin in Charleston Township, John Hunter in Newtown Township, and Anthony Wayne in Easttown Township. William Albin resided possibly in Newtown Township as well. His sister, Elizabeth Albin Bennett, resided in Chester County and is buried in Concord Township.[40]

---

[40]*Chester County Pennsylvania Maps*, accessed March 18, 2015, www.chester.pa-roots.com.

CHAPTER III

William Albin Sr. (1710?-1765)

Pennsylvania and Virginia

The Right Honorable Thomas Lord Fairfax ...Proprietor of the Northern Neck of Virginia ...Do give grant & confirm unto William Albion of Frederick County a certain tract of ungranted land on Red Bud Run, a branch of the Opeckon in the said County....

> From a Deed for 189 acres,
> Thomas Lord Fairfax to
> William Albin, May 14, 1764

Only look to Frederick [County], & see what Fortunes were made by the Hite's & first takers up of those Lands. Nay how the greatest Estates we have in this Colony [Virginia] were made; Was it not by taking up & purchasing at very low rates the rich back Lands which were thought nothing of in those days, but are now the most valuable Lands we possess?

> George Washington to John Posey
> June 24, 1767

Because one may hold here as much property as one wishes, also pay for it when one desires, everybody hurries to take up some property. One may choose where he pleases. The farther one goes, the better it is.

> Letter of Christopher Sower,
> written in 1724, describing Con-
> ditions in Philadelphia and vicin-
> ity[1]

It can be said that Sower's description of Pennsylvania land acquisition in 1724 mirrored that of Virginia's Shenandoah

---

[1]Corbly, *Letters, Journals, & Diaries*, 103.

Valley a decade later. For William Albin, Sower's last sentence proved to be remarkably accurate.

    The life of William Albin during his time in Chester County remains a mystery. As a teenager he probably lived with his siblings temporarily under the care of the Hunters. It is possible he may have served as one of Hunter's redemptionists or became an indentured servant as mentioned earlier. By William's twenty-first birthday, in approximately 1731-1733, his indenture would likely have been fulfilled providing him with a much deserved freedman status after a decade or more of servitude. Subsequently, in either 1734 or 1735, possibly spurred by his new freedom and coinciding with Hunter's death in April 1734, William decided to leave Pennsylvania and set out on his own.

    In search of land and a new life, William chose to move to western Virginia. This relatively unsettled wilderness region stood in stark contrast to both the more populated Chester County and to the eastern part of the Virginia colony with its established plantations and institutions like the House of Burgesses and William and Mary College. In so doing he left his brothers and sister behind in Chester County. His sad farewell to his siblings and the Hunter family probably was accompanied by a sincere dose of gratitude to his Aunt Margaret for having initially taken care of him in Ireland and then in America. As it turned out, William's departure from Chester County marked the last time he would ever see any of these family members.

    William's journey to Virginia probably was not a solo venture. He had would have quite naturally joined other Chester County pioneers also bound for the same destination, the fertile Shenandoah Valley. William may have traveled with his widowed cousin, Elizabeth Hunter Steel, the daughter of John and Margaret Hunter. She is known to have left Chester County about the same time as William, perhaps with her second husband, Josiah Harvey.[2]

---

[2]In her father's will, written in January 1734, Elizabeth Hunter "Steel" is mentioned. Her second husband, Josiah Harvey, must have died in Virginia because on June 14, 1738, in the Hopewell Meeting House (Quaker), Frederick County, Virginia, Elizabeth married for a third time. Her new husband, Benjamin Beeson, was a devout Quaker (as was Elizabeth by then) and the son of one of the "Fa-

The route that members of William's group followed during their epic 250-mile journey from Chester County to Frederick County, Virginia, began just north of the Hunter home in Newtown. It soon linked up with an east-west road from Philadelphia. Whites called it the Great Wagon Road. Originally an old Indian trail, the Native Americans knew it as The Great Warriors Path. By the time of William's journey, it still retained every sign of its rugged backwoods characteristics. In many places it was but one horse track wide. Settlers trekking along the occasionally obstructed pathway were often compelled to hack out crude pathways to ease the burdens of their struggling horses or oxen that pulled thoughtlessly overloaded wooden wagons. Eventually, this challenging route became a more manageable thoroughfare that would bring many thousands of settlers into the western part of Virginia and beyond.

Heading west on The Great Wagon Road the party would have passed through the towns of Lancaster and York in southeastern Pennsylvania. Soon, the group forded the Susquesahanock (Susquehanna) River, then Antietam Creek, and later the Patowmack (Potomac) River. As they left these landmarks behind, Albin and others might have seen the last of any Europeans until they reached their destination. Turning southwest the travelers next experienced the excitement of seeing for the first time the Shenandoah Valley. Its numerous small streams and rivers unfolded picturesquely before them. Bordered by the Allegheny Mountains on the west and the Blue Ridge Mountains on the east, it resembled an open park, green and expansive. The valley acted as the gateway to Fredericktown, later renamed Winchester, Virginia, and the party's endpoint. Depending upon the weather and the obstacles encountered along the way, the journey could have taken two months or longer.

Years later, one of the main organizers of settlements in the area recalled a similar journey he and his followers had undertaken in 1732 (at nearly the same time as William Albin's group)

---

thers of the Quaker Colony" in Frederick County, Richard Beeson. John Weyland, *Hopewell Friends History, 1734-1934, Frederick County, Virginia: Records of Hopewell Monthly Meetings and Meetings Reporting to Hopewell*, (Westminster, Maryland: Heritage Books, 2007), vol. 1, 21. Hopewell is just a few miles north of Winchester near where William Albin would eventually settle.

from Pennsylvania into the Shenandoah Valley where they settled at Opequon Creek (shown as Opeckon on Map 7):

> For the greatest and most difficult parts of the way they [the settlers] were obliged to make roads and once settled obliged to live in their Waggons [sic] till they built small huts to shelter themselves from the inclemency of the weather.[3]

Map 7
A 1736-7 survey map of the Northern Neck of Virginia showing a portion of the "Waggon" Road on which William Albin must have traveled to Winchester

The writer then described how provisions or "necessaries" could scarcely be procured "nearer than from Pennsylvania or Fredericksburg" approximately 200 miles away.

The history of white settlement in the region began in the late 1720s and early 1730s. Quaker land speculators Morgan Bryan and Alexander Ross (a Scotsman by way of Ireland) both of Chester County, along with Joist Hite, and Robert McKay (also a Scottish Quaker) acquired land grants for thousands of acres in the

---

[3] Joist Hite in Warren Hofstra, *The Planting of New Virginia, Settlement and Landscape in the Shenandoah Valley,* (Baltimore: Johns Hopkins University Press, 2006), 98, 116 and Cecil O'Dell, *Pioneers of Old Frederick County, Virginia,* (Westminster, Maryland: Heritage Books, 2007), 19.

Shenandoah Valley provided they could settle a specified number of families there.[4] To encourage settlements that would provide a buffer zone between the French and the rest of the colony, Virginia's Colonial Lt. Governor Sir William Gooch had offered grants to those who promised to live in the Valley. Gooch instructed Ross and Bryan to survey: ". . . one thousand acres of land for each of seventy families brought in by them [Ross and Bryan] to Our said colony and settled upon the lands. . . ."[5]

In accordance with Gooch's directive, Ross and Bryan promised the Virginia government on April 23, 1735, that they could fulfill the requirement of placing each of seventy families on the aforementioned 1,000-acre tracts.[6] Subsequently, these grants procured by Ross and Bryan, along with those of Hite and McKay, resulted in an escalating migration to the virgin Shenandoah Valley throughout the next decade.

Numerous families in the initial Ross/Bryan contingent hailed from Chester County, perhaps as many as twenty-two including both Ross and Bryan. Many of these newcomers were Quakers, resulting in the growth of a large Quaker population in the Lower Shenandoah Valley in Frederick County.[7] Of the original seventy families Ross and Bryan conveyed, only thirty-six patents (grants) issued to thirty-four families have been located. Thus, it is very possible that in those families unaccounted for there were additional Chester County citizens.

Though William Albin is not shown on the list of early patent recipients, it appears he arrived with the so-called seventy families group. Others had arrived to the area earlier, but Wil-

---

[4]Albin, *Virginia Albins,* Chapter 1, i, fn 2. Briefly put, Jost or Joist Hite first obtained 40,000 acres of land in the Valley of Virginia from his cousins John and Isaac VanMeter on August 5, 1731. The Van Meters had previously secured their conditional grants under orders of the governor and council, dated June 17, 1730. (Morgan Bryan's granddaughter Rebecca would later marry Daniel Boone.)
[5]Weyland, *Hopewell Friends History*, 12-13.
[6]Hofstra, *Planting of New Virginia* 29-30. See also, O'Dell, *Pioneers of Old Frederick County, Virginia,* 11. Ross/Bryan had originally promised to settle *100* families.
[7]Weyland, *Hopewell Friends History*, 14-34. See also Grace L. Tracey, and John Philip Dern, *Pioneers of Old Monocacy: The Early Settlement of Frederick County, Maryland, 1721-1743*, (Baltimore: Genealogical Publishing Co., 1987), 87.

liam's group was among the first to settle in Frederick County, an area then situated at the very edge of civilization. William selected a tract of land just west of the meandering Opequon Creek. Issued under the seal of the Colony of Virginia, the patents to this land near and on the Opequon were considered Royal grants supposedly free of any encumbrances of "the Fairfax Family who claimed the land as lords and proprietors of the Northern Neck of Virginia." Significantly, land patents for the identifiable families in the group of seventy were all dated November 12, 1735. Because the process to realize a patent entailed several time consuming steps, William Albin's arrival in Frederick County most likely occurred in 1734 or approximately one year prior to his land purchase.[8]

For William and others, a patent was the last step in a four-part process for acquiring land in some colonies. The first step, entry or claim, meant the buyer had notified the government agency of his intention to purchase and had paid the entry fee. Step two, receiving the warrant, allowed the holder to have the acreage surveyed (step three) which likewise required a fee. After the survey was completed, the grant or patent was made and the deed issued. Therefore, by November 1735, William had likely completed the four-step process, and at age twenty-five, he had become a landowner, a nearly impossible accomplishment had he remained in Ireland. (In Ireland an orphan like William with virtually no chance to obtain land would most likely have remained a landless farmer working for the landowner.) Here in America, then, was William's chance of a lifetime, as landownership meant the difference between potential success and none at all.[9]

---

[8]George W. Vale, *Genealogy of the Vale, Walker, Littler, and Other Related Families,* (Winter Park, Florida: Cowart's Rollins Press, Inc., 1973), 281.

[9]I have based William Albin's arrival date in Frederick County (and hence his departure date from Chester County) on the fact William's neighbor and in law Hugh Parrell had his patent completed on November 12, 1735, with the original survey completed in 1734. Additionally, John Bruce, William's future father-in-law, had a survey completed in 1735 or 1736 on land adjacent to William. In Parrell's case Robert Brooke completed his survey for a tract of 466 acres on October 28, 1734, and then another survey was completed on March 10, 1735, for 402 acres "on the Opequon." (Parrell's land was not located on the Opequon River, but on Red Bud Run.) William's survey, it is assumed, may have commenced on or near those dates as well given the fact that all three men had purchased land in proximity to one another. Further research may uncover his exact

As William soon learned, the source of Opequon Creek lies northwest of today's town of Opequon in Frederick County. It then flows east to Clarke County where it bends and runs north into West Virginia, eventually emptying into the Potomac River. By the time of William's arrival in about 1734, land matters had been set in motion in and around the Opequon at least three years earlier.

As previously mentioned, Albin most likely arrived in Virginia with the Ross/Bryan group. William, perhaps, had become acquainted with Ross during their years in Chester County. He and several Quaker families (*no* Quaker records show any Albins up to this time belonging to that religious group), some were Scotch-Irish or English like himself, also settled on Red Bud (a kind of tree) Run Creek. The creek was one of three tributaries that fed into the larger Opequon Creek about 2 miles east of present day Winchester. Today's real estate agents would have truthfully promoted it then as "a prime location in the heart of the Shenandoah Valley."

Joist Hite, considered the father of early Shenandoah Valley settlement, was also familiar with the area. In 1732 he had stopped at a place called Red Bud (Run) – the same location where William Albin eventually settled - with sixteen Pennsylvania pioneer families before proceeding to another tract situated along Opequon Creek between today's Winchester and Stephens City.[10]

Whether these early settlers and those who followed them into the Valley were aware that their presence was part of Lt. Governor Gooch's grand settlement scheme remains unknown. Surely though, anyone able to read a map of the area in 1732 had to realize that if the rival and expansion-minded French planned an eastward incursion into the English claims in the Shenandoah Valley, Frederick County would lie directly in their path.

---

arrival date in Frederick County, but until then we may assume that William arrived in approximately 1734. See Louis Des Cognet, *English Duplicates of Lost Virginia Land Records*, (Baltimore: Genealogical Publishing Company, 1958), 118 and 120, for information on early land surveys in the Opequon area including those of Parrell and his father-in-law John Calvert (mentioned below).

[10]No author, *Men of West Virginia*, (Chicago: Biographical Publishing Company, 1903), Vol. II, 678, accessed March 23, 2009, http://books.google.com/books?id=eqki8LI8mfUC&printsec=titlepage.

By November 1735, approximately thirteen months after arriving in Frederick County, William resided on the Red Bud Run land *he now owned*. (According to researcher Violet Bruce, by 1735 fifty-four families had settled near Winchester.)[11] William, surprisingly, was able to afford more than a modest sized tract. In fact, he ended up purchasing a total of four separate sites totaling *1,078* acres, at a cost of perhaps three pounds per one hundred acres.[12] Since Albin's acquisition of 1,078 acres exceeded the 1,000 acres specified in the Ross/Bryan agreement with Lt. Governor Gooch for their seventy-family group, his purchase may indicate that William indeed had joined Ross and Bryan upon leaving Chester County.

How William as an orphaned, twenty-five year old former servant or farmer acquired the approximately £30 required for his land purchase and also the additional filing costs is unknown. Perhaps he had reached an agreement with the sellers to finance the balance after making an initial down payment. In his will John Hunter had left his entire estate to his wife and children, so William would have inherited nothing from his uncle.[13] It is also highly unlikely that William's deceased father or grandfather in Ireland had bequeathed money to him and his siblings. Another explanation regarding the source for William's funds may be linked to the end of his supposed indenture. It was customary for the master at the expiration of a contract to provide clothing, land, and a modest amount of cash to the departing servant. Perhaps, then, William had received enough money by the end of his term to help him afford the land parcels on and near Red Bud Run. Regardless of the method by which he had acquired the funds, upon his arrival in Frederick County William had been financially able to make the first land purchase of his life.

---

[11]Violet Bruce, *John Bruce of the Shenandoah*, (Decorah, Iowa: Anundsen Publishing, 1987), 2.

[12]Albin,*Virginia Albins*,14-15. For the price per acre see Edward Price, *Dividing the Land: Early American Beginnings of Our Private Property Mosaic,* (Chicago: University of Chicago Press, 1995), 153, fn 42. The cost today would equal perhaps $2,070.

[13]The will of John Hunter probated on May 19, 1736.

William Albin's neighbors (many of which would become his in-laws when he married) at the time he settled near Winchester were John Bruce (his future father-in-law, whose land was originally surveyed in 1735 or 1736), John Calvert Jr. (of Chester County, Pennsylvania, arrived in 1732, land surveyed 1732, October 1734, and March 1736), Hugh Parrell (surveyed October 1734 and March 1735) and the Carters. Calvert and Parrell were the great grandfather and grandfather respectively of Mary Bruce, (William's future wife), and were, among others, considered "fathers of the Quaker colony" in the Winchester area. Like the Albins the Calvert line hailed from England. However, in the 1660s because of the religious persecution they had suffered there on account of their Quaker beliefs, they had resettled in Ireland – another case of an English family assuming an Irish geographic identity while apparently retaining their English bloodline through subsequent generations.

Not only did familial connections abound within this expanding group, but also geographic links existed between them encompassing Scotland, Ireland, Chester County, Pennsylvania, and now Frederick County, Virginia.[14] Yet, despite this web of family connections between the Bruces, Parrells, and Calverts, none of them were William Albin's actual blood relatives. Hereditarily, William in Virginia stood alone as the only Albin family member present. His cousin Elizabeth Hunter Steel Beeson mentioned above may have moved to North Carolina in the early 1740s and would have been his nearest geographic relative.

---

[14]Hugh Parrell and John Bruce had both lived in the same northern area of Scotland. Parrell married Ann Calvert, the daughter of John Calvert Jr. Their daughter, Sarah Parrell, married John Bruce. The couple produced a daughter, Mary Bruce, who married William Albin, initiating the Scottish link in this Albin family tree. John and Sarah Bruce's other daughter, Ann, was perhaps born in Ireland (1724 or 1725?), though she may have come from Scotland and merely lived in Ireland for a time. See Franklin Ellis, ed., *History of Fayette County, Pennsylvania*, (Philadelphia: L. H. Everts & Co., 1882), 681. Ellis states that Ann Bruce settled in America when she was twelve. That would mean Ann and her parents, John and Sarah Parrell Bruce, arrived in America in approximately 1736 or 1737. (The original survey for Bruce's Frederick County land, however, occurred in 1735 or 1736 according to historian Peggy Joyner.) Yet, another historian suggests the Bruces may have spent time in Chester County prior to their arrival in Virginia. If any connection between the Albins and Bruces in Ireland or Chester County did occur, it is so far undiscovered.

Early settlers like William Albin who arrived in Frederick
County and the Shenandoah Valley, naturally chose the most desirous sites for their homesteads, namely those that bordered a
stream or claimed river access for water and transportation. William would have coveted a location sufficiently clear to allow him
to quickly plant crops and for the grazing of his livestock, thus
avoiding months or even years of hard labor felling trees and removing stumps. At the same time, William would have sought a
tract near a substantial grove of timber for both firewood and for
the wood necessary for the construction of his cabin and a barn.
On Red Bud Run, William had found just such a site.

Located near the spot he had chosen was the timber, and
running through part of William's land and separating it from that
of his father-in-law John Bruce was the water supply (Red Bud
Run). In this markedly pristine location, William Albin established
his Virginia roots, which in the ensuing decades would result in
generations of his descendants inhabiting various areas of Frederick County in and near Winchester.

Life in the Early Winchester Area

At the time of William's arrival, Virginians in the more
civilized areas of the colony regarded the Shenandoah Valley as
Virginia's backcountry. Yet, the Valley's isolation and unspoiled,
untamed uniqueness offered a challenging existence for recent
settlers like William Albin who were determined to create a new
life for themselves and their families. Diversity developed almost
immediately in Frederick County with the arrival of different religions and ethnicities - Quakers, Presbyterians, Germans, Irish,
Scottish, and English. Within this mix were various social levels,
including servants, slaves, freemen, and a few men of means. Life
proved difficult for all, though even harder for some, in the Shenandoah Valley. Long hours spent clearing the land, building
homes, planting crops, and generally creating those items necessary to eke out a living in the wilderness – everything from household articles to clothing and tools – became the settlers' routine.
Not only were the primitive conditions a difficult enough challenge, but citizens also faced a fragile and precarious Indian presence. Every freeman living in the area essentially stood as a sol-

dier first. In contrast to the established planters of Virginia's Tidewater and Piedmont areas, these hardy citizens of the back-country faced day-to-day survival in decidedly demanding surroundings.

Before Hite, Ross, and other speculators arrived, the Senedo tribe (the origin of the word Shenandoah possibly derived from these people) may have inhabited the Valley. They, however, may have been exterminated in battles with the rival Catawbas. Subsequently, a treaty concluded in Albany, New York, in 1722 allowed whites to settle east of the Blue Ridge Mountains (but not in the Shenandoah Valley) while the Iroquois and their allies agreed to remain west of the mountains. The French also inhabited these distant western lands coexisting to a degree with the Indian tribes. By 1732 the Valley had been virtually without human habitation except for wandering Indian hunting parties that roamed its vast prairie in search of the abundant buffalo, elk, deer, and bear. Earlier, in approximately 1728, just before trespassing whites in violation of the Albany Treaty began to arrive, the area along a trail near today's city of Winchester had been used as a Shawnee Indian camping ground or village.

The trickling arrival of a few Germans into the Valley during this time gave way to a flood of Quaker settlers and others, heralding the onset of a dramatic population increase. However, despite this surge, as late as September 1744 the Virginia House of Burgesses considered providing rewards for the killing of wolves in Frederick County, suggesting that the area still retained its wilderness identity.[15]

On December 21, 1738, shortly after William's arrival, members of the Virginia House of Burgesses renamed territories west of the Blue Ridge Mountains. From land previously belonging to other counties, they had formed Frederick County, named after the Prince of Wales. James Wood, the surveyor of neighboring Orange County, chose the site for the new county seat. Rejecting its original designation, Frederick Town, Wood renamed it

---

[15]H.R. McIlwaine, ed., *Journals of the House of Burgesses, 1742-1747, 1748-1749*, (Richmond: Colonial Press, E Waddey, Co., 1909), Vol. 7, 106. Later that month the proposal passed.

Winchester, after his place of birth in England and the site of the old Norman capital there. It thus became the first English city west of the Blue Ridge Mountains. The "city" itself consisted of 26 half-acre lots and three streets situated within its 1,300 acres. At that time Winchester had but two log cabins "near the run."[16]

After settling on Red Bud Run, William Albin married. In about 1738 he and Mary Bruce (the author's fifth great grand-mother), the daughter of Sarah Parrell Bruce and John Bruce, wed in Frederick County.[17] For William the marriage to Mary meant that many of his neighbors on Red Bud Run now became his rela-tives. All - the Bruces, Calverts, Parrells and Albins - lived in close proximity to one another. For at least the next two genera-tions following William Albin and Mary Bruce's marriage, and extending into the nineteenth century, their male descendants would marry female descendants in the Bruce clan.

Mary Bruce was born on June 3, 1715, in Peterhead (ac-cording to Ethel Albin) north of Aberdeen on the coast, in Aber-deenshire, Scotland. Her parents, both born in Scotland, may have come to America by way of Ireland. Upon their arrival the Bruces possibly resided in Chester County, perhaps with their Calvert rel-atives, before settling near Winchester in approximately 1735.[18] However, there is no record of William Albin encountering a young Mary Bruce while he resided in Chester County.

---

[16]Samuel Kercheval, *History of the Valley of Virginia*, (Winchester: Samuel H. Davis Publishing, 1833), 238. Wood's son, James Wood Jr., later became Virgin-ia's fourth state governor in 1796.

[17]Cartmell, *Shenandoah Valley Pioneers*, 9, *places the Bruces' arrival between 1737 and 1740.* See the footnote below for a contrasting arrival year. Some sources indicate William and Mary Albin were married in "Spotsylvania, Freder-ick County." Spotsylvania, between 1722-1734, comprised land that extended into the middle of the Shenandoah Valley. In 1734 it gave rise to Orange County, and in 1738 Frederick County, too, was formed from a portion of Spotsylvania County. Perhaps, then, the Albins were indeed married in Spotsylvania County in 1738 near the time of the formation of Frederick County.

[18]Bruce, *John Bruce of the Shenandoah*, 3, 4. Peggy Joyner, compiler, *Abstracts of Virginia's Northern Neck Warrants and Surveys, Frederick County 1747-1780*, (Portsmouth,Virginia: Peggy Joyner, 1985), Vol. 2, 21. *Joyner writes that the original survey for John Bruce's land occurred in 1735-6.* See Wilmer Kerns, *Historical Records of Old Frederick and Hampshire Counties, Virginia*, (Bowie, Maryland: Heritage Books, 1992), 128 where he mentions the Bruces in Chester County.

The following diagram shows the family of Mary Bruce Albin, William Albin's wife:

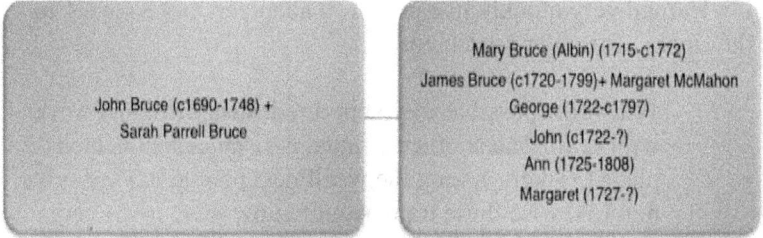

John Bruce (c1690-1748) +
Sarah Parrell Bruce

Mary Bruce (Albin) (1715-c1772)
James Bruce (c1720-1799)+ Margaret McMahon
George (1722-c1797)
John (c1722-?)
Ann (1725-1808)
Margaret (1727-?)

According to the historian Cartmell, the Bruces arrived in Frederick County under the guidance of Hite's sons.[19] Near Winchester John Bruce and his wife Sarah Parrell Bruce claimed approximately 315 acres next to Mary Bruce Albin's grandfather, Hugh Parrell, who originally owned approximately 712 acres. Both families' land adjoined that of William Albin's acreage, which was situated on the south side of Red Bud Run, with a portion extending to the north side. The twenty-five year old William's ownership of 1,078 acres - he was the youngest of the four heads of family - eclipsed that claimed by John Bruce, the Parrell families, and Mary's great grandfather John Calvert who claimed 752 acres.[20] (See Map 8 below.)

Mary Albin's grandfather, Hugh Parrell, lived along a path that ran southwest to northeast near the acreage claimed by the Albins. As recently as just a year or two before William arrived, perhaps in 1732 or 1733, small bands of Catawbas and Delaware had called peacefully at Parrell's house using the same path. By

---

[19]Cartmell, *Shenandoah Valley Pioneers*, 9.
[20]See "Surveys of the Ross Patents" in Albin, *Virginia Albins*, following p. 20. Because his land was first surveyed in 1732, Calvert must have been one of the county's earliest settlers.

1741 this path had been converted to a public road.[21] Moreover, on the west side of Opequon Creek between Albin's and Joseph Carter's land stood a grove of trees and also a limestone spring where 200 or 300 Indians would remain for weeks.[22] Thus, in the early stages of the area's development, William, Mary, and their neighbors had direct, peaceful contact with local Indians.

From the Parrells and the Calverts, William Albin probably learned very quickly just how well adapted Quakers were to the rigors of frontier settlement:

> Whenever possible they supported, sustained, and worked with or for one another. Mutual assistance had helped place Quakers among the wealthiest people in Pennsylvania. Likewise these traits would allow them to do very well in Virginia. Quakers also possessed a profound respect for the original inhabitants of the land [Native Americans].[23]

Connected by marriage and blood, the Albin, Bruce, Parrell, and Calvert families contributed significantly to the early growth of the Winchester community. Their fellow citizens must have respected them as several served in positions of great civic responsibility. Mary Bruce Albin's father John Bruce, a carpenter by trade, built the first stocks and pillory in Winchester in 1744 for a fee of 1,840 pounds of tobacco.[24] John Bruce also operated a successful gristmill (a mill for grinding grain), sawing mills, and fulling mills (mills that cleansed woolen cloth) approximately seven miles northeast of Winchester. (Next to the farmer, the millwright was the most essential member of the community.) Bruce ran the mill with Mary Ross Littler (formerly of Chester County,

---

[21]Hofstra, *Planting of New Virginia*, 31. Hofstra, on this and succeeding pages, generates an excellent discussion of the land and people living at that time along the Opequon and Red Bud Run Creek.

[22]Kercheval, *History of the Valley of Virginia*, 74.

[23]Hofstra, *Planting of New Virginia*, 30.

[24]Cartmell, *Shenandoah Valley Pioneers*, 24. Hofstra writes that John Bruce and his neighbor William McMachen (McMahon) were ordered to "agree with Workmen for Erecting a Pillory Stocks and Whipping post." Hofstra, *Planting of New Virginia*, 183. In that same year, 1744, McMahon's daughter Margaret married James Bruce, John Bruce's son and William Albin's brother-in-law.

Pennsylvania, and the daughter of Alexander Ross), his son George Bruce's mother in law.[25] Later, modern day Brucetown would develop on the site of the mill. John Bruce, with his son James (Mary's Albin's brother), along with Morgan Bryan, John Hite, and Francis Ross served on one of the county's first juries sometime after April 1744, perhaps hearing the case of Jonathan Curtis indicted for "plowing on Sunday." Likewise, Hugh Parrell served on the first grand jury also in 1744. The following year in October 1745, James Bruce earned sixty-four pounds of tobacco for mending seats in the courthouse.[26] Later, county officials placed William Albin on several occasions and his brothers-in-law George and James Bruce in dozens of other instances in charge of road and bridge construction projects at various sites within the county over a span of many years.

Various religions were represented among these early settlers and also within the Albin and Bruce clans in Frederick County. Though Mary Bruce Albin's grandparents, the Parrells and the Calverts, were Quakers, her father was a member of the Church of Scotland (Presbyterian).[27] William Albin may also have been of that faith. Because William's sons later became involved in (Methodist) church life, we may assume that as parents William and Mary must have promoted a religious atmosphere within the family, practicing their faith when time and circumstance allowed. Similar to their Quaker neighbors, Presbyterians in the Opequon area had worked quickly in the early years to establish "meeting places."[28] Later, Presbyterians built one such place in Winchester in close proximity to the Bruce and Albin cabins.

Despite an absence of any specific description of the Albin residence on Red Bud Run, an imperfect image of their cabin may still be gleaned from a variety of sources. In 1738 a female observer noted just "two small log cabins" existed in Winchester

---

[25]O'Dell, *Pioneers of Old Frederick County*, 246. George Bruce (1722-c1797) married Rachel Littler. The mill with a tavern was first called New Design. Weyland, *Hopewell Friends*, 33.

[26]Cartmell, *Shenandoah Valley Pioneers*, 25.

[27]Albin, *Virginia Albins*, 3. John Bruce's wife, Sarah Parrell, may have been a Quaker like her father and grandfather.

[28]Hofstra, *Planting of New Virginia*, 185.

and "those near the run", so the Albin's cabin, probably built before 1740, would have been one of the earliest in the area.[29] According to Hofstra,

> Dwellings along the Opequon [and on Red Bud Run] stood about every one-quarter to one-half mile apart on tracts that were all roughly rectangular. Archaeological remains of foundation stones or earthen mounds indicate that these structures were small, approximately square, and between sixteen to twenty feet on a side [400 square feet or less]. They were by all accounts single room cabins.[30]

An area resident at the turn of the century (1800) provided another description of these early structures while observing some of the remaining cabins from William's time:

> The first houses erected by the primitive settlers [of the 18th century] were log cabins, with covers of split clapboards, and weight poles to keep them in place. They were frequently seen with earthen floors; or if wood floors were used they were made of split puncheons, a little smoothed with the broad axe.[31]

Conversely, Hofstra writes that "Despite the log cabin myth of the early frontier, many of the earliest structures were built of stone," many with thatched roofs.[32] The abundance of limestone in the Winchester area made it feasible for settlers (like William Albin) to replicate the stone structures they knew in England, Ireland, or Scotland. But, regardless of whether the Albin home was constructed of stone or logs, it offered shelter but few conveniences.

Most pioneers made do with "windows" that were often nothing more than greased paper. Such a situation presented a challenge to inhabitants during the long, cold Virginia winters. If

---

[29]Sperry, cited in Kercheval, *History of the Valley of Virginia*, 238fn.
[30]Hofstra, *Planting of New Virginia*, 38.
[31]Kercheval, *History of the Valley of Virginia*, 151.
[32]Hofstra, *Planting of New Virginia*, 38.

window glass could be afforded and imported, it had to come from the East. Likewise, a one room, 400 foot square cabin housing as many as seven people made life all the more difficult. In the case of William and Mary's dwelling, expansion beyond these small dimensions described by Hofstra may have occurred out of necessity, as their family continued to grow in the decade after their cabin was first constructed.

Surrounding the house would have been "a patchwork of small fields" containing gardens or crops. Seen growing in the Opequon area were wheat, rye, barley, corn, and oats. On lands already cleared, roamed sheep, cattle, hogs, and horses in unfenced meadows.[33]

Outdoor wells and Red Bud Run Creek provided water for the Albins and most of their neighbors living in the vicinity.

Near the Albins were the mills of the Carters and Lewis Neill. In addition to the their flourmill, located on Abraham's Creek where it drained into the Opequon River, the Carters also operated a distillery on the same site, on the west side of the Opequon River. It provided them with the alcohol they served to area residents in their tavern.[34] Because of the proximity of the Carters to his land, William likely had his grain milled there, perhaps enjoying a drink at the tavern before returning home.[35]

Throughout Frederick County by 1744, tobacco had become a significant crop (as it had in the more established parts of the colony) and citizens often used it as legal tender. Many residents even paid their annual taxes in units of tobacco, which would remain an accepted form of exchange in Virginia until 1794. Mary Albin's grandfather Parrell in 1744 and William's brother-in-law James Bruce in 1757 along with dozens of Frederick County's taxpayers appear on County Clerk Fees Lists paying

---

[33]Ibid.
[34]Weyland, *Hopewell Friends History*, 169.
[35]Neill's mill, situated upstream near where Red Bud Run spilled into the Opequon, provided residents living to the north of William Albin's property with another convenient site to have their grains milled.

levies in tobacco in lieu of hard currency.[36] William Albin is also known to have grown it as a cash crop as confirmed by a court order that specified he repay a debt with 125 pounds of tobacco. The growth of tobacco as a cash crop in Frederick County resulted in a corresponding reliance on slave labor. Though slavery existed in Frederick County at the time of William Albin's arrival, *initially* the use of slaves had been minimal as compared to the older counties in Virginia's easternmost areas. However, to claim that his arrival in Virginia marked William's first exposure to slave labor would probably be mistaken.

Growing up in the 1720s in Chester County, William probably had little direct contact visual or otherwise with Negro slaves due to their limited number. In fact, during the period 1729-1758 only 104 slaves had resided in the entire county.[37] However, during the 1730s more residents began using slave labor, so William may have occasionally observed slaves working at various jobs in and around Newtown in the years just prior to his departure for Virginia (a sight that he would never have witnessed in Ireland).[38]

By the time William arrived in Frederick County, slavery had just begun its spread west over the mountains and into the Shenandoah Valley. The irrepressible institution brought wealth to slave owners much like indentured servitude had done earlier in colonial Virginia's history. William should not have been surprised, therefore, to find some of his new neighbors in Frederick County utilizing slave labor in their fields along Red Bud Run and

---

[36]"1744 Frederick County Clerk Fees", *VAGenWeb*, accessed February 16, 2014, http://www.genealogenie.net/vafreder/1744.shtml and "1757 Frederick County Clerk Fees", http://www.genealogenie.net/vafreder/1757.shtml.
On these extensive tax lists for 1744 and 1757, William Albin's name does not appear though he resided in Frederick County at the time. Parrell's and Bruce's names are shown with each entry followed by their assessed tax fees listed in pounds of tobacco. Clothing and sundries also played a vital role in the Valley's ongoing exchange based economy.
[37]Carol Berkin, *First Generations: Women in Colonial America*, (New York: Hill and Wang, 1996), 98. According to Berkin Quakers owned most of these slaves.
[38]Gary Nash, *Freedom by Degrees: Emancipation in Pennsylvania and Its Aftermath*, (New York: Oxford University Press, 1991), 67. While William's uncle John Hunter probably made use of indentured servants, it is doubtful he owned slaves.

elsewhere. Some like William McMachen, William Albin's neighbor to the west, claimed only house slaves.[39] The prominent James Wood Sr., Winchester's founder, its first court clerk, and an active political figure in Frederick County, owned three slaves.[40]

Moreover, it was not unusual *in the early years* for several of Frederick County's Quakers, who maintained a strong presence in the Valley, to claim slaves. One of the county's more prominent residents, none other than the Quaker Alexander Ross a "founding father of the Valley", held slaves from an early date. Nevertheless, other Quakers avoided owning slaves altogether, and later a new generation of Quakers in the Valley and elsewhere gradually came to view the institution of slavery as contrary to their beliefs.[41]

In contrast, during the ensuing years while Quaker aversion toward slavery steadily grew, other Frederick County non-Quaker planters, driven by the lure of greater profits, expanded their land holdings. In turn, the county's increasing number and size of its tobacco farms and plantations required additional slave labor, a formula that imitated a trend that had already developed in eastern Virginia and the established agricultural areas in other Southern colonies. By 1754 a Frederick County census recorded a white population of nearly 8,700 and 680 slaves.[42] But, slavery and tobacco production in the grain and livestock oriented Shenandoah Valley did not reach the levels seen in eastern Virginia.

---

[39]Paul Heinegg, *Free African Americans of North Carolina, Virginia, and South Carolina from the Colonial Period to about 1820,* (Baltimore: Genealogical Publishing Co., 2005), Vol. 1, 658. Specifically, McMachen owned Rosamond Hughes, and her two young children, a mulatto girl named Elizabeth born about 1745 and Luke born about 1740.

[40]Wood claimed a black woman, Sat, and her two infant mulatto children. Hofstra, *Planting of New Virginia,* 201.

[41]Weyland, *Hopewell Friends History,* 16. In his will, Ross requested that his slaves not be sold but held in the family.

[42]Hofstra, *Planting of New Virginia,* 221. The census included a count of Frederick County's titheables, those Virginians in the seventeenth and eighteenth century who paid one of the taxes levied by the General Assembly. In colonial Virginia, the tax could be a poll tax assessed on any free white males, African American slaves, or Native American servants (both male and female) sixteen or older. Owners and masters paid these taxes assessed on their slaves and servants.

Many new arrivals emigrating from Pennsylvania into the Shenandoah Valley had an aversion to slavery based on their religious and/or personal beliefs. William Albin's reason for not holding slaves may have fit into one or both categories. We may assume that though William was not rich, his purchase of more than 1,000 acres on Red Bud Run suggests that had he chosen to do so he could have afforded to acquire at least a small number of slaves. Perhaps his faith and his time spent as a supposed indentured servant in Chester County had weighed heavily on him influencing his decision to avoid any use of slave labor.

Furthermore, William's rejection of slavery launched a lasting and admirable legacy in the Albin family. William's descendants, regardless of the slaveholding colonies (and later the states) in which they lived, spurned slavery despite the presence of significant numbers of slaveholders in their communities. During the Civil War, William's grandson and a non slaveholder living in a slave state, Kentucky, but too old to serve in the active Army, sided with the anti-slavery North and joined his local Home Guard.

In the years after their marriage, William and Mary produced five children, all males. In either 1739 or 1740, their first son John was born. (The traditional naming pattern of the first-born son usually receiving the given name of his father is absent.) Four additional sons were born in the ensuing years: Robert in 1743, William (Jr.) in 1746, James in c1756, and finally George in 1758.[43] Though they were the first of this Albin family's descendants born in America, all five were of English and Scottish blood.

William had seen to the construction of the house (likely with the help of his neighbors as was the custom on the frontier) before the children were born. Still, additional tasks accomplished so easily and thoughtlessly today consumed much of the family's time. Preparing the soil for planting without a plow (they probably dragged a knotty log over the earth), sowing the seed, stitching clothing from skins, laundering, making soap, shoes, furniture, and chopping the endless supply of wood needed for warmth and

---

[43]Albin, *Virginia Albins*, 20. No other Albins are known to have resided in the Winchester area during this time.

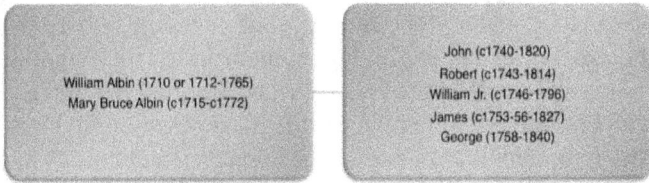

William Albin (1710 or 1712-1765)
Mary Bruce Albin (c1715-c1772)

John (c1740-1820)
Robert (c1743-1814)
William Jr. (c1746-1796)
James (c1753-56-1827)
George (1758-1840)

cooking were but some of the essential duties confronting frontier families. Moreover, the county's adult male family members were required to assist in building roads for the common good.

Backwoods conditions on rural eighteenth century American farms dictated that pioneer women be possessed of a hardy constitution. The expectation for Mary Bruce Albin would have been no different. The burdens Mary and other pioneer women faced amounted to spending hours of repetitious daily toil - cooking, cleaning, sewing, mothering, and perhaps tending to the livestock - regardless of the season or their health on any given day. Such a tiring regimen was bound to wear down even the strongest constitution. Perhaps if a picture of Mary did exist, it might show a rather tired looking woman in a crude, homemade dress of no particular color, perhaps with two or more children at her feet, pitchfork in hand, with chickens feeding on the grain she had recently scattered in the dirt in front of the family's windowless and rudimentary one room log cabin.

Education for the five Albin children, as for most of the area's youngsters, was not an option. Schools and teachers were mostly non-existent in Winchester's early years. Certainly the illiterate William Sr. could not have been expected to further the boys' book learning. Mary, even if she could read and write, would have found it difficult to provide even a rudimentary education for her five children given the formidable and time consuming daily labor burden she faced. In addition, the boys would have been expected to help out with the vital, everyday tasks associated with farm life on the family's 1,000-acre homestead. As a result, survival inevitably won out over education. A will created in 1814 bearing their second oldest son Robert's mark shows that he remained illiterate for his entire life. It is safe to assume that each of Robert's four brothers also lacked the ability to read and write. As they matured the five boys, of necessity, would have become expert woodsmen. Living on the frontier, their hunting and fishing skills would provide food and clothing (from the animal's fur) for the Albin family. Furthermore, each of the boys most likely became highly proficient horsemen and one, William's youngest son George, later became an express rider for George Washington in the early stages of the Revolutionary War.

With families like the Albins, Bruces, and Calverts arriving steadily during the late 1730s and into the 1740s, the population of Frederick County increased rapidly. By 1745 the number of settlers had risen to 4,300. By 1754 that total had more than doubled to 9,300 (counting slaves). Nine years later, at the end of the French and Indian War, the count had risen to 11,000 residents.

Hofstra suggests that by 1746 Winchester (Frederick Town) may not have conformed to the popular notion of the materially backward frontier town. While trading between neighbors became common, the local "store" where customers could find an array of goods like broadcloth, soap, claret, snuff, sugar, silk, shalloon (a lightweight wool fabric), and local country produce served, but not always reliably, the area's residents.[44] At what exchange rate these goods, many of which had to be imported from eastern Virginia, "sold" for is difficult to determine in the area's barter-based economy. Whether or not the Albins could have availed themselves of the more luxurious items offered is unknown.

In addition to local stores, the Winchester town charter of 1752 authorized trading fairs twice yearly.[45] Since roads to the eastern parts of the colony could not accommodate wagons, early Shenandoah Valley farmers rarely were able to trade with tidewater and piedmont Virginia.[46] The trading fairs served to fill this void. Opening on the third Wednesday of June and October, the fairs lasted two days. Traveling merchants and peddlers would

---

[44]Hofstra, *Planting of New Virginia*, 192.
[45]Frederic Morton, *The Story of Winchester, Virginia, The Oldest Town in the Shenandoah Valley,* (Winchester: Shenandoah Publishing House, 1925), 50.
[46]Later, in the 1750s and 1760s, roads linking the Shenandoah Valley to eastern Virginia were constructed.

gather at specific sites in Winchester eager to sell their wares. In turn, enthusiastic locals willing to buy, trade, or simply browse met the vendors at their stalls. One can imagine an excited Albin family walking or riding horseback the two or three miles into Winchester on the specified Wednesday or Thursday anticipating what the peddlers might have to offer. Not only was it a shopping and trading trip, but the fair also offered opportunities for neighborly socialization and the exchange the news of the day. These fairs remained a regular feature of Winchester life and helped make the city a commercial center of the Shenandoah Valley.

Despite this hint of civilization, remote Winchester during the 1740s and early 1750s was not to be confused with cities like Willamsburg in "old" Virginia. As Hofstra writes, Winchester possessed "only a scattering of stone and log buildings... streets obstructed by stumps, and many uncleared private lots" with perhaps sixty poorly built houses and a city population of only a few hundred as late as 1753.[47] But, with the growth of town and country settlements like Winchester, and as others emerged on the expanding frontier, collectively they came to epitomize the notion of Middle America.

As the population increased, though, there came additional civic responsibilities for William and his neighbors. In November 1743, Frederick County's first court official was sworn in, and in September 1745 William Albin declared himself titheable (taxable): "On the motion of William Albon [sic], it's ordered that he be added to the List of Titheables for this year."[48] Soon, these titheables were called on to provide labor for road construction and other public works projects within the county.

The county government, to serve such purposes, issued "Road orders". These orders directed individuals, usually under the authority of one of their neighbors, to "open" a road from one place to another. By becoming part of the historical record, the road orders provide not only an indispensable chronology of pro-

---

[47]Hofstra, *Planting of New Virginia*, 193.
[48]Frederick County, Virginia, *Court Order Book* I (1743-1745) September 3, 1745, cited in Albin, *Virginia Albins*, Chapter 2, iii, fn 16. See also page 14. Three years later in August 1748, David Crockett, grandfather of the legendary woodsman and adventurer of the same name, declared himself a titheable in Frederick County.

gress in Frederick and other counties, but also they present the opportunity to view the fascinating minutiae that constituted daily community life. Contained among the first Road Orders cited were the names of William Albin and two others who were tasked in 1746 with connecting a road from Opequon Creek to the recently constructed Winchester Courthouse. (William had no way to foresee that in the coming years he would often make the trip from his home to the Courthouse using this road he helped construct.) The following road orders were transcribed from the originals:[49]

> Ordered that . . . Hugh Perill [Parrell] William Albin & Simeon Taylor View Mark & lay of[f] a Road from the part of the said Creek [Opequon] . . . the Nearest & best Way to the Courthouse & that they make report thereof to the next Court. [7 May 1746]

> It is ordered that William Albin John Parrell Peter Shipley [Shepler] and Joseph Parrell or any three of them being first sworn do View the Ground from Lewis Neills mill into Perry's road and make [a] Report of the Conveniences and Inconveniences attending opening a Road from the said Mill to the said Road at the Next Court. [2 November 1763]

At its next meeting, the court appointed William Albin the overseer of this 1763 road project with instructions that the titheables on each side of the proposed road work under Albin's guidance.[50]

---

[49]G. Luckman and A.B. Miller, *Frederick County Road Orders 1743-1772*, (Richmond: Virginia Department of Transportation, 2005), Accessed March 20, 2017, http://www.virginiadot.org/vtrc/main/online_reports/pdf/05-r32.pdf, Keyword-"Albin", 20, 119, 120. The road orders begin in 1743 the same month as the Frederick County courthouse and records system was established. Peter Shipley (Peter Shepler, 2 November 1763) is actually a neighbor and the future brother-in-law of William Albin Jr. The Parrells, of course, are William's in-laws through his wife Mary's family. The names of William's brothers-in-law George and James Bruce also appear many times in these road orders over the years.
[50]Ibid., 3 January 1764.

In 1748 an unspecified illness seems to have struck Frederick County resulting in the deaths of many notable early Frederick County settlers. Among those succumbing, perhaps in an epidemic of smallpox, in the Winchester area were Abraham (his mother was a Calvert) and Ann Hollingsworth, Dr. Daniel Hart (one of the earliest physicians in the Shenandoah Valley), Josiah Ballinger (an associate of Alexander Ross and with Ross an early promoter of Quaker settlement in the Valley) Alexander Ross, his sons David and John, Ross's son in law John Littler, George Littler, Richard Beeson Jr., Morgan Bryan's wife, and many others. For the Albins death struck particularly close as Hugh Parrell, Mary Albin's grandfather died in October 1748, and prior to that, on September 23, Mary's father (and William's father-in-law) John Bruce passed away.

In his will, dated November 4, 1747, John Bruce bequeathed to his son James Bruce his 150 acre plantation, to his other son George another 150 acres of "ye remaining tract of land" and to "my son-in-law William Albin my suit of linen clothes and to my daughter . . . Mary Albin ten shillings [approximately $32 in the year 2000] of currency . . . to be paid in grain."[51]

Financial Hardship and War

In 1747 Thomas Lord Fairfax returned to Virginia from England. The aftermath of his arrival would soon cast a pall over many of the county's landowners similar to the gloom that lingered countywide during the dying of 1748. By 1749 Fairfax resided in the Shenandoah Valley, a few miles west of the Shenandoah River. His arrival in Virginia was the culmination of years of effort he had devoted to reclaiming disputed tracts of Virginia land. In Virginia Fairfax had legally reaffirmed his right to more

---

[51]Weyland, *Hopewell Friends History*, 16. See also, Albin, *Virginia Albins,* 5. An outbreak of smallpox struck Williamsburg in 1747 and continued into 1748. In May 1748 in Augusta County, only seventy-five miles south of Frederick County, "Eleanor Rutledge not summoned as a witness because she was where the smallpox was." No author, *Chronicles of the Scotch-Irish Settlement in Virginia,* (Augusta County, Va: Commonwealth Printing Company, 1912), I, 299. John Bruce is the author's sixth great grandfather. See Appendix II for the text of Bruce's entire will.

than 5,000,000 acres up to the North Branch of the Potomac as a result of charters and decrees set forth by Kings Charles II and James II of England.[52] Fairfax soon commissioned surveyors, including a youthful George Washington, to survey his expansive holdings.[53]

For William Albin and dozens of other local Winchester landowners residing on the disputed tracts, Fairfax's claim inflicted a financial gash in their collective economic souls. Imagine the panic and frustration felt among these people, for the land William and others thought they owned was now the property of another! And, Fairfax now lived in Virginia and the Winchester area, all the while supervising the prosecution of his claims. As a result of the Fairfax claim, in the years 1746 and 1747 William and Mary Albin suffered a severe financial setback the lingering effects of which would haunt them for years.

The solution for all the affected settlers, though extremely disagreeable, was very simple, either repurchase the disputed land or lose it and move on. William, like many of his neighbors, relatives, and Quaker friends, elected to pay the filing fees to receive warrants from Fairfax. Next, the land would have to be resurveyed which would result in a further expense.[54] William obtained warrants for four plots of land:

> The first plot for which he obtained a warrant (copy missing) was for [400] acres on Red Bud Run and joining Hugh Parrell. He then sold this plot to Thomas Sperry/Perry who had it surveyed 14th March 1750-1751. The

[52]Jost Hite, one of the original Frederick County settlers, eventually sued Fairfax to recover his land. The first judgment, favored Fairfax, but Hite appealed. In 1786, a judgment was returned in favor of the Hites. A final settlement was reached around 1802, but by then all of the principals in the case had died.
[53]Washington and the others began the surveying project in 1747 and completed it one year later. Washington would continue to maintain a survey office in Winchester for the next seventeen years. During that time he was elected to the House of Burgesses in 1758 representing Frederick County. Both William Albin and Washington had dealings with Lord Fairfax. Because of Washington's nearly two-decade association with the citizens of Winchester, it is highly probable that both he and Albin met. Later, General Washington would select William's son George as a member of his personal bodyguard during the Revolutionary War.
[54]Albin, *Virginia Albins*, 14-15.

second warrant was dated February 15, 1752 for 200 acres, which he sold to James Agen/Hagen, who in turn sold it to George Meret, who had it surveyed on March 26, 1754. The survey showed 239 acres. The third plot was for [250] acres, lying just northeast of the first. This warrant dated March 27, 1753, he sold to Earnest Andrews who had it surveyed on 26 March 1754. These plots surrounded on three sides the 189 acres William kept for himself, [presumably the site of the Albin cabin] (Map 8).[55]

Thus, out of the original 1,078 acres he had purchased on his arrival in Frederick County some years earlier, William now could afford to retain only a mere 189 acres, having sold the remainder to presumably help finance his "repurchase" from Fairfax. Albin received the patent or grant for this last remaining plot years later on May 14, 1764, from Lord Fairfax for "189a[acres] on Red Bud [Run]."[56] The deed reveals that John Bayliss surveyed the land, and since the document is dated 1764 we know it represents William's repurchase of the land due to Fairfax's claim. Extinguished now was Albin's original dream of providing a substantial legacy of land, perhaps 200 acres, to *each* of his five sons.

William and others had been compelled to pay Fairfax for the land itself and also for the cost of the second survey. But in addition Fairfax similarly assessed William and the other deed holders a "quit rent" of approximately one shilling per 50 acres yearly due on the feast day of St. Michael (September 29). Though the fee represented a very nominal amount, it was a payment nonetheless.[57] The deed also specified that if William failed to pay the quit rent for two consecutive years, Fairfax could reclaim the land.[58] Thus, Fairfax had just regranted the land, then sold it back

---

[55]Ibid., 14, and Joyner, *Abstracts of Virginia's Northern Neck Warrants and Surveys,* 1, 3, and 122. Ethel Winifred Albin mistakenly records the size of the third plot as 256 acres.

[56]Albin, *Virginia Albins*, 15,

[57]About $6.40 in today's money for the 100 acres and a bit less for the eighty-nine acres. A quit rent is a fixed rent paid by a freeman in lieu of services required of him.

[58]*Land Office Patents and Grants/Northern Neck Grants and Surveys, Virginia,* "Library of Virginia", accessed November 1, 2015, http://lva1.hosted.exlibrisgroup.com/F/6GU12171GVMMTRJU2SXPJP7YDG9P

to the original purchasers who would not own it entirely because of the quit rent.[59]

As a result of this unforeseen development, by the late 1740s and early 1750s, the fortunes of William Albin, his family, and many of his neighbors had taken a fateful turn for the worse. Albin's unexpected expenses meant that any wealth, particularly in land, he had worked so hard to gain in the more than two decades since arriving from Ireland had now been irreversibly diminished.

If his monetary problems created by the Fairfax claims were not enough, William found himself having to fend off money demands from a different source. In October 1751 the illiterate William Albin had co-signed a note for a William Taylor. Apparently Taylor had purchased some buckram (a coarse cotton fabric heavily sized with glue and used for stiffening garments and in bookbinding), thread, and other items. When the note came due, Taylor could not be located. As a result, the court held William, as the co-signer, responsible for the entire repayment. Unfortunately for William, the note was almost twice the cost of the items purchased.

3CTSI97YM2IJY78P3U2ANV-61136?func=find-b&request=william+albion&find_code=WRD&adjacent=N&x=36&y=6, s.v. William Albion, 1764. This website is an excellent source for eighteenth century Virginia deeds and countless other Virginia historical papers.

[59]Long after Fairfax died, conflicting claims to his land reached the United States Supreme Court in 1816, when it agreed to hear arguments in *Martin v. Hunter's Lessee,* one of the landmark cases in United States legal history. In brief, Thomas Bryan Martin, a Fairfax heir, claimed he was the rightful owner of a grant to the Fairfax land in Virginia known as the Northern Neck. On the other side, David Hunter claimed the land, as Virginia had confiscated it during the American Revolution as loyalist holdings (Fairfax was a loyalist) and ownership had passed to Hunter. In a unanimous decision, the Supreme Court ruled in favor of Martin. Justice Story declared that states (in this case Virginia) must recognize the authority of the Supreme Court, and if that were not so then each state would be able to interpret the Constitution as it pleased. Story's ruling thereby asserted the landmark principle establishing the primacy of federal over state courts.

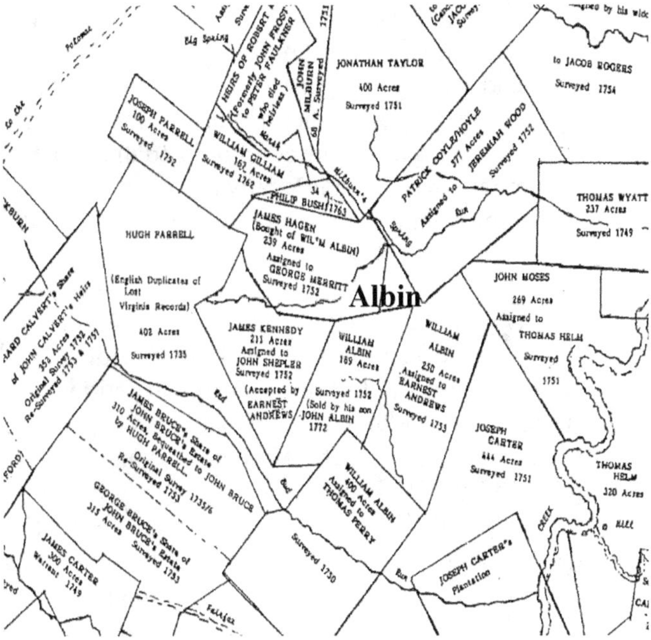

Map 8
Original Surveys of Patent Land on Red Bud Run and the Opequon, Frederick
County, Virginia, granted by the Proprietor Thomas Lord Fairfax, 1750-1764.
Albin's four parcels are shown along with those of the Bruces, Hugh Parrell, and
John Shepler. Copyright 1989 by Ethel Albin

William subsequently filed suit against Taylor. The court
ruled on February 14, 1752: "William Albin vs. William Taylor on
attachment (William was trying to obtain a judgment to attach
Taylor's wages?), this suit ordered dismissed neither party appearing."[60] Why William had failed to appear for a hearing regarding a
lawsuit he had initiated is unknown.

Four months later, on June 3 and again on June 4 the court
heard that Taylor owed William 10 pounds "current money" but
he (Taylor) had "absconded" and could not be prosecuted.[61] Ap-

---

[60]Albin, *Virginia Albins*, 16. Before this October 1751 court appearance, William
had been called as a witness in a murder case on February 16, 1751. Robert Bird
had stood accused of "feloniously murdering his own child", but he was found
not guilty.
[61]Ibid.

proximately 1 month later, on July 7, 1752, William learned to his dismay that Taylor was deemed an insolvent debtor (bankrupt) and that he now resided in "gaol" (jail) because of another lawsuit brought against him by yet another debtor. Taylor swore to his insolvency, and subsequently the court ordered the sheriff to release him from jail. With Taylor legally absolved of the debt, approximately eight months later attention refocused on William Albin:

> Fryday [sic] the 9th day of March 1753. William Cocks [debtor] agt [against] William Taylor and William Albin, defts. [defendants]. On petition. The sheriff having returned that he had left a copy of the summons at the deft. Albin's usual place of abode [on Red Bud Run] and the sdd [said] deft. being solemnly called & *failing to appear* [italics mine] the plt [plaintiff] in court made oath to his accounts ft[?] the deft. for four pounds eight shillings & three pence half penny court money [fees]. It is thereupon considered by the court that these pltf. recover agt thee deft Albin the sd sum of four pounds eight shillings & three pence half penny curt [current] money and costs and the said deft in mercy & the sheriff having returned the deft. Taylor not found, this suit against him is ordered to be dismisd[sic].[62]

William was now held responsible for the entire debt, approximately $288 in year 2000 currency, a considerable sum considering William's tenuous financial position. Perhaps this debt had compelled William to sell the 256-acre plot he owned on Red Bud Run. On March 27, 1753, just 18 days after the court's decision, he sold a warrant for that acreage in the easternmost section of his holdings to Earnest Andrews for an unknown amount (see above). That transaction, however, did not cause William to cease attempting to raise money through the courts during these difficult times.

---

[62]Albin, *Virginia Albins*, 16.

Approximately five months later, on "Saturday, the 11th day of August, 1753", Albin reappeared before a Frederick County judge. This time the court awarded him a judgment for an unspecified reason in the amount of four pounds and court costs against James Lemon, who had failed to appear. Later, Lemon did appear, but by that time it was too late and the court refused to hear his argument. Apparently, Lemon continued to press the matter, but he never could produce any evidence to support his case. His last petition against William was dismissed because Lemon had died in the interim.[63]

Just as William's financial situation seemed to be improving, one of Mary Albin's relatives, Richard Calvert (1727-1770), her grandmother Ann Calvert's nephew, appeared in court on September 4, 1753, with a claim against William. Apparently Calvert had appeared for five days (!) as a witness for William in the Lemon case and he was now seeking compensation (strained family relations?). The court agreed: "It is ordered that the said William pay him [Calvert] one hundred twenty five pounds of tobacco, the same according to law."[64]

Eleven months later William Albin made yet another court appearance, this time as a plaintiff against William Cocks, a prominent local citizen and soldier and the same man who had won a judgment against William back in March 1753. On August 8, 1754,

> William Albin produced a certificate under the [h?]and of William Cocks, Gent, dated the 22nd day of June 1754 for taking up a servant belonging to Samuel Hammon of [nearby] Prince William County about ten miles from his said master's house and the said William Albin having made the oath that he has received no satisfaction for his said claim it is ordered to be certified.[65]

By initiating this claim in a court, Albin was pursuing apparently the only remedy possible to recover his reward for securing the runaway indentured servant. At the same time, William's

---

[63] Ibid.
[64] Ibid.
[65] Ibid.

efforts to obtain his payment reveal the financial impact his mounting debts had produced. The record does not indicate what settlement, if any, Albin received for his latest encounter with the Frederick County legal system.

William Albin's precarious financial situation and his numerous court appearances were not unique during this "Fairfax" time. Records show that unpaid debt suits were common in Frederick County courts. Neighbors sued neighbors for debts large or small.[66] In short, no one had any money except Lord Fairfax.

In the wake of the Fairfax's successful claim, citizens were scrambling to save the land they had received in prior grants, and every shilling mattered. Adding to their income woes was the difficulty in getting their money crops to markets inland. In Frederick County transportation difficulties had always existed due to poor roads and insufficient water routes, but then with the onset of a more serious menace the problem only worsened.

As Albin and others were struggling to stay financially solvent, British relations with their French adversaries in North America worsened. Along the exposed Pennsylvania and Virginia borders, tensions rose between these two competing world superpowers. Soon, Virginia and the other twelve colonies would experience one of the most devastating wars in North American history.

---

[66]Ibid., *Virginia Albins*, 7, 17.

Original Deed to William "Albion" (Albin) - May 14, 1764, from Lord Fairfax
for 189 acres on Red Bud Run.[67]

In early April 1754, twenty-one year old George Washington, Lord Fairfax's trusted surveyor and a Winchester resident, embarked on a sensitive military expedition. Acting on instructions from the British government to resist French encroachments in the Ohio Valley just west of Virginia, Virginia's Governor Robert Dinwiddie had sent Major (later Colonel) Washington and

[67]*Land Office Patents and Grants/Northern Neck Grants and Surveys, Virginia,* "Library of Virginia", 273.

William Albin Sr.

a group of soldiers from the Virginia Regiment on a critical mission to the French commander in western Pennsylvania. Acting as Dinwiddie's emissary, Washington was to convey to the French a protest against any incursions they might make into the disputed territory. One thing led to another, and in July Washington's force met a French detachment in the forest near present-day Pittsburgh (then Ft. Duquesne) in a brief but bloody engagement. Days later, outnumbered and far from any immediate help, Washington surrendered to the French on July 4, 1754.[68] By firing on the French, Washington had unwittingly triggered a bloody conflict between France and England - the French and Indian War. Later, English politician Horace Walpole wrote, "The volley fired by a young Virginian in the backwoods of America set the world on fire."

As a result of Washington's engagement, hostilities continued for two tumultuous years but remained local until 1756 when the French and English governments declared war on each other, formally launching a final battle for North American supremacy. Known in European history as the Seven Years War (1756-1763), the conflict expanded into a world war that threatened, from our perspective, Britain's North American colonies for its duration. Ultimately, the war's impact on the global balance of power, the map of North America, and the lives of not only British and French colonists but also those of the Native American tribes involved in the struggle would be monumental.

The onset of war meant dire peril for the thousands of British colonists living in or near the western "buffer areas" as they were in the path of any invading French and Indian forces. Locally, fear of the French and their Indian allies and the specter of the musket, hatchet, and scalping knife haunted the Albins and every family residing in Winchester, on Opequon Creek, Red Bud Run, and the hundreds of isolated farms scattered across the Valley. Until this time the settlers in the Shenandoah Valley had coexisted in relative peace with the Indians. Both lived in close proximity to one another - the Indians maintained their traditional lifestyle while the colonists developed farms, raised families, and grew crops. Now, inhabitants of western Virginia and elsewhere

---

[68]Soon, the French generously released Washington who had promised he would not return for one year.

on the colonial frontier faced the threat of surprise attack by a marauding and merciless enemy. Shortly after the French released him near Ft. Duquesne in July 1754, Washington returned to Winchester and established his headquarters there. One year later following the British General Braddock's devastating defeat near Ft. Duquesne in July 1755, the entire frontier appeared even more threatened if that was possible. "Everyday," wrote Washington, "we have accounts of such cruelties and barbarities as are shocking to human nature. Such numbers of French and Indians are all around that no road is safe."[69] In Winchester on October 10, 1755, Washington found ". . . every thing in the greatest hurry and confusion, by the back [country] Inhabitants flocking in, and those of the Town removing out. . . ." With such fear and panic existing in Winchester, his attempts to enlist the neighboring militia were futile.[70] The men remaining in and near Winchester simply refused to leave their homes unprotected to foray against the Indians, choosing instead " . . . to die, with their wives and Familys [sic]."[71] Six months later, in April 1756, Washington wrote from Winchester, "The Blue Ridge [Mts.] is now our frontier, no men being left in this county, except a few, who keep close with a number of women and children in Forts. . . ."[72] Indeed, the war's impact became even more apparent as Frederick County's population soon declined by almost one-

---

[69]George Washington in Francis Parkman, *France and England in North America* (New York: Literary Classics of the United States Inc., 1983), II, 1071-1072.
[70]George Washington in John C. Fitzpatrick (ed.), *The Writings of George Washington,* (Washington, D.C.: United States Government Printing Office, 1931), I, 200. In his journal Captain Charles Lewis recorded during successive days in mid-October 1755 while marching with his company from Winchester northwest to Ft. Cumberland the number of deserted houses and empty fields brought on by fear of the French and Indians. During the expedition his company was joined by Colonel George Washington. R.A. Brock, editor, Charles Lewis, "Journal of Charles Lewis of the Virginia Regiment Commanded by Colonel George Washington in the Expedition Against the French," *Collections of the Virginia Historical Society,* (1892), 208.
[71]Ibid., Fitzpatrick, 201.
[72]George Washington to Governor Robert Dinwiddie in Albin, *Virginia Albins,* 18.

third as frightened residents launched hasty escapes east to the safer parts of Virginia.[73]

From his Winchester headquarters, the newly commissioned Colonel Washington, as Commander in Chief of the colonial forces, was responsible for securing the nearly 350 miles of open Virginia frontier against both French and Indian intrusion and attacks. Locally, Washington, in command of between 1,000 and 1,500 men, reacted to the daunting task before him by ordering, planning, and then supervising the construction of Ft. Loudon (today it is located in downtown Winchester).

Ostensibly the fort, covering one-half acre, would protect Washington's garrison, serve as his headquarters, and provide a rallying point for colonial forces in the area. Moreover, Ft. Loudon would offer a safe haven for the area's remaining residents in the event of a raid by the French and Indians on Winchester or its environs. Constructed of logs packed with earth, the fort could accommodate 450 men in its barracks and featured fourteen artillery pieces. Not completed until December 1756, Ft. Loudon was but one in a chain of British defenses extending from the Potomac River to the North Carolina border all hurriedly constructed that year.

Despite these strengthened defensive arrangements, not everyone felt safe. As the war progressed, frightened citizens continued to abandon their farms and homesteads. (Perhaps some were spurred to leave because of debt.) In a letter to Governor Dinwiddie, Washington expressed concern that Augusta, Frederick, and Hampshire Counties would soon be depopulated, as the residents evacuated. The French commander Marquis de Montcalm wrote on May 11, 1756, "I can only tell you that...the savages have made great havoc in Pennsylvania and Virginia and carried off, according to their custom, men, women, and children."[74] "In Virginia," wrote another contemporary, "they [Indians] have committed unheard of cruelties, carried off families, burned a great many houses, and killed an infinity of people."[75]

---

[73]Matthew Ward, *Breaking the Back Country, The Seven Years War in Virginia and Pennsylvania, 1754-1765,* (Pittsburgh: University of Pittsburg Press, 2004), 72.
[74]Montcalm letter in Parkman, *France and England*, II, 1094.
[75]Ibid., M. Duchat letter, July 15, 1756, 1103.

From 1754 to 1758, heavy Indians attacks occurred
in the Shenandoah Valley in Virginia....These assaults
had a considerable effect upon southward movement.
From October, 1754, to the end of 1756 at least 68
persons were killed by the Shawnees and Delawares
in the Shenandoah Valley. During the same period, 13
were wounded and an additional 75 taken prisoner.
In the Shenandoah Valley in 1757 and 1758, 49 settlers were slain, five wounded, and 86 taken prisoner.[76]

In the midst of this milieu of war, fear, and panic, and despite the threat to their safety, William Albin and his family, unlike many of their frightened neighbors, apparently decided to remain in Frederick County for the duration of the war. William's
choice at first glance may appear foolhardy. However, because the
Albin cabin was only two or three miles from the refuge offered
by the heavily manned and well-fortified Fort Loudon, it may have
been a rational decision. Despite the Albin family's proximity to
the fort, William Albin must have maintained a special vigilance
as he and his two oldest sons (John and Robert were both in their
teens) worked daily in their fields.

Conversely, unlike many of their remaining neighbors,
most Quakers were determined not to fight because of their commitment to non-violence. This righteous Quaker pacifism was not
as well tolerated in Virginia or in Frederick County as it had been
in Quaker-dominated Pennsylvania due to the fact that Virginia
remained primarily an Anglican colony. Soon, local officials in
Winchester had a jail constructed that periodically held Quakers
from many parts of Virginia who protested the French and Indian
War and who also refused to pay taxes to the Anglican parish.[77]

George Washington, from his Winchester headquarters

---

[76]Robert Wayne Ramsay, *Carolina Cradle: Settlement of the Northwest Carolina
Frontier, 1747-1762,* (Chapel Hill: University of North Carolina Press, 1964),
193.

[77]For the extent of Quaker pacifism, see Parkman, *France and England in North
America* volume II, 677, where he reports that "The Pennsylvania Assembly,
controlled by Quaker non-combatants, would give no soldiers" for the proposed
British invasion of French Canada during the French and Indian War.

noted on August 4, 1756, "I could by no means bring the Quakers to any terms. They chose rather to be whipped to death than to bear arms, or lend us any assistance whatever upon the fort, [Loudon?] or anything for self-defence."[78] Instead of flogging, Washington later thought it best to release the Quakers and wait for Governor Dinwiddie's decision on the matter.

As the war continued and amidst reports of persistent Indian depredations against whites, William and Mary Albin stood steadfast in their decision to remain in their home. Furthermore, it appears the last two of their five sons were born in the Red Bud Run cabin during the hostilities, James in approximately 1756, and George on February 15, 1758.[79]

Further evidence that the Albins remained in Winchester is found in the local courts records. They show William Sr. in the Winchester courts at least five times *during the war,* still attempting to recover debts or fend off legal claims made against him.

On August 3, 1756, just one day prior to Washington's comments regarding the Quakers written in his Ft. Loudon headquarters, a case against William was being settled nearby in the Frederick County Courthouse. This time John Bayliss, the surveyor William had hired back on March 27, 1754, to survey land he had sold to Andrews on March 27, 1753, sued Albin. Apparently, William had neglected to pay Bayliss for his work, and he also failed to appear to answer the claim. In William's absence the court ruled,

> "The Dft failing to appear, the plt [Bayliss] produced his note, whereupon judgment is granted agt [against] him [Albin] for forty three shillings [a little more than two

---

[78]Colonel George Washington: "Difficulties of the War against the French" (Extracts from Washington's correspondence, 1755-1756) in Howard Walter Caldwell, *A Source History of the United States: From Discovery (1492) to the End of Reconstruction,* (Chicago: Ainsworth and Co.,1909), 134.

[79]The Albin's first three sons John, Robert, and William Jr. were all born in Winchester prior to the war.

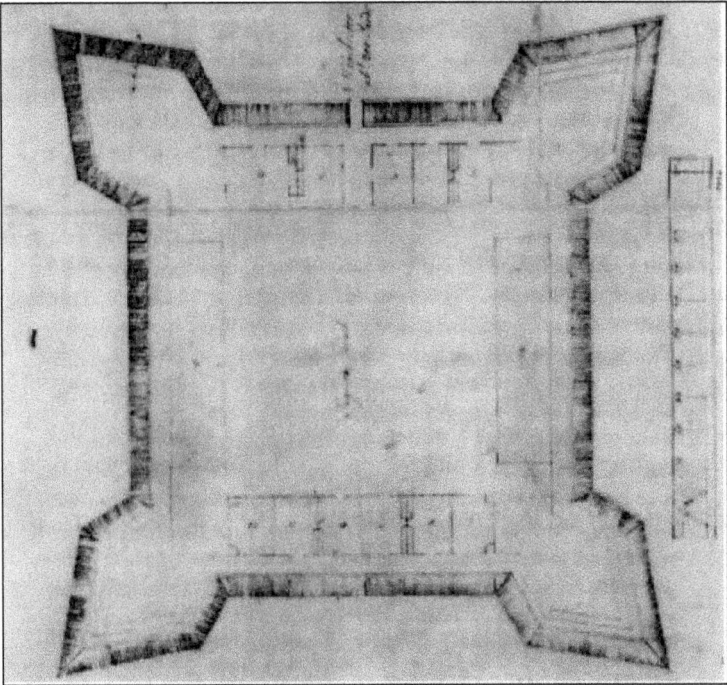

1756 plan of Ft. Loudon in Winchester, Virginia, drawn by George Washington.
The fort was located just a few miles from the Albin home.
Library of Congress Washington, D.C.
During the war Fort Loudon was never attacked.

two pounds] from the 27 day of March 1754 until
paid and costs."[80]

Albin's legal and financial misadventures continued into
1757. On February 1 he agreed to post a bond (from where did he
get the money?) for a neighbor, Jonathan Taylor.[81] Later that same

---

[80]Albin, *Virginia Albins*, 17.
[81]Ibid. Taylor lived on 400 acres just north of the Albin property. On May 4,
1757, in the Frederick County court, a grand jury could not be seated "occasioned
by the commotions in the county on account of the Indians." Frederick County
Court minutes cited in *Virginia Albins*, 18.

year in another case, the same Jonathan Taylor assumed an obligation for William.

On Tuesday, August 2, 1757, William and Stephen Pilcher, a local resident, appeared as defendants in a case where it seems either William or both men had possibly co-signed another note, this time for George Martin, deceased. The executors of Martin's estate were suing William for some unknown debt. With the arrival of his fourth son in 1756, and with Mary expecting another child in February 1758, William could ill afford another financial setback. (One would think that William would have by now learned the dangers of being a co-signatory.) At this point Taylor and James Carter (the brother of Albin's brother-in-law, Richard Carter) fortunately stepped forward and agreed to "pay the condemnation" of the court.[82] At least in this case, it was refreshing to see William's family provide help, though questions about William's judgment must have lingered in the minds of all parties concerned.

As William struggled with his legal and financial burdens, the French and Indian War continued to rage. By 1758 Virginia was making greater efforts to raise troops to defend the colony. Volunteer companies formed. A separate group, the Virginia regulars, mustered 2,000 men. These units merged into two separate regiments - Colonel Washington commanded the first Virginia Militia, and Colonel William Byrd, of the famous Byrd family of Virginia, led the second Virginia Militia.[83] Despite this increase in troop strength Washington, in the summer of 1758 while en route to his home at Mt. Vernon, found Winchester jammed with more frightened settlers bound for the safer confines of the East.

In the midst of the conflict, Washington had good reason to return to his plantation, family, and to Williamsburg briefly during that summer of 1758. In the previous ten years, Washington had spent more nights in Winchester than any other place except Mt. Vernon. Moreover, on July 24, 1758, his fellow Frederick County citizens, including George Bruce, Mary Albin's brother,

---

[82]Ibid., 17. Richard Carter had married Mary Bruce Albin's sister Margaret Bruce.

[83]H.J. Eckenrode, (archivist), *List of the Colonial Soldiers of Virginia, Special Report of the Department of Archives and History for 1913,* (Richmond: Public Printing Office, 1917), 12.

had elected him to his first public office position as a member of
the Virginia House of Burgesses, the oldest representative body in
the colonies then seated at Williamsburg, Virginia, near Mt.
Vernon. (Three years later both George and his brother James
Bruce (my gggg grandfather) voted for Washington in the May 18,
1761, election, his second successful run at the House seat for
Frederick County.)[84] Upon his return in 1758 to Frederick County,
Colonel Washington would soon engage in another struggle not
for votes but instead on a battlefield opposing the French nearly
two hundred miles from his Winchester post. One of the Albin
sons would serve in the sister regiment that marched and fought
with Washington.

Perhaps to the dismay of Mary and William, John, their
oldest son at eighteen, joined the colonial army. The question, now
answered, had probably been lingering in their minds for some
time: Should John be allowed to fight in the militia if the time
came? John was assigned to Colonel Byrd's second Virginia regiment in Captain Hancock Eustace's company.[85] On August 3,
1758, at Ft. Cumberland, Byrd's unit numbered 859 men.

When outdoorsmen like John and others reported for duty
they were equipped to fight though most lacked any battlefield
experience. Each militiaman had to provide himself with a well-
fixed firelock, bayonet and double cartridge box. All were ordered
to have a pound of gunpowder and four pounds of musket balls
fitted to a musket.

Four months after his visit to Mt. Vernon, Washington
commanded a contingent of militia that participated in the capture
of the vital French outpost at Fort Duquesne, near the location
where the French had held him prisoner four years earlier. On November 26, 1758, the fort had surrendered to the combined forces
of Colonels Washington and Byrd under overall command of
General Forbes. No records were found that point to John Albin's
role in the battle, but it is known that Captain Eustace's company

---

[84]Murtie Clark, *Colonial Soldiers of the South*, (Baltimore: Genealogical Publishing Company, 1983), 513, 546, 549. William Albin's name does not appear in
any of the poll lists for either election. Years later, when Washington became the
nation's first President, the Bruces could both boast their votes in these two elec-
tions had helped launch the political career of their neighbor George Washington.
[85]Albin, *Virginia Albins,* 18.

(John's unit) was engaged in the attack. Despite this significant victory and though the French later lost another pivotal battle at Quebec in September 1759 virtually guaranteeing an English victory in the war, the conflict endured for another five years.

By 1763 the English had finally defeated the French, driving their centuries-old antagonist from North America and winning control of not only Canada, but all French claims as far west as the Mississippi River including the long-coveted Ohio River Valley. Grateful, British colonists now joyously accepted an outcome that only years earlier had seemed unlikely. However, the Indian tribes previously allied with the French still remained.

Returning to his family following the war, John Albin may have been viewed as a conquering hero especially by his younger brothers. Ironically, years later on June 20, 1771, *The Virginia Gazette* printed a notice advising John Albin and thirteen other veterans that balances were due them for service "in the second Virginia Regiment, and of Captain Hancock Eustace's company, in the year 1758, and who, being dispersed... never made any application for those balances."[86] The notice added, "Some of the balances are considerable." Whether or not John applied for this windfall is unknown.

John Albin returned to a Virginia reeling from the debilitating financial effects of a nearly nine-year long conflict. By 1765 Virginia had spent so much money on war-related expenses that the colony suffered from a financial panic.[87] For the Albins and others, the end of the war would have been a welcome event, but perhaps their feelings of happiness were tempered to a degree by the reality of the ongoing difficult financial situation they faced. During these hard times, lasting more than a decade, John's father again sought the help of the local court as a collection agent.

Sometime in either 1763 or 1764, William Albin attempted to recover money owed him by Stephen Pilcher. Pilcher had been a defendant along with William in a case back in 1757, and while the cause of this new debt is uncertain, William asked the

---

[86]*Virginia Gazette*: Rind, June 20, 1771, 3, col. 2., accessed April 11, 2014, http://research.history.org/CWDLImages/VA_GAZET/Images/R/1771/0057hi.jpg.
[87]Eckenrode, *List of the Colonial Soldiers of Virginia*, 14.

court to attach Pilcher's wages to satisfy the liability. In the ensuing proceeding, a Henry Heth appeared and informed the court that he owed Pilcher forty shillings. Inasmuch as Pilcher, who was not in court, owed William Albin ten pounds the court allowed Albin to accept the forty shillings that Heth owed "toward satisfying this judgment."[88] It is not clear whether or not William ever collected the remaining money owed him.

Following the French and Indian War many citizens of Virginia and Pennsylvania expected an era of peace to ensue. Almost at the same time as the peace treaty to end the war was being signed, Pontiac's War broke out in the spring of 1764. Chief Pontiac's forces besieged Fort Detroit and later the Indian offensive spread along the Great Lakes and east into the Ohio Valley. Native warriors forced many of the English colonial soldiers to leave the region. In a year of vicious fighting, Indians conducted raids as far east as Winchester. Concern about the Indians' ability to strike anywhere at any time caused Virginia to maintain over 1,000 militia on duty as a first line of defense. Perhaps John Albin, with experience in the French and Indian War, or even his younger brother Robert, who would have been of military age in 1763, were called to defend the colony. By 1764 the fighting essentially ended, and Winchester citizens could return to somewhat normal lives after ten years of warfare.

Just two years after the war with France ended, on June 2, 1765, William Albin died at the age of fifty-five.[89] It is unclear whether Mary preceded her husband in death. Some sources indicate she died in 1765 as well, but perhaps she passed on in 1772. Since William died intestate, under existing law John Albin, the eldest son, inherited the family's property, including both the land and the cabin. John's inherited acreage was the last remaining tract of land William had repurchased years earlier.

With William's death an era had ended in the Albin family history. Of the four Albin orphans who had arrived in America with the Hunter family back in 1722, William had outlived two of his siblings who had resided in Chester County. His oldest brother

---

[88]Albin, *Virginia Albins*, 17.

[89]Ironically, George Washington's seventeen-year affiliation with Winchester ended that same year.

James had died on September 29, 1750 and sister Elizabeth Albin Bennett had passed away on May 23, 1748. His other brother, John Albin, is last shown in the Chester County tax records for 1765, so he may have passed away at about the same time as William.

William Albin had arrived in America presumably with very little money or possessions and most likely began his new life in the Pennsylvania colony as an indentured servant. He must have been adventuresome, ambitious, and industrious to later abandon the relative comfort and security of civilized Chester County for a new start in wild and unpredictable Frederick County. Settling in a frontier land bordering Indian country and near the French in the 1730s, he acquired land, married, and raised a family. In the turbulent, dangerous times during the French and Indian War, he chose to remain in the home he had built near Winchester, prepared and willing to defend his family and property. For William, however, selling some of that same land to meet the monetary demands of the Fairfax claim in the 1740s had been as mentally straining as safeguarding his home from attack in the 1750s. William Albin the progenitor of this line of the Albin family in America and his wife Mary left five sons to carry on the Albin name and legacy.

CHAPTER IV

William Albin Jr. (1748 - 1796)

Mathias Shepler of the County of Westmoreland and state of Pennsylvania...in consideration of the sum of twenty pounds of lawful money [paid] to me in hand paid by William Albin....

> From a land deed to William Albin Jr.
> from his brother-in-law Mathias Shepler
> February 24, 1783

Virginia and Pennsylvania

Following the deaths of both William and Mary Albin, their oldest son John had inherited the family's 189-acre farm on Red Bud Run. It is unknown if both John and his brothers shared the responsibilities on the family farm or if John managed it alone. It is clear that William Jr. understood that his older brother John's inheritance of the property rendered him dispossessed. At the same time, he realized the limited prospects for acquiring his own land parcel in Frederick County. As a result, William Albin Jr., at twenty-three the third oldest of the five Albin brothers, left his boyhood home in Frederick County, probably in 1771, bound for the backwoods country of western Pennsylvania. One year later, in August 1772, John ended up selling the Red Bud Run property and soon moved to Harrison County, Virginia.[1] Perhaps the land on the Albin homestead had simply worn out after having been subjected to more than thirty years of harvests particularly the soil-depleting tobacco crops the Albins had grown.

William Albin Jr.'s departure from Virginia resembled a similar trek his father had initiated from Chester County to Frederick County thirty-five years earlier. The identical twin desires to acquire land and start a new life combined with a bold spirit that had defined his father now surfaced in his son. William Jr. pro-

---

[1]Albin, *Virginia Albins*, 22 and Chapter 3, fn 1, p.i. By 1772 Mary Albin was most likely deceased, as her name did not appear on the sales document for the land her son John had sold.

ceeded northwest some 160 miles from Winchester. Bound not for
Pennsylvania's more settled eastern regions of his father's childhood, William was instead attracted to an untamed area in the colony's southwestern region – now free of the French menace - not
quite as far north as Ft. Pitt (Pittsburgh). He settled in what would
soon become Westmoreland County.

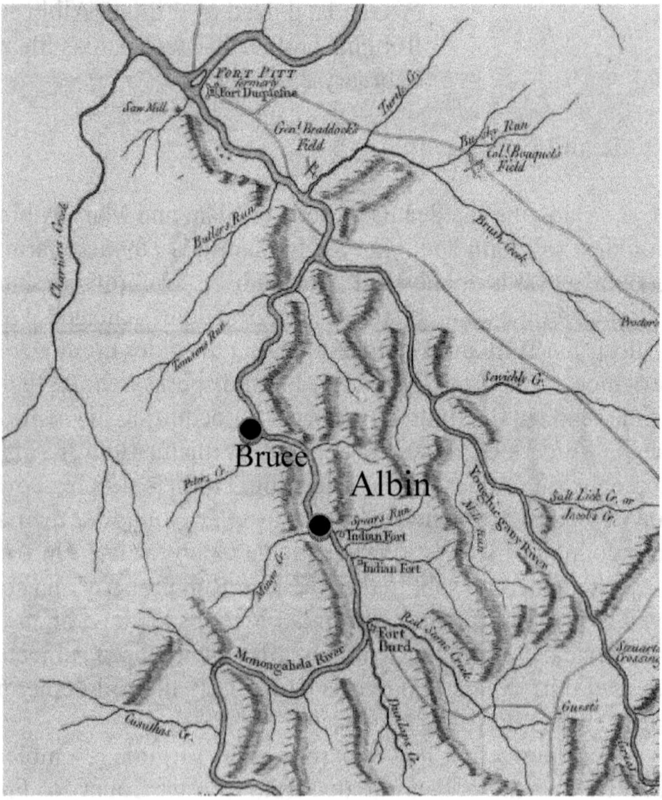

Map 9
An original 1777 map showing the approximate location of the Albin
and Bruce lands in Westmoreland County and Washington County respectively,
south of Ft. Pitt (Pittsburgh) both on or near the Monongahela River. The Albins
lived on Speers (Spears) Run and the Bruces on Peters Creek.

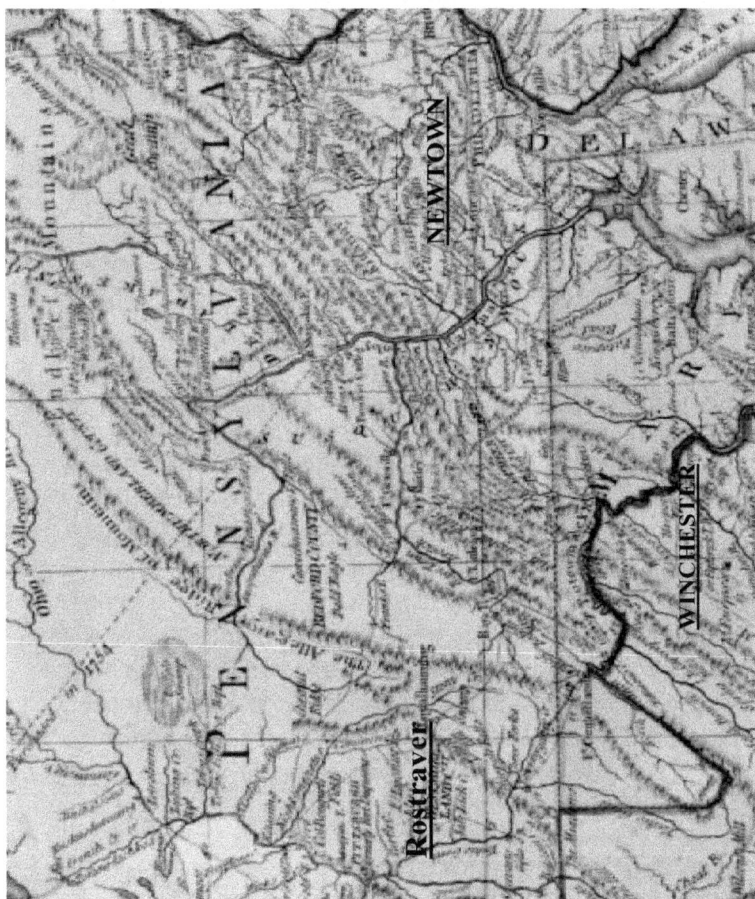

Map 10
The early Albins in North America, 1722-1791
1794 Map[2] showing **Newtown**, Chester County, **PA**, **Winchester**, Frederick
County, VA and **Rostraver Township**, Westmoreland County, PA.

---

[2]*A New and General Map of the Middle Dominions Belonging to the United
States of America*, published May 12, 1794, by Laurie and Whittle, 53 Fleet St.,
London, England, accessed November 11, 2015,
https://www.raremaps.com/gallery/enlarge/15675.

William Jr. may have joined with other Virginians, maybe even some from Frederick County and the Winchester area, on the trek to Pennsylvania. Perhaps, like William, they too were young and sought affordable land in this vast, uninhabited region of western Pennsylvania. Their journey would have followed nearly the same course as British General Braddock's ill-fated army in 1755 when it marched to attack Ft. Duquesne during the French and Indian War. From our vantage point of nearly 250 years, William's epic journey placed him in the vanguard of nothing less than a historic migration - by Virginians and others to western Pennsylvania - that eventually would expand the colonial frontier into and beyond this, the site of the former French realm in North America. In leaving Virginia, it appears likely that William Jr., like his father before him upon his departure from Chester County, never again saw his siblings.

Regarded as Indian country then, the western Pennsylvania region attracted few settlers before the 1760s. However, a treaty agreed to at Fort Stanwix, near present day Rome, New York, between Great Britain and the Six Nations, Delaware, and Shawnee Indians in 1768 finally permitted settlement west of the Allegheny Mountains beginning in April 1769. Following the signing of the treaty, and with their heads overflowing with fabulous descriptions of this virgin Pennsylvania region reported by traders, trappers, and veterans who had fought there in the French and Indian War a few years earlier, pioneers migrated there en masse. (Perhaps it was due to John Albin's glowing accounts of a fertile, forested Pennsylvania that he had observed back in '58 during his march to Ft. Duquesne that inspired his brother William to resettle near the same area.) These newcomers, some landless and disinherited like William, sensed an opportunity to begin a new life just across Virginia's border.

Drawing part of its land from neighboring Bedford County, Westmoreland County, on February 26, 1773, became the first county established in Pennsylvania west of the Alleghenies. It extended as far north as Ft. Pitt until the late 1780s when Pittsburgh became a part of a new county, Allegheny. When Westmoreland County was officially organized on April 5, 1773, Rostraver became one of its original townships. It was there that William Albin would remain for approximately the next two decades.

Located in the extreme western part of Westmoreland
County, Rostraver lies some fifteen miles south of Pittsburgh. Its
western boundary touches on the winding Monongahela River.
The source of the river's name, Monongahela, originated from the
name given to the river by the Native American Delaware tribe,
"river with the sliding banks."
The topography of the Rostraver Township is diversified.
High bluffs overlook the streams, while the land in the interior is
level in most spots.[3] Additionally, evidence of ancient civilizations
appeared in various locales across the Rostraver landscape.
Among the earliest inhabitants were various groups of
long-forgotten Native-Americans. The ancient Adena people supposedly occupied the land from 1000 BC to 700 AD. They had
constructed earthen mounds in the area for ceremonies or burials.
One such mound still exists in Rostraver on the land that once belonged to the Shepler family.[4] Moreover, long before the arrival of
whites, Indians had built at least nine separate "forts" within the
area that would eventually comprise Rostraver Township. Some
were situated at sites on the few hilltops in the area. One of these
structures was constructed on Shepler Hill, at 1,416 feet the highest point in the area.[5] Another Indian fort had stood at the mouth
of Speers Run (Map 9) where it emptied into the Monongahela
River (currently near where the I-70 Bridge crosses the Monongahela).
Following the French and Indian War, when Rostraver's
early settlers first arrived, they found no Native American towns
or villages despite a centuries-long presence by various tribes.
Thus, at first William and his neighbors may have been unac-
quainted with the specific Native American history of the area
even though they may have occasionally discovered random arti-
facts of an early Indian presence in their fields or elsewhere.
In Rostraver Township William Albin Jr. may have lived

---

[3]John Newton Boucher and John W. Jordan, *History of Westmoreland County,
Pennsylvania,* (New York: Lewis Publishing Co. 1906), I, 519.
[4]Cassandra Vivian, *Monessen: A Typical Steel Country Town,* (Charleston, South
Carolina: Arcadia Publishing, 2002), 11. Vivian also reports that in later times
four separate Indian villages had existed on what would become Shepler's Hill.
[5]Shepler Hill bears the surname of the family of William Jr.'s future wife, Magdalina Shepler.

at first with one of his three brothers-in-law known to have settled there. Eventually, he established his own farm not far from the aforementioned location of the ancient Indian fort at the drains of Speers Run but farther inland.

In approximately 1767, not long after his father's death and some years before leaving for Pennsylvania, nineteen-year old William Jr. had married. He wed a fifteen-year old, Magdalina or "Delina" or "Linney" Shepler, born in approximately 1752 in New Jersey or Virginia.[6] William Jr. and Magdalina undoubtedly had met because of the proximity of their two families on Red Bud Run where the Albins and Sheplers shared a common property line. This union of William and Magdalina formally united the two neighboring families, and it also introduced the first German blood into the heretofore exclusively Scottish-English Albin lineage.

Magdalina's parents, John and Magdalene Shepler, and her three brothers had likely emigrated from the Heidelberg area, in Germany's Rhenish Palatinate, then settled in East Jersey (New Jersey) in the mid-1750s. Later they settled near Winchester.[7] On April 29, 1760, the Sheplers purchased 211 acres on Red Bud Run adjacent to the Albin property. From that point the two families apparently became close friends. One of the Shepler's sons, Peter Shepler, and William Albin Sr. must have gotten along well, as they shared responsibility for planning a road within Frederick County in November 1763.

In 1768 William Jr. and Magdalina's first child, William III, was born, probably in Virginia, as Westmoreland County was then not open to legal settlement. Later, and possibly aware that the Treaty of Fort Stanwix allowed settlement west of the Allegheny Mountains (and thus in Westmoreland County), William II decided to move to Pennsylvania. Like others, he realized that the treaty would provide a legal basis to occupy the land there, but he may have also hoped it would bring peace to the region and thereby security for his family.

---

[6]*Ancestry.com. "U.S. and International Marriage Records, 1560-1900,,"*(Provo, Utah: Yates Publishing Company, 2004).

[7]Joyner, *Abstracts of Virginia's Northern Neck Warrants and Surveys, Frederick County 1747-1780*, 140. See Map 8 above for Frederick County landholders including the Sheplers on Red Bud Run and the Opequon.

The Albins arrived in Westmoreland County prior to or in 1771. That year Magdalena Albin gave birth to a second son, George Henry in November. (The 1880 census record shows George's daughter Sarah Albin Smith resided in Webster Township, Harrison County, Indiana, and it corroborates the birth of her father George in Pennsylvania.) Thus, it appears the Albins may have arrived in Pennsylvania earlier than the Sheplers, but the possibility exists the three Shepler brothers may have traveled with the Albin family.

In Rostraver Township William and Magdalina joined her three brothers, Peter, Matthias, and Philip Shepler in establishing homesteads. The Sheplers and the Albins were thus among the earliest settlers to arrive in Westmoreland County.[8]

Arriving from Winchester the Sheplers first appear in the Westmoreland County Record on November 20, 1772. On that date Matthias and Peter signed a deed with John Beans then of Cumberland County. Witnessing the signing were their neighbors living just to the east of the Sheplers' land, Joseph Hill Sr., Joseph Jr., and Joseph Sr.'s son in law Casper Geyer, a fellow countryman of the Sheplers from Germany. Part of the Shepler brothers' 600-acre purchase fronted the Monongahela River, while the remaining acreage extended inland in the direction of Shepler's Hill.[9] The two Sheplers paid £200 "lawful money of Pennsylvania" for the land, naming their tract Fairfield. That their purchase was situated along the Monongahela and thus provided a coveted water access underscores the notion that the Sheplers had arrived in Rostraver Township early on. Conversely, settlers arriving in subsequent years would find these more desirable riverfront plots already surveyed and settled.

The Albins made no land purchases during this early peri-

[8]Boucher and Jordan, *History of Westmoreland County, Pennsylvania*, 519. The authors do not mention William Albin's arrival in Westmoreland County nor do they mention the Sheplers.

[9]See Map 12 below. A copy of this original deed is in the author's possession found in *Deed Book A*, 308, Westmoreland County, Greensburg, Pennsylvania, Recorder of Deeds. Despite appearing in the Westmoreland County Land Records in 1772, the Sheplers (and the Albins) are not shown on the 1773 tax rolls for Rostraver Township, then a part of Bedford County even though many of their neighbors are listed.

od. The absence in the local deed books of any Albin-related land transactions may support the belief that the Albin family resided at first on land owned by the Sheplers.

Besides the Sheplers, many other German families inhabited the area near Shepler's Hill where the Albins lived, probably much to the delight of Magdalina Albin. Casper Geyer, the Barkhammers, Peter Reasoner, the Rhinelander Matthew Beazell, and his immediate neighbor to the east Henry Speers Sr. (sometimes spelled Spears) and his wife Regina who arrived in Rostraver in 1772 were all of German extraction.

The Speers had left Germany and settled originally in Frederick County, Virginia, before they moved to Pennsylvania.[10] In Rostraver Township they occupied a tract of land near the Albins and Sheplers adjacent to Edward Cook's property on the banks of the Monongahela River. Later, a small creek running through Albin's property and parts of his neighbors' tracts became known as Speers Mill Run shown on maps then as Speers Run.

Quite probably, William Albin's family had known the Speers family in Virginia. Perhaps, too, Magdalina and Regina Speers had already met - their common German heritage perhaps facilitating a friendship. Later, they may have become reacquainted in Pennsylvania possibly sharing recollections, perhaps in German, of life in Frederick County. It was probably at this same time in Virginia that the Albins also became acquainted with young Henry Speers Jr., born July 8, 1756. In 1773, only a year after his arrival in Rostraver, Henry Speers Sr. died. It would be his son Henry Jr., though, who would have the greatest impact on the local inhabitants. He operated an Indian canoe ferry across the Monongahela near the Albins' and Sheplers' land. Speers eventually became a preacher in the local Baptist Church at Enon in Washington County that William attended.[11]

In addition to this German link between many of William's neighbors, there was also a Frederick County and Winchester, Virginia, connection. Near William in Rostraver, there were

---

[10]In the Frederick County Road Orders from 1754 to 1762, Henry Speers is mentioned repeatedly. See 2 February 1762, p. 360 for one example. His wife Regina inherited their Rostraver land upon Henry's death.

[11]Boyd Crumrine, Ed., *The History of Washington County, Pennsylvania,* (Philadelphia: Everts and Company, 1882), 649-650.

no less than nine families from the Winchester area, ten if we include the Van Meters who lived in eastern Rostraver, not far from the Albins. Including William and Magdalina Albin, there were, of course, the three Shepler families, and later in 1770 the James Bruce Sr. family (the Bruces would first settle in Washington County, see below) - all from the Red Bud Run area. Van Swearingen, Dorsey Pentecost, the Speers, William Richey (Frederick County north), and Peter Reasoner all hailed from the Winchester area or near it as well. There could be others, but as of this writing these families remain the principal former Frederick County families identified in Rostraver Township near the Albins.

This link to Frederick County is significant. It is quite possible that many of these Virginia neighbors had traveled to western Pennsylvania together, because many arrived in Westmoreland County at nearly the same time, in approximately the late 60's or early 70's. Dorsey Pentecost is found in Westmoreland County in March 1771, followed by the Albins that same year (and perhaps the Sheplers?). Then, the Van Swearingen, Speers, Van Meter, and Shepler (?) families soon followed. However, it seems the earliest of these Virginians to arrive may have been Peter Reasoner, in 1763 or 1764. Once these families set foot in Rostraver Township, their common Frederick County roots might have influenced them to settle near each other for support, socialization, and protection.[12] Time and again we see frontier families of this era understanding the value of strength in numbers particularly in an unfamiliar and demanding wilderness setting.

As time passed, William Albin Jr. eventually reunited with additional family members in the area near Rostraver Township. Years earlier in Virginia in 1763, Mary Bruce Albin's brother James Bruce Sr., his wife Margaret (McMahon) Bruce, and their sons William, James, and George left Winchester. Bruce had sold

---

[12]Barely twelve miles south of Rostraver, another Virginian known to William and many others purchased land at about the same time. George Washington in April 1769 purchased nearly 1,900 acres in southern Westmoreland County (now Fayette County) along the trails he had marched in the early and middle stages of the French and Indian War back in the 1750s. Unlike his neighbors Washington would not reside in Pennsylvania, but instead he would assume the role of an absentee landowner visiting Pennsylvania and Rostraver Township after the Revolutionary War had ended.

William Albin Jr.

his acreage adjoining the Albin land on Red Bud Run on March
20, 1763.[13] Because of the continuing Indian menace and because
the large migration from Virginia to Pennsylvania had not yet begun, it remains doubtful the Bruces moved to Pennsylvania that
year. Instead, they may have lived temporarily in Maryland, according to a Bruce descendant.

Eventually, in June 1770 the Bruces settled in Pennsylvania. They resided just north of Westmoreland County, but *on the
west side* of the Monongahela River in Washington County. They
settled on perhaps 400 acres near William McMahon (Margaret
McMahon Bruce's brother) close to where William Albin Jr. and
the Sheplers would settle approximately one year later. Though
one description erroneously places the Bruce clan about fourteen
miles above Pittsburgh, they actually lived about that same distance but *below* Pittsburgh, on Peter's Creek near Elizabeth (Map
9 above). (Years later the branch of Peter's Creek where the
Bruces settled became known as Bruce's Run, which emptied into
the Monongahela River.) William Bruce recalled that because of
an Indian threat in the area, his two sisters were born inside a fort
in Elizabeth just after the Revolutionary War broke out in 1776.[14]
Thus, even though William Albin Jr. and his family had left Winchester far behind when they relocated to Pennsylvania, they
would end up living in proximity to William's uncle and aunt,
James Bruce Sr. and Margaret, William's cousins, and his three
Shepler brothers-in-law.

As the decade of the 1770's progressed, relations between
England and her restless American colonies steadily deteriorated.
Taxes, assessed by an increasingly hostile Parliament in London
on their equally hostile and unreceptive American colonies, lack of
colonial representation in Parliament, and the Rights of Man were
all issues of the day. Undoubtedly, William Albin and his neighbors were aware of Parliament's efforts to raise money from its
American colonies with its passage of the Stamp and Sugar Acts.
Westmorelanders would also have been aware of the British im-

---

[13]O'Dell, *Pioneers of Old Frederick County,* 247 and Frederick County, Virginia,
Deed Book 8, 365.

[14]William Bruce, is the uncle of Piety Bruce Albin, the author's ggg grandmother).

posed, yet economically harmless but assertive Declaratory Act and the punitive Intolerable Acts levied on the citizens of Massachusetts. Colonial cries of "no taxation without representation" would likewise have extended to western Pennsylvania.

In April 1775 the die had been cast in Massachusetts at Lexington Green and at Concord Bridge when colonial militia and British regulars exchanged those celebrated musket shots heard round the world. Rebellion would soon spread to the other twelve colonies impacting the Albin family and their neighbors. Each of the five Albin brothers, the four residing in Virginia and William in Pennsylvania, would serve the colonial side pitted against the mother country - traitors in the eyes of the English, patriots in the eyes of most of their neighbors.

Unlike the Albins who had already resolved to support the colonial cause, other colonists felt unsure about their allegiance. Where did their allegiance rest, with a King and Parliament in a distant country they had never seen or with many of their colonial neighbors who supported independence? While considering their relationship with England, some may also have questioned their own identity. Am I an Englishman or an American? The answers to these vexing questions determined the path, loyalist or rebel, they would follow during the war. For the citizens of Westmoreland County the question was formally answered in May 1775.

On May 16, 1775, approximately one month following the initial shots of the Revolutionary War, Westmoreland County citizens gathered at a unique meeting in Hanna's Town. Labeled the Westmoreland Resolves or the Hanna's Town Resolves, the document they created declared:

> 3d. That should our country be invaded by a foreign
> enemy, or should troops be sent from Great Britain
> to enforce the late arbitrary Acts of its Parliament,
> we will cheerfully submit to military discipline, and to
> the utmost of our power resist and oppose them, or
> either of them, and will coincide with any plan
> that may be formed for the defence of America in

general, or Pennsylvania in particular.[15]

Item "4th" declared that the citizens did not "wish or desire any innovation, but only the things that may be restored to, and go on in the same way as before the Stamp Act...."[16] Then, the Resolves emphatically pronounced that only when "British Parliament shall have repealed their obnoxious Statutes, and shall recede from any claim to tax us...our Association shall be dissolved."[17] Collectively, these were very bold declarations indeed from colonists residing in a relatively isolated locale so susceptible to British and/or Indian raids. Not quite a declaration of independence but threatening a call to armed resistance, the Resolves left no doubt as to its signers' intentions. And, they meant every word.

Due to his youth, William had avoided service in the French and Indian War. Yet, he was probably quite familiar with the frontier warfare the county was about to experience. As William was growing up in Virginia, he undoubtedly had heard stories of the bloodshed and depredations committed by both sides from his older brother John who had served in the French and Indian War.

With remembrances such as these embedded in their minds, Westmorelanders prepared for the kind of warfare the British and their Indian allies would soon wage in the colonial backwoods. Sudden, violent, often brief ambushes or encounters in forests or full-scale attacks on soldiers or civilians in their homes and fields would be commonplace. Vigilance would become a commandment for survival. The law of the musket and tomahawk would guide each man, both white and red.

In 1777-1778 with the war well under way, as expected Indians in the area, some acting independently and some acting at the behest of the British, threatened civilians and militia alike in Westmoreland County and other nearby settlements in adjacent counties. To make matters even worse, General Washington in

---

[15]Thomas Montgomery, Ed., *Pennsylvania Archives*, (Harrisburg: J. Severns & Co.,1906), Vol. II, 263. The original of the document was destroyed when the British and Indians attacked and burned Hanna's Town on July 13, 1782. Apparently, the town was never rebuilt.
[16]Ibid.
[17]Ibid.

December 1776 had ordered 680 men of the crack Westmoreland 8th Pennsylvania Regiment east thus depriving the county of six companies desperately needed for local defense. During 1777-1778 numerous Indian attacks occurred all along the Pennsylvania border. Applying tactics hauntingly similar to those used in the French and Indian War, Indians seemed to be lurking in every thicket, behind every tree, and along every stream. In response, the Westmoreland County council issued a proclamation encouraging young men to join small ranging companies to combat "Indian style" both the Redcoats and Indians. These units would utilize unconventional tactics suited to wilderness combat, a vastly different strategy from the European style on-line assaults across an open battlefield that colonial defenders at Boston's Bunker Hill had just recently withstood during repeated and coordinated British advances.

This call to arms conjured up notions of adventure that appealed to many of the county's energetic young men.[18] At about this time, perhaps in March of 1778, thirty-year old William Albin Jr., enlisted either in the Westmoreland County militia or the Frontier Rangers. Pay receipts and an undated roster of William's unit (see below) confirm that he spent time in the militia. However, he later served, along with his Shepler brothers-in-law, as a Westmoreland Ranger of the Frontier from 1778 to 1783.[19]

Albin had entered the service as a private, assigned first to John Van Meter's third company, fourth battalion. (Whether it was a militia unit at that time or a ranger unit is unclear.) Apparently, only weeks later, on April 2, 1778, Albin earned a promotion to Ensign, the lowest ranking commissioned officer (somewhat like a second lieutenant today) while serving in Van Meter's company.[20]

---

[18]Boucher and Jordan, *History of Westmoreland County, Pennsylvania,* vol. 1, 87.

[19]William Engle, ed., *Pennsylvania Archives, Third Series,* (Harrisburg: William Ray, 1897), Vol. XXIII, 282, 314. In the transcribed roster of William "Albion's" 3rd company, the Shepler brothers appear as "Shepley" or Shippley. They, like William, were illiterate so someone incorrectly spelled their names for them. Later, Albin appears on the roster of Andrew Robb's fifth Company, fourth battalion.

[20]William Albin's surname is spelled Albion or Alben in some of the records of the Revolutionary War era. See Thomas Lynch Montgomery ed., *Muster Rolls, Etc., 1743-1787, Pennsylvania Archives, Sixth Series* (Harrisburg: Harrisburg Publishing, 1906), II, 285, 290 for "Alben's" name, accessed April 11, 2014,

This sudden promotion from private to officer rank in such a short time indicates William must have clearly demonstrated great soldierly skills as well as leadership ability.[21]

No matter what the unit type, militia or rangers, he served with, William would have put his backwoods experience to good use. Years spent roaming the wild forests of Virginia, hunting, and trapping with his father and brothers rendered Albin particularly skilled to undertake the challenging missions the Westmoreland volunteers would soon encounter.

Westmoreland County's eight Ranger companies mustered nearly 300 soldiers. Each company was usually comprised of neighbors or men who were well acquainted with each other and who lived in proximity to their Ranger captain. For example, in William's 3rd Ranger Company his neighbor, Captain John Van Meter, acted as the company commander, and William's three brothers in law, Peter, Phillip, and Mathias Shepler served as privates.

Assembled into efficient, approximately forty man companies, rangers worked together, sometimes even in smaller-sized units depending on the situation. They had no uniforms. Instead, rangers braved the wilderness in homespun clothing. Equipped at his own expense, each man carried a musket or rifle, a knife, and hatchet. Armed with these weapons and their wilderness experience, rangers proved to be formidable light infantry fighters. Relying heavily for survival on their hearing, eyesight, physical abilities, stamina, and instincts, they could remain in the woods and

---

Google Books,
https://books.google.com/books?id=ED4OAAAAIAAJ&printsec=frontcover&dq=joseph+beckett+westmoreland+county+pa&hl=en#v=onepage&q&f=false.
[21] Albin, *Virginia Albins*, 239 and fn. 2 following p. 280. Transcribed Pennsylvania pay certificates are in the author's possession from the "Pennsylvania State Archives", *Revolutionary War Military Abstract Card File*, for Ensign "Albion, Wm" (William Albin) in the amounts of 1 pound 10 shillings (the author in *Virginia Albins* erroneously reports that this warrant was **10** pounds 10 shillings), certificate 7651, and 2 pounds 12 shillings, certificate 7600, for service in the Pennsylvania Militia, apparently for the periods 2 August to 3 September 1778 and November to December 1778 respectively. Two of the certificates seem to represent back pay, as they are dated December 1785. Accessed April 11, 2014, items 35-37. Item 37 shows Albin's ensign rank apparently as of April 2, 1778, http://www.digitalarchives.state.pa.us/archive.asp?view=ArchiveItems&ArchiveID=13&FID=421275&LID=421374&FL=&Page=3.

mountains for long periods, sometimes without food. Always fearful of an Indian ambush, rangers likewise dreaded capture which usually meant a slow and agonizing death by torture.

Ranger company rosters often remained in a state of flux due to deaths, wounds, captures, or men having to return home to take care of their families and farms. Though it seems William was able to return home at different intervals during the course of the war, Magdalena was often alone left to care for the children including two new arrivals James in 1775 and Absalom in 1778.

Looking after her six children, the oldest being ten-year old William III, as well as managing the farm during the times when William served with his ranger Company must have been a daunting task for Magdalina. Fortunately, she could rely on her Shepler sisters-in-law who resided nearby on adjoining farms for support. (Their husbands, too, were serving in the militia or rangers.) Magdalina's concern for the safety of her husband, the welfare of her children, and the very real threat of Indian attack undoubtedly resulted in a great deal of stress for her and others in Westmoreland County during these wartime years - none more so than during the early months of 1779.

In February 1779, rumors spread in Westmoreland County that British Colonel Butler with a force of 300 Loyalist rangers planned to canoe down the Allegheny River in the spring or early summer and attack the county's "defenseless inhabitants."[22] On February 26 the British and their Indian allies from the upper Allegheny River area struck at Turtle Creek, approximately twenty miles east of Ft. Pitt. Eighteen people were either killed or carried off into captivity.[23] Inhabitants of Westmoreland County, as a result, prepared to leave (Magdalina and the children too?). About this time the county lieutenant called out or raised two companies of Westmoreland Rangers to protect the settlement and patrol likely "warpaths by which the invaders came."[24] Later, additional enemy raids east and south of Fort Pitt occurred. The proposed British strike deep into Westmoreland County, however, never followed that spring perhaps due to the Rangers' vigilance.

---

[22]Louise Phelps Kellogg, *Frontier Advance on the Upper Ohio, 1778-1779*, (Madison, Wisconsin: The Society, 1916), 34.
[23]Ibid.
[24]Ibid.

A RETURN OF THE OFFICERS OF THE 4TH BATALION
OF WESTMORELAND COUNTY MILITIA WITH THE NO.
OF THE COMPANY.

Field Officers.

Benjn Davis 1st Col'o.
John McClellen, 2nd.
Samuel Wilson, Maj.

1st.

William Sparks, Capt.
John Allen, 1st Lt.
Andrew Arnal, 2nd.
James Cravin, Ens'n.

2d Company.

William Conwell, Capt.
Jesse Rude, 1st Lt.
John Armstrong, 2nd.
Saml. Adams, Ens'n.

3rd.

John Vanmeter, Capt.
John Reed, 1st Lieut.
William Morgan, 2nd.
William Albion, Ens'n.

4th.

John Kyle, Capt.
Peter Wedel, 1st Lt.
Joseph Pearce, 2nd Lt.
Lewes Pearce, Ens'n.

5th.

Andrew Robb, Capt.
Hugh Gilmore, 1st Lt. accused with Toryism.
Thomas McKibbins, 2nd Lt.
William Frame, Ens'n.

6th

Edw'd Morton, Capt.
Wm. Moore, 1st Lt.
Wm. Banker, 2nd.
Philip Howel, Ens'n.

William (Albion) Albin shown on the roll of the Westmoreland County militia during the Revolutionary War, date unknown.[25]

Hostile raiding parties, nevertheless, continued to threaten area settlements during the ensuing months.

Following what may have been Pennsylvania's coldest winter in decades (for Westmorelanders heavy snows had provided a sort of tenuous respite from attack while simultaneously producing food shortages among locals), one of the more unusual

---

[25]Montgomery ed., *Muster Rolls, Etc., (Pennsylvania Archives)*, 285.

events during William's time in Westmoreland County occurred.[26] In the summer of 1780, as the war continued to rage, a movement that had begun in 1776 resurfaced. Nearly 2,000 citizens living in Southwest Pennsylvania in Fayette, Washington, Westmoreland, and Greene Counties, and perhaps the Virginia counties of Ohio and Monongalia considered a petition calling for the addition of a fourteenth state to the recently formed Union. Ill feelings that had been simmering for years between Virginia and Pennsylvania's citizens over disputed tracts of land in their western regions had finally reached the boiling point. So much so, that by 1780 this unresolved quarrel threatened to escalate into widespread violence.

Specifically, the petition advocated for the establishment of "the Provinse [sic] and Government of Westsylvania," a new state to be formed in the disputed territory encompassing portions of what is now Ohio, West Virginia, Virginia, and Pennsylvania (Map 11). Westmoreland County along with Washington County would have been included as part of Westsylvania.

During that summer Albin joined hundreds of his Westmoreland County neighbors including his brother-in-law Mathias Shepler, Colonel Benjamin Davis, Casper "Giger' (Geyer), Joseph Hill Sr. and Jr., Michael Springer, Peter Reasoner, Henry Spears, John Burkhame (Barkhammer), and from Washington County William McMahon (Margaret McMahon Bruce's brother) in signing the petition then circulating through the area. Directing their appeal to the Second Continental Congress, signees declared their support for the formation of Westsylvania.[27]

The two opposing factions contesting this radical idea were so at odds that the American war effort in Pennsylvania was hindered for a time. Dissident pro Westsylvania leaders even argued that settlers should refuse to pay Pennsylvania taxes. "In Westmoreland and Washington Counties armed bands drove off

---

[26]Edgar Hassler, *Old Westmoreland, A History of Western Pennsylvania During the Revolution*, (Pittsburgh: J.R. Weldin & Company, 1900), 103. Hassler writes that the snow was four feet deep in the woods and mountains of Westmoreland County with exceedingly cold weather for two months.
[27]Howard Leckey, *The Ten Mile Country and Its Pioneer Families*, (Apollo, Pennsylvania: Closson Press, 1993), 141-152. William Albin's name appears on page 151. Mathias Shepler is found on page 143. The petition was located in the Papers of the Continental Congress, no. 48, Folios 251-256, pgs. 89-96.

tax collectors and refused to take the oath to the Quaker commonwealth."[28]

The extent of William's involvement in the tax protest
other than signing the petition is unknown. Whether the Continental Congress ever considered the disgruntled settlers' petition is
likewise unknown. Later, a ruling by the state of Pennsylvania in
1782 deemed such petitions treasonous resulting in the discontinu-
ation of any further agitation for Westsylvania statehood and thus
averting the violence many had feared. Nonetheless, the disagree-
ments between states and the subsequent agitation for establishing
Westsylvania portended the local and national struggles the postwar United States would confront as its leaders sought to create a
government agreeable to all thirteen states.

Though William Jr. had served in the defense of Westmoreland County for some five years, he and other rangers returned to their homes periodically as circumstances allowed. An-
swering the need to look after their families and tend to their farms
during the war, these rangers often lived at home while "on call."
Neither William's name nor the names of the Sheplers appear on
the payroll records of Van Meter's company for June 1782, "for
running the line between this state [Pennsylvania] and Virginia"
lending credence to the belief that they were not on active duty for
that period.[29] William is shown, though, on a document dated "ye
8th of August, 1782," and titled "A Return of the Second, Third,
and Fourth Classes Ordered on Duty." William "Alben" appeared
in the "class 4th."[30] Apparently, William and others on the list had
been granted a leave and were now being recalled to duty. Perhaps
William had returned home during this period for the birth of his
second daughter, Sarah, who was born in approximately 1782.
Previously, Magdalina had also given birth to a sixth son, Isaac, in
about 1780.

---

[28]Jack Sosin, *The Revolutionary Frontier 1763-1783*, (New York: Holt, Rinehart
and Winston, 1967), 163. William's famous neighbor living only two farms
away, Reverend James Finley, played a significant role in this episode. Acting as
a secret agent for Pennsylvania, he used his prestige to convince settlers that separation was ill advised.
[29]Montgomery ed., *Muster Rolls, Etc., (Pennsylvania Archives)*, 288-289.
[30]Ibid., 290.

Map 11
The proposed fourteenth state, "Westsylvania", advocated for in a petition signed
by William Albin and others in 1780. Later, during the Civil War parts of this
area would emerge as the new state of West Virginia. (Westmoreland County lies
approximately between Ft. Pitt and Redstone.)[31]

On October 19, 1781, the British commander, Lord Cornwallis, in a dramatic move that "turned the world upside down"
surrendered his entire besieged army to General Washington at
Yorktown, Virginia. While Cornwallis' surrender appeared to be a
knockout blow for the British, fighting still continued at various
locations throughout the colonies. Because the treaty ending the
war would not be signed until 1783, skirmishes on the frontier
erupted sporadically. In July 1782, in one of the final acts of the
War, British-allied Indians attacked and destroyed Hannastown in
eastern Westmoreland County not far from William Albin's home.

---

[31]Wikipedia, "Westsylvania Map," accessed April 22, 2014,
http://en.wikipedia.org/wiki/File:Westsylvaniamap.png.

As a result, William and other Rangers remained on duty in western Pennsylvania into 1782 and 1783 despite Cornwallis' surrender.

As the long conflict drew to a close, civilians all recognized the Rangers and militia's indispensable contributions to the local war effort during their five years of active duty. Accustomed to the wilderness, these farmers turned fighters had sought out roving bands of Indians who were then attacking areas south and east of the Allegheny River. They warned settlers of impending attacks and escorted women and children to safety in forts or fortified houses. No matter what the season, they conducted countless, tedious patrols in the dense forests of Pennsylvania always on the alert for a sudden Indian ambush or for telltale signs of the enemy. Some performed the unenviable task of being kept out as "spies" on the frontier to give advance notice of an approaching enemy. Others guarded prisoners of war and garrisoned the forts that served as sanctuaries for their families and neighbors. Rangers and local militia had proven repeatedly to be the saviors of Westmoreland County's non-combatants whose lives depended on their vigilance and bravery.[32] They had held the rear line against the Indians just as others in the colonial army held the front line against the British Redcoats. Thus, at war's end William Albin, the Sheplers, and others who had taken up arms in the defense of their homeland could take great pride in knowing they had accomplished their mission against an enemy focused on their destruction and thus helped strike a blow for American independence.[33]

On December 3, 1785, and five days later on December 8 William "Albion" received back pay for two separate tours of active duty each approximately one month in length that he had

---

[32]Boucher and Jordan, *History of Westmoreland County, Pennsylvania*, I, 88.

[33]On May 10, 2008, Ed Smock, a Shepler descendant still residing in Westmoreland County, Pennsylvania, contacted the author and provided the following information regarding his 2002 visit to Philip Shepler's gravesite in Fells Cemetery, Fellsburg, Pa: "To the immediate left of Abraham Smock's grave is the grave of "Jacob Shepler." To Jacob's left (plus one empty space), is the grave of: "Philip Shepler" Died May 22, 1829, aged 88 yrs. (b.1741). There is an American flag with a Revolutionary War bronze emblem/holder attached near to Philip's headstone commemorating his service in the American Army. This Philip was married to Mary Hill."

completed seven years earlier in 1778. The payments amounted to almost four pounds.[34] Though not a great sum, the money was nonetheless welcomed by William and his large family. These payments to William and other veterans occurred at the same time that money in each of the thirteen states remained scarce due to the nation's overwhelming war debt. In light of the country's dire financial circumstances, this admirable monetary commitment to those veterans who had fought for the country's independence seemed very appropriate.

Though Washington's stunning victory over Lord Cornwallis at Yorktown in October 1781 had all but ended the Revolutionary War, the conflict did not officially end until both Great Britain and the United States of America signed the Treaty of Paris on September 3, 1783. Under the terms of the Treaty, Great Britain recognized her former thirteen colonies as free and sovereign states, although Great Britain would be allowed to retain control of Canada. For the first time since Englishmen settled at Jamestown in 1607, these former British subjects now citizens of the world's newest country would be under the rule of neither a King or Parliament. Having just defeated the world's greatest military power, the United States was now free to pursue its own destiny, as were its citizens in each of its thirteen states.

Seven months prior to the signing of the Treaty of Paris and with the war winding down William Albin continued to reside with Magdalena and their children in Westmoreland County. On February 24, 1783, William purchased from his brother-in-law and fellow Westmoreland County Ranger Mathias Shepler 150 acres on the east side of the Monongahela River close to today's Belle Vernon. William paid "twenty-one pounds lawful money of Pennsylvania" for the land.[35] To facilitate the purchase, the three Shepler brothers generously divided their approximately 600 acres into

---

[34]Albin, *Virginia Albins*, Chapter 6, p. 1 fn. 2. Ethel Albin incorrectly shows the amount for the period 2 August to 3 September 1778 as 10.10 (ten pounds, ten shillings). A transcribed copy of the original pay certificate #7651, issued 8 December 1785, for that period in the author's possession shows the amount to be 1.10 (one pound ten shillings).
[35]Ibid., Chapter 6, p. i, fn 3. Since 1777 the Articles of Confederation had governed the fledgling United States of America. It allowed each of the thirteen states to issue its own currency.

four equal shares. A census document recorded later in the year revealed that each of the Sheplers and William Albin now claimed exactly 150 acres.[36] As part of the plan and in order to equalize the division of Sheplers' property, Peter Shepler had sold 150 of his 300 acres to his brother Philip for £29 the next day (February 25). William Albin and Colonel Joseph Beeler (another former Frederick County resident of German heritage) had acted as witnesses to the transaction.

It should be noted that Philip Shepler paid £8 more for his 150 acres than did William. Possibly William's acreage had sold for less because it was situated inland and lacked access to the Monongahela River. (The Sheplers had originally purchased the 600 acres for £200, or £50 per 150-acre plot, more than twice as much what they charged William.)

Map 12 clearly shows the location of the "Shepley's" land extending to the banks of the Monongahela River, while William "Albon's" tract is situated inland from the river bordering Mathias Shepler on two sides.[37] Today, this site is located just off the Vance DeiCas Highway and the intersection of State Route 3009, southeast of the Donora-Monessen Bridge that spans the Monongahela River. Despite its distance from the river, proximity to water was not a problem for William, because on a separate survey map in the author's possession Speers Mill Run is shown flowing through a portion of the Albin property.

For the Sheplers to arrange this transaction at such a generous price in order to accommodate William indicates a close bond existed between the four men. When a disinherited William

---

[36]William Henry Egle, *Return of Taxables for the Counties of Bedford (1773-1784), Huntington (1788), Westmoreland (1783,1786), Fayette (1785-1786), Allegheny (1791), Washington (1786), And Census of Bedford (1784) and Westmoreland (1783)*, (Harrisburg, Pennsylvania: William S. Ray, 1898), 369, 378. Copies of the deeds for these sales between the Sheplers and Albin are in the author's possession.

[37]This survey is but one of hundreds found at an extraordinary website of the Pennsylvania State Archives. Though it takes some navigating, the website provides historic land records for all Pennsylvania counties. *Pennsylvania Historical and Museum Collection*, accessed April 11, 2014, http://www.phmc.state.pa.us/bah/dam/rg/di/r17-114CopiedSurveyBooks/Books%20C1-C234/Book%20C198/Book%20C-198%20pg%20411.pdf.

arrived with Magdalena in Westmoreland County (in 1771?) he probably did not have the means to purchase any land. Given the absence in Westmoreland County's Land Records of any land transactions prior to 1783 in William Albin's name, it is reasonable to assume this land purchase was his first. Now, thanks to his brothers-in-law, William had become a legitimate landowner.

Put into perspective, the same 1783 Rostraver Township tax records referenced above reveal 2,350 white inhabitants with approximately 503 listed as heads of household. Of those, less than half, only 231, claimed land. Of that number only 180 possessed 150 acres or more like William. With his land purchase from the Shepler family William, by no means a rich man, had just emerged as one of Rostraver's more significant property-owners.

Depending on how many acres they had cleared in the years since their arrival, the Albins and Sheplers may have been better off compared to other landowners in various sections of western Pennsylvania. According to one source, most settlers residing there in the 1780's were living at a subsistence level with the median cleared acreage per farm being twenty acres. (Some studies suggest forty acres would have been necessary to support an average family.) Later, when the newer areas of Westmoreland and other counties became more thickly settled a marked decline in the size of individual land holdings occurred. Subsequently, by the 1790s tax records reveal that the majority of persons in Fayette and Washington Counties (both located near Westmoreland County) were landless. The Sheplers and Albins could not have avoided noticing this trend and most likely regarded themselves as fortunate to not only own land but also to be able to claim tracts situated along the Monongahela River.[38]

Among the landowners residing near the Albins and Sheplers were some of the county's elite citizens. All were influential, affluent, and highly respected, but perhaps not as well off in the

---

[38]No author, *Whiskey Rebellion Resources in Southwestern Pennsylvania*, (Washington: National Register of Historic Places, United States Department of the Interior, 1992), 6, accessed April 24, 2014, http://www.phmc.state.pa.us/Portal/Communities/BHP/MPDFs/Whiskey_Rebelli on_Resources_in_Southwestern_PA.pdf.

William Albin Jr.

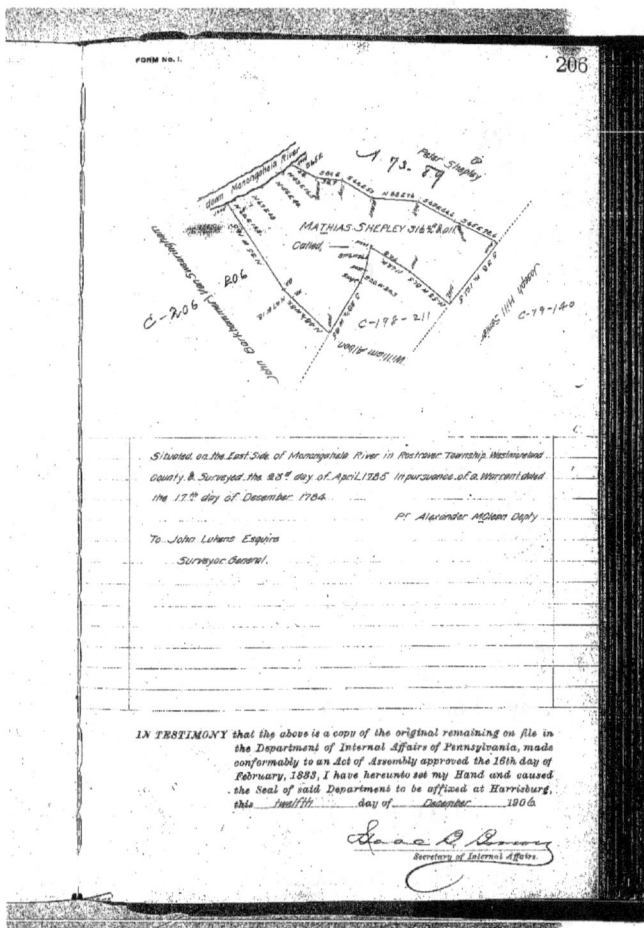

Map 12
Copy of the original survey of the Albin and Shepler Land in Rostraver Town-
ship, Westmoreland County, Pennsylvania, 1785 on the Monongahela River.
Albin's name appears inverted on the map.

postwar era as they had been in 1775. Living on land adjacent to
the Albins was Joseph Hill Sr., said to be the first settler in Rostraver Township. He had arrived in 1754 as an eighteen year old.

Another of William's neighbors was the Irish-born Reverend James Finley the celebrated minister, Pennsylvania agent in
the Westsylvania movement and in 1772 the first to bring orga-

nized Presbyterianism to the Alleghenies when he established the Rehoboth Church very near to William's property. Colonel Dorsey Pentecost, a rich and influential native of Frederick County, Virginia, who owned several tracts of land in Westmoreland County, resided near the Albin family in the county's early years. Wealthy Michael Springer owned hundreds of acres in both Westmoreland and Allegheny Counties, some near Speers Run close to the Albins and Sheplers. The noted Revolutionary War soldier and William's neighbor to the west, Captain Van Swearingen, owned two plots of land in Westmoreland, while Joseph Beckett claimed three separate tracts. None, however, could surpass the elevated standing of the affluent Colonel Edward Cook whose land bordered the western edge of Albin's property.

Cook, a friend to George Washington, in June 1776 became a Westmoreland County Deputy to the Provincial Conference of Committees held at Carpenter's Hall, Philadelphia. Later, the committee's work resulted in a declaration of independence delivered to Congress on June 25, 1776. Cook claimed least 3,000 acres in Washington, Westmoreland, and Fayette Counties, and he also owned for a time the nearest store where William and his neighbors could hope to find any necessities.[39]

Lastly, another of Albin's neighbors was Benjamin Fell who resided just east of William on a hill overlooking the Monongahela River. Fell likewise was a close friend to Washington and had participated in one of the first conventions assembled at Independence Hall in Philadelphia.[40]

---

[39]By 1776 Cook had constructed a mansion of limestone on his land adjacent to that of William Albin. Pretentious for its time, the two-storied structure stood out among all the log cabins of Cook's neighbors. Cook had served as a lieutenant in the Westmoreland County Rangers in William's battalion responsible for payroll and reimbursement. Later in 1784, following the Revolutionary War, General George Washington made a tour westward to the Monongahela River where he visited with Cook and delivered an impromptu speech on Cook's porch to a group of soldiers. Ellis, *History of Fayette County*, 807. Was Cook's neighbor, William Albin, in attendance that day during Washington's address? If so, might Albin have spoken with the General, reminding him of the old days when the Albins and Washington both resided in Winchester, Virginia? Colonel Cook is buried in Rehoboth Cemetery, Westmoreland County, near the Rehoboth Church established by his neighbor Reverend James Finley.

[40]Fell had lived in Bucks County, Pennsylvania, and worked as a tanner prior to residing in Rostraver Township in March 1782. According to tradition Fell of-

William Albin Jr.

Significantly, many of these men were slaveholders.

Slavery in Westmoreland County

As Westmoreland's postwar population continued to increase, local leaders, probably beginning in the late spring or early summer of 1783, conducted a countywide census. The record shows Will'm "Alben" (Albin) and seven additional but unnamed family members living on his recently acquired 150 acres in Rostraver Township. Given his father's aversion to slavery, William Jr. held no slaves, but he did own two horses, three cattle and five sheep. His Shepler in-laws also appeared in the census.[41] The entire township counted 2,350 whites and 107 blacks. Most of these blacks were slaves who worked in Rostraver's agriculture-based economy.

Despite the number of blacks counted in the 1783 census, the attitude regarding slavery across Pennsylvania as well as in Westmoreland County had been undergoing a gradual, but decided change since approximately 1780. In March of that year, during the height of the Revolutionary War and under pressure from its strong anti-slavery Quaker population, Pennsylvania passed "An Act for the Gradual Abolishment of Slavery" which allowed for the future potential emancipation of blacks. Pursuant to that Act, any master who held Negroes or mulattoes as slaves was compelled to document with the county in which he resided the number, names, age, and sex of each of his slaves. These master-created slave inventories thus provided a valuable accounting of

---

fered the contents of his tannery to General Washington's troops to make shoes for the Continental Army at Valley Forge. See John Boucher, *The Old and New Westmoreland*, (Pittsburgh: University of Pittsburgh Digital Research Library, 1999), Vol. 3, 141, accessed January 6, 2018,
https://babel.hathitrust.org/cgi/pt?id=pst.000003844946;view=1up;seq=221.
[41]Egle, *Return of Taxables*, 369, and for the Sheplers, 378:

Peter "Shipler"	150 acres	3 horses	3 cattle	8 sheep	10 whites	0 blacks
Mathias Shipler	150 acres	3 horses	5 cattle	8 sheep	7 whites	0 blacks
Philip Shipler	150 acres	3 horses	5 cattle	5 sheep	5 whites	0 blacks

Revolutionary War era slavery as well as a more personal look at the individuals involved, both slave and free.[42]

The following slaveholders and the numbers of slaves each held are derived from these lists and represent *only those Westmoreland County slave masters who were immediate neighbors of William Albin* in the years they reported their holdings, that is from October 12, 1780, to December 31, 1782. The men were part of the upper echelon of Westmoreland's society:

Colonel Edward Cook (8 slaves)
Reverend James Finley (9)
Van Swearingen (13)
Colonel Dorsey Pentecost (15)
Joseph Becket (7)
Joseph Hill (7)
Reverend Henry Speers (20)
Peter Reasoner (1)
Casper Geyer (1)[43]

Despite living among these slaveholders, neither Albin nor the Sheplers held slaves. William Jr.'s opposition to slavery likely was based on moral grounds. His presumed aversion to slavery echoed those sentiments advanced by his parents in Virginia years earlier. Later, while living in Kentucky, William rejected any slave purchases even though he then possessed sufficient money to do so. Furthermore, he went one step further in his refusal and aligned himself with an anti-slavery Baptist clergyman.

---

[42]Boucher, *The Old and New Westmoreland*, Vol. 1, Chapter XXII, "The Work of the Early Courts", 197, 198, 200-204, accessed September 24, 2013, https://babel.hathitrust.org/cgi/pt?id=wu.89065990392;view=1up;seq=226.

[43]Ibid. These of course are abbreviated entries. A typical slave list entry in the documents contained more information. For example: "Date reported: December 10, 1781, Owner: Van Swearingen: Slave: Male, Harry. **Age**: 24." Many slaves had no last names. The age range for the slaves owned by William's neighbors was 2 years three months to 39 years. In addition, these slaveholders may have owned indentured servants. Then Colonel George Washington (through his agent) sold two indentured servants, Peter Miller and John Wood, to Edward Cook in late July 1774 for forty-five pounds. Boucher, *Old and New Westmoreland*, Volume 1, 196.

Because of his stance on slavery, the question arises as to how William interacted with his many slaveholding neighbors in Rostraver Township. Albin must have found support and comfort in the knowledge that Magdalina's three brothers had also resisted the temptations of slaveholding. It is quite possible that William simply accepted the fact that though immoral, holding people in bondage remained the choice of each individual, and that the pro-slavery views held by his neighbors were their right as it was his right to reject slavery.

Perhaps, though, a perceptive William also saw through the hypocrisy of the situation. Americans had just fought an eight-year war against England to secure their precious liberty while at the same time some of his neighbors and other colonists, including Washington at Mount Vernon and Jefferson at Monticello, continued to own slaves. Perhaps the 1775 query of the prominent Englishman Dr. Samuel Johnson would have made perfect sense to William, "How is it we hear the loudest yelps for liberty among the drivers of Negroes?"

The aftermath of the war brought considerable change to the United States and its citizens. Gone were the King's Redcoats, while the king himself and Parliament could no longer exercise any control over their American subjects as they had done since 1607. Postwar Americans set about adjusting to life under a recently ratified Constitution, written miraculously and under great pressure in just a few months during a steamy Philadelphia summer in 1787. All realized that the Constitution, though not understood by everyone, was a document of their own making. Furthermore, American voters soon replaced one George with another. England witnessed the replacement of King George as the ruler of its former American colonies while Virginia's own George Washington assumed office as the nation's *democratically elected* President.

A glance at a map of the infant United States in 1790 revealed other significant changes. The United States' western

Map 13
The site of the land previously held by William B. Albin and the Sheplers in a
2008 aerial view of Rostraver Township,
Westmoreland County, Pennsylvania.
The Monongahela River is in the upper left.

boundary now extended to the Mississippi River. Beyond that
stretched a vast, unexplored wilderness claimed, along with Florida, by the King of Spain. More backwoods country lay tantalizing-
ly closer west of the Allegheny Mountains extending into Ohio
and Kentucky. While the nation's center of population was situated east of Baltimore, New Yorkers took pride that with the ratifi-
cation of the Constitution their city now served as the nation's official capital. (Washington, D.C. in 1790 existed only in the planning stage.) The nation's three most populated cities were New

William Albin Jr.

York with 33,131 people, Philadelphia at 28,522, and Boston with 18,320 persons.[44]

ROSTRAVER TOWNSHIP.

	Acres.	Horses.	Cattle.	Sheep.	Inhabitants. White.	Inhabitants. Black.
Allen, David, ...	..	2	2	3	5	..
Allen, Benja'n, ...	..	4	2	3	5	..
Andrews, Will'm, ...	200	3	3	6	8	..
Alben, Will'm, ...	150	2	3	5	8	..
Armstrong, Tho's, ...	..	2	2	..	4	..
Alexander, Adam, ...	..	2	2	..	7	..
Archer, Joseph, ...	..	1	2	..	3	..
Applegate, Dan'l, ...	275	4	6	4	10	..
Applegate, Sam'l, ...	..	1	2	2	6	..
Applegate, Benj'n, ...	300	2	4	10	6	..
Anderson, Will'm, ...	..	1	1	..	3	..
Allen, Will'm, ...	..	1	1	..	5	..
Applegate, Will'm, ...	300	3	5	8	11	..
Adair, Will'm, single, ..	..	..	..	..	1	..
Blakeley, Rob't, ...	300	3	3	6	5	..
Burns, Sam'l, ...	300	..	..	..	..	..
Baker, And'w, ...	100	2	1	..	7	..
Burgess, Ann, ...	70	1	1	..	7	2
Brownlow, James, ...	..	3	4	..	7	..
Becket, Mary, ...	400	2	4	5	3	..
Burgan, Dan'l, ...	..	2	1	4	6	..
Baxter, Sam'l, ...	..	2	2	..	10	..
Bovel, John, ...	50	1	4	6	8	..
Briggs, John, ...	..	2	1	..	3	..
Barrackman, George, ...	100	2	3	2	5	..
Barrackhamer, John, ...	70	2	3	4	7	..
Burch, John, ...	..	1	1	..	8	..
Burges, Richard, single,.	..	1	..	..	1	..
Brownlow, Thomas, ...	..	..	..	..	1	..

William Albin (Alben) in the 1783 Westmoreland County Census showing the 150 acres he had purchased from Mathias Shepler earlier that year.[45]

---

[44] *Heads of Families Census at the First Census of the United States Taken in the Year 1790, Pennsylvania*, (Washington, D.C.: Government Printing Office, 1908), Introduction, 5, accessed April 30, 2014, http://www2.census.gov/prod2/decennial/documents/1790g-02.pdf.

[45] Engle, *Return of Taxables*, 369.

The country's first *Federal* census began on Monday, August 2, 1790. The document showed the William Albin Jr. family still lived in Westmoreland County, Pennsylvania. Specifically, it listed "Wm. Albon" as the head of a family consisting of *one* free white male over age sixteen (William), *five* free white males under sixteen (the children), *one* free white female over sixteen (Magdalina), and no slaves. In this census format, only the name of the head of household appeared.[46]

Rostraver Township then counted a total population of 1,088 people, just about seven percent of Westmoreland's total population of 16,018. Rostraver also claimed forty-nine slaves in its total population, more than any other township in Westmoreland County but significantly less than half the 107 slaves it had counted in 1783. (The complete elimination of slavery in Pennsylvania had proven to be a gradual process.) If the totals are correct, Rostraver Township's population was declining. It had lost a total of 1,262 whites and fifty-eight blacks since the 1783 county census.[47]

During the years following the Albin family's arrival nearly two decades earlier, Westmoreland County had gradually assumed a more civilized character. By 1790, for the most part, the threat of Indian attacks had diminished. Churches of different denominations flourished. New settlers continued to arrive but not enough to offset the number who had departed. Fields were cultivated and banks and stores emerged.

Until approximately 1790 William and other citizens of Rostraver had confronted a nagging problem of how to acquire certain necessities for their families. Much of the food that William and his neighbors consumed was grown on their farms,

---

[46]The children of Magdalina and William and their approximate birth dates are: William Jr. (III) 1768, George 1771, John (born in Pennsylvania) between 1770-1780 (the 1830 Harrison County Indiana, federal census lists John as between 60-70 years old), Mary Elizabeth 1774, James 1775, Absalom 1778, Isaac 1780, Sarah 1782, Phillip 1784, and Joshua Carman 1794.

[47]Many citizens of Rostraver Township and Pennsylvania had abandoned their state in favor of the West, specifically Kentucky. Some slaveholders had moved to Maryland or Virginia taking their slaves with them rather than manumit them under the terms of Pennsylvania's 1780 "Act for the Gradual Abolishment of Slavery".

caught in streams and rivers, or hunted in the vast forests surrounding Rostraver Township. However, there were certain items that the Albins and others required but could not always easily purchase. Rostraver's citizens coveted sugar, flour, superfine cloth, and blankets, for example, but such goods were difficult to obtain. Some of these commodities were not available at all in the early days. As the years passed, though, William and other Rostraver citizens were able to find most of these items at a convenient general store operated by one of their neighbors.

In approximately 1790 David Furnier, a Frenchman who had moved to the area near Speers Run in 1771 or 1772, operated a store and flour mill in Belle Vernon close to Albin's land on the banks of the Monongahela River, just below where Speers' Run drains into the river. Attached to the store was also a distillery, and collectively the store, mill, and distillery were known as "The Barter Mills." It became probably "the largest business firm in the valley at that time."[48] It was this proximity of the Barter Mills store to William's cabin near Speers Run, however, that allowed him to trade there.[49] Perhaps, too, William found that The Barter Mills offered a better selection and perhaps better prices than the store once run by Edward Cook. Comparative shopping had come to Rostraver – another sign of advancing civilization.

Furnier owned two other stores, one at Pittsburgh and another at Devore's Ferry in "the substantial log mansion house" of Joseph Beckett on the river opposite the town of Monongahela seven miles north of William Albin's land. (This store located at Beckett's near the river was less than a mile from the Albin's relatives George and later James Bruce.) Furnier stocked both his

---

[48]John S. Van Voorhis, *The Old and New Monongahela*, (Pittsburgh: Nicholson, 1893), 445-446. It is possible that Furnier's *other* store near Devore's Ferry at Beckett's cabin opened in 1785. Deed of William Witherow, August 25, 1785, accessed April 14, 2014, "Pennsylvania State Archives Land Records," Copied Surveys, C-232-183: http://www.phmc.state.pa.us/bah/dam/rg/di/r17-114CopiedSurveyBooks/Books%20C1-C234/Book%20C232/Book%20C-232%20pg%20365.pdf. On Witherow's deed there is a reference to his property being located "near the New Store on Monongahela River in Rostraver Township."

[49]J.H. Beers, *Commemorative Biographical Record of Washington County, Pennsylvania*, (Chicago; J. H. Beers & Co., 1893), 1093. See also, Van Voorhis, *The Old and New Monongahela*, 312, and 444-446.

Pittsburgh store and the other two with various goods including groceries. As would be expected, each of the three did a thriving business; one transaction alone in the Pittsburgh store on July 2, 1791, accounted for 142 barrels of fine flour, 84 do [?] of superfine [cloth] 5 quarts of whiskey, 10 pounds of bacon, 1 tin cup, 16 pounds of bread, and 1 blanket.[50]

A portion of the 1790 Federal Census enumeration in Westmoreland County, Rostraver Township. "Albon's" name is preceded by the names of several Sheplers (shown as Shipler), specifically Philip, Mathias, and Peter and perhaps William's father-in-law John.[51]

Conversely, local grain producers found Furnier an eager customer. Much of the vast quantities of rye supplied by local farmers (perhaps some grown by William Albin?) Furnier converted into whiskey at his distillery.

A record book kept in 1790-1791 by Furnier's bookkeeper, Jacob Bowman, lists the names of people doing business at the

[50]Ibid., Van Voorhis, *The Old and New Monongahela*, 445. The total cost of the transaction was £323 or $1,615 in federal money according to the store's records. One pound apparently equaled five federal dollars.

[51]1790 United States Census, Westmoreland County, Pennsylvania, s.v. "William Albon," accessed through *Heritage Quest*, April 18, 2011.

William Albin Jr.

Barter Mills in Belle Vernon. Shown were Albin, Shepler, and their neighbors Speers, Cook, Hill, Barkhammer, Reasoner, Fell, Springer, and many other citizens of Rostraver Township.[52]

By the end of the decade of the 1780s, or before, William Albin had associated himself with the local Baptist Church and possibly assumed a leadership role within the congregation. On March 19, 1791, area Baptists including William "Allen" joined to form the Baptist Church Enan, which later evolved into the Maple Baptist Church. Located in a log cabin across the river on the *west* side of the Monongahela near the mouth of Maple Creek, the "church" stood some distance from Albin's Rostraver cabin on the river's east side opposite the village of Belle Vernon. William's German neighbor, Henry Speers Jr., who had since moved from Rostraver near William across the Monongahela River to Fallow-field Township, Washington County, helped found the church located near his property there.[53] Speers apparently had belonged to the Baptist church for quite some time and "his earnestness as a worker and his consistency as a Christian gave him a power and prestige among the early settlers that few men possessed."[54] After prayer on that March day, the congregation proceeded with the business of selecting key members to leadership positions.

A little more than a year later, on May 5, 1792, the Enon Church congregation licensed Speers "to Exercise his gift in preaching the word" and formally approved him to the ministry. Among the ten select church representatives whose names appeared at the bottom of a document signifying their endorsement of Speers was that of William Albin. As Albin was, at this time, residing in Kentucky, he must have allowed his name to be added in his absence.[55]

---

[52]Van Voorhis, *The Old and New Monongahela*, 445-446. According to Van Voorhis, the daybook was in his possession in 1893. Since Edward Cook traded at The Barter Mills, it is possible he had ceased operation of his own store at some point.

[53]Crumrine, *The History of Washington County, Pennsylvania*, 649, 650, 794. On page 794 Crumrine refers to William Albin as William "Allen", but on page 650 he mentions William Albin.

[54]Ibid., 650.

[55]The possibility exists that the William Albin referenced here could be William and Magdalina Albin's son, William Albin III, born in 1768. However, in 1791,

Following the Federal census in August 1790 or early in 1791, the urge to head westward, conspicuous in William Albin Sr., resurfaced again in his son William. Now forty-three years old William, with Magdalina and the children, had decided to relocate to Kentucky. Given the distance involved and the complexities associated with traveling there, this venture would prove much more challenging than William Jr.'s previous move in the 1770s from Winchester to Westmoreland County. A prime factor in William's decision to relocate westward was perhaps again the availability of vast virgin tracts of land. Perhaps, too, the woodsman and adventurer in William sensed that an increasingly populated Westmoreland County would eventually engulf him, turning him into a passive city dweller.

His analytic thinking aside, William's decision to leave Pennsylvania must have been a difficult one. After spending more than twenty years in Westmoreland County, the Albins would be severing ties with numerous friends and neighbors. Weighing particularly heavy on William and his family was the thought of forsaking their relatives, the three Shepler families. The strong bonds to each dated back decades to Frederick County. Later, the mutual hardships the Albins and Sheplers endured in early Westmoreland County and more recently during the seemingly endless Revolutionary War had reinforced those attachments. The Albins would never return to Pennsylvania and would never again see Magdalina's parents, her brothers, nor their many nieces and nephews. The memories of twenty years spent living near one another in Rostraver Township would have to sustain them forever.[56]

In preparation for the move, William sold his acreage to John Shepler Sr. He and his wife Magdalen (further evidence they were the parents of Magdalena Albin) had sold their 211 acres on Red Bud Run in Virginia on March 24, 1783. They had since lived in Westmoreland County, probably in the vicinity of their three sons, the Albins, and their many grandchildren, as evidenced by

---

at the time of the meeting referenced above, William Albin III would have been just twenty-three and probably far too young to be considered a voting elder of the church.

[56]The three Shepler brothers remained in Rostraver Township, their offspring marrying into local families there. The Shepler name is still seen in Westmoreland County today.

the proximity of their names to each other on the census sheet of 1790 (above).[57] Later, a May 1794 survey reveals that John "Shiplor" claimed the same tract formerly owned by William Albin (Map 14).[58]

It is estimated that the Albins left Pennsylvania on their westward journey within a narrow time frame, between August 1790 and early 1791. Census and tax records help confirm these dates and point to a more probable 1791 departure. As stated earlier Albin had been counted in Pennsylvania's 1790 census (the enumeration began on August 2, 1790, and ended in May 1791). Later, in 1791 William Albin's name appears on a Nelson County, Kentucky, tax roll. The Albins, therefore, would have most likely departed, not in the late fall or winter of 1790 from Pennsylvania, but instead in 1791 after the spring thaw occurred thus opening the Ohio River to easier navigation.

It may seem that these Kentucky-bound settlers would have loaded their possessions and children into covered wagons for the long journey ahead, conjuring up an 1840s Oregon Trail like vision of a westward bound pioneer wagon train. The reality was, however, quite different. Given the absence of roads linking Pennsylvania to their Nelson County, Kentucky, destination, the Albins made the journey in a flatboat as their relative William Bruce Sr.'s family had done in 1784.[59]

The Albins would have begun the first leg of their water journey on the nearby Monongahela River, heading toward Pittsburg just north of Rostraver. At Pittsburgh they may have joined a

---

[57]Albin, *Virginia Albins*, 239, and Chapter 6, footnote 3, p. i.

[58]Pennsylvania State Archives. Search under Copied Surveys, in Volume C-198-211 referenced above. Shepler named his tract Smyrna.

[59]William Bruce, "Memoirs of the Bruce Family," *The Indiana Magazine of History*, (1927), Volume 23, 63-72, accessed January 4, 2016, http://scholarworks.iu.edu/journals/index.php/imh/article/view/6407/6535. William Bruce Jr. (1776-1853) penned these recollections on August 6, 1851, at age 75. He died two years later in Bruceville, Indiana. Bruce Jr. recalled that his family "landed at the mouth of the Bear Grass" [now the site of Louisville] on the Ohio River at the end of their trip from Pennsylvania in 1784. He was a second cousin to William Albin Jr. For a description of flatboats on the Ohio in the 1780s see Alfred Pirtle, *James Chenoweth, The Story of One of the Earliest Boys of Louisville and Where Louisville Started*, (Louisville: The Standard Printing Company, 1921), 5-9.

flotilla of flatboats or "Kentucky boats" as they were called. Each craft held other eager Pennsylvanians all well-prepared for the long trip down the Ohio River.

These flatboats presented a curious sight. Farm animals had been carefully lashed to railings onboard. Sharing space with the livestock, furniture had also been strapped alongside the deck, atop the small cabins, or stowed inside. William and others would have also secured their plows, harnesses, and agricultural tools for use in Kentucky in whatever appropriate places they could find.

Traveling by day the flatboats drifted slowly, as reliable deckhands propelled each craft with oars in deep water or used large poles that touched bottom in shallow areas. Steering was accomplished with the use of a large oar mounted on the stern. Also, in the rear was a fireplace built on a bed of dirt and stones where cooking could be done in rainy weather or when the boat could not land. Firing ports were constructed on each side of the vessel for defense in case of Indian attack. When darkness came, the travellers would land, tie their boats along the bank, and camp for the night. Alert guards stood watch onboard and in the woods outside the campsite at this particularly vulnerable time. The journey would have taken the Albins and others a month or longer depending on the water's depth and if blockages were encountered on the river.[60]

Some 590 miles later, the Albin family disembarked at or near present day Louisville, perhaps at the mouth of the Bear Grass Creek near the Falls of the Ohio. From there they made the short journey south to Nelson County perhaps with the help of their Bruce relatives who had probably been eagerly awaiting their arrival.[61]

---

[60]Soon, 1,000 flatboats would float down the Ohio from Pittsburgh each year. John Van Houten Dippel, *Race to the Frontier: White Flight and Westward Expansion,* (New York: Algora Publishing, 2005), 77.

[61]Flatboats, built to go downstream only, were in the early years of Kentucky settlement the lifeblood of commerce and transportation. These wooden flat bottoms were easy to build and operate, and at the end of the water journey they provided wood for constructing a cabin. They could be anywhere from twenty to sixty feet long with a lengthy rear oar and two side oars. The hazards travelers faced came from pirates, Indians, illness, poor construction and poor piloting. Nonetheless, more than a million immigrants floated down the Ohio into the Ohio River Valley prior to the advent of passenger steamboat travel in approximately

Located in the west central part of Kentucky, Nelson County had been formed from a portion of Hardin County. The first explorers arrived in 1775-6, and by 1780 the first settlements arose. Shortly thereafter, the first elements of the Bruce had clan arrived.

The Bruce Family

In perhaps late 1784, several years prior to William Albin's arrival in Kentucky, his cousins William Bruce Sr. and George Bruce, along with their sixty-five year old father James Bruce Sr. and his wife Margaret (McMahon) Bruce, approximately fifty-six, had moved to Kentucky from Allegheny County, Pennsylvania. (James Sr. and Margaret were of course William Albin's uncle and aunt.) It appears that the Bruce's third son remained in Pennsylvania, intending to join the family later in Kentucky.[62]

James Bruce Jr. had chosen to remain behind possibly due to his concern for his wife Mary "Polly" (Runyan) and their newborn daughter. In March 1784 Mary had given birth to Piety (later Piety Bruce Albin the author's ggg grandmother) in the Bruce cabin (near Elizabeth?) in Allegheny County. Thus, when possibly confronted in late 1784 with the prospect of subjecting his family and the infant Piety to a lengthy and arduous early winter trip down the Ohio River to Kentucky, James Jr. may have wisely chosen to wait until Piety was older.

James Jr. had purchased land from his brother George in Rostraver Township near William Albin prior to George's departure. By January 1786 survey records show the 259 acres George owned in Rostraver Township had passed to James. A search of

---

1817. See John Kleber, *The Kentucky Encyclopedia*, (Lexington: University of Kentucky Press, 1992), 324 for a further discussion of flatboats on the Ohio.
[62]Albin, *Virginia Albins*, 4. The author bases this assumption on the fact that the names of James Sr., George, and William Bruce all appear for the first time in the Nelson County Titheables List for 1785, while James Jr. first appears in 1786. "Nelson County Tithes 1785-1791," accessed May 8, 2014, http://files.usgwarchives.net/ky/nelson/taxlists/taxes/nelson2.txt.

the surveys by the author yielded the location of the Bruce land north of the Albin property.[63]

It is likely that James Bruce Jr. had chosen to move to Rostraver Township after residing for years in Washington and Allegheny Counties because of the proximity of his relatives William and Magdalina Albin. Possibly during the Bruces' residence in Rostraver, William's son, six-year old Absalom Albin, gazed for the first time at his infant cousin Piety Bruce, unaware that the two would later marry and travel life's road together for nearly fifty years.[64]

Beginning at the Albin property shown on Map 13 above and passing through the Mathias and Peter Shepler land following the Monongahela River "up", one would next come to the tracts of George Martin and Peter Rothwell, (not shown on the map) both adjoining the river. Next, after Rothwell's land would be that of James Bruce, also fronting the Monongahela. These surveys, therefore, reveal that both of my gggg grandfathers James Bruce Jr. and William Albin Jr. lived in close proximity to each other, probably less than two miles apart during a short span from 1785 until 1786. However, in 1786 James Bruce left Rostraver for good, joining his father and brothers in Kentucky.

With the Albins' arrival in Kentucky in 1791, the two families were once again reunited. Most likely in a prearranged undertaking the Albins, upon landing in Kentucky, would have logically joined their Bruce relatives, at least temporarily until a cabin could be constructed. As had been the case ever since William Albin Sr. married Mary Bruce Albin in Frederick County, Virginia, in the late 1730s, the Bruce and Albin families maintained their close relationship.

---

[63]In the author's possession are copies from the Pennsylvania State Archive website for Rostraver, Westmoreland County, showing the same 259 acre tract of land first with George Bruce's name, then on the second copy James Bruce's name appears. See Pennsylvania State Archives, *Copied Survey Books*, Volume A-29, pgs. 78, 79 for George Bruce.

[64]In 1786 after James Sr., George, and William Bruce had settled in Kentucky, a 1786 Return of State Tax record shows William "Albon" paid four pounds six shillings tax while his cousin James Bruce Jr. paid seven pounds eight shillings tax in Rostraver Township, Egle, *Return of Taxables*, 473-474.

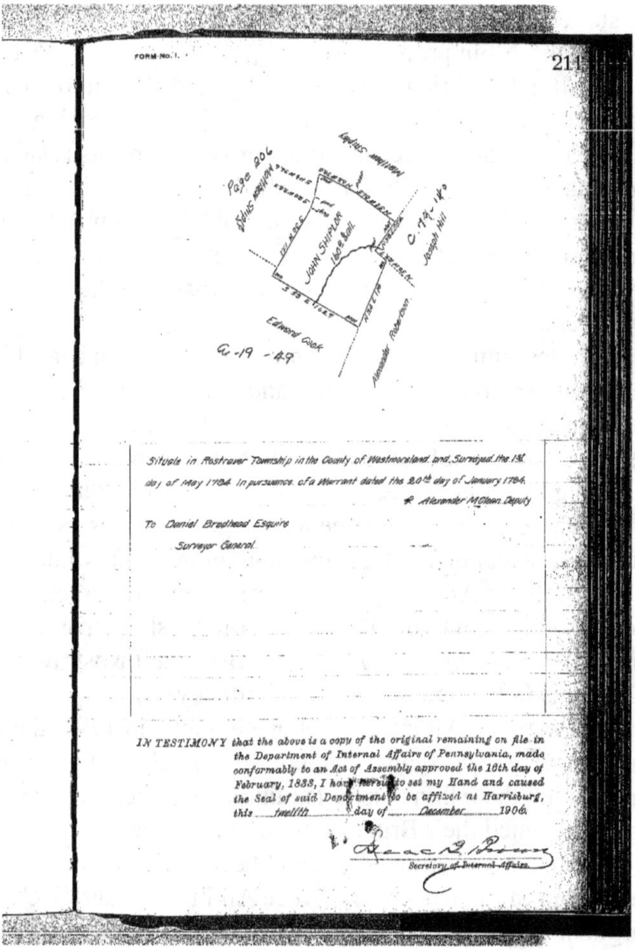

Situate in Rostraver Township in the County of Westmoreland and Surveyed the 1st day of May 1784 In pursuance of a Warrant dated the 20th day of January 1784.

℞ Alexander McClean Deputy

To Daniel Brodhead Esquire
Surveyor General

IN TESTIMONY that the above is a copy of the original remaining on file in the Department of Internal Affairs of Pennsylvania, made conformably to an Act of Assembly approved the 16th day of February, 1833, I have hereunto set my Hand and caused the Seal of said Department to be affixed at Harrisburg, this twelfth day of December 1906.

Secretary of Internal Affairs.

Map 14
A 1794 survey drawing showing John "Shiplor" occupying land formerly owned by William Albin. Compare to Map 12 above where William Albin's name appears but in 1783.

CHAPTER V

Nelson County, Kentucky

A man that stays in the valley always wonders what is on the other side of the mountain, he can guess but never knows for sure.

Daniel Boone in *The Crist Account Book*, May 26, 1778[1]

By the early 1790s, with the elimination of the Indian threat in the eastern Ohio Valley, America's frontier had shifted westward beyond Pennsylvania. The Albin and the Bruce families during this expansionist period became part of a general migration trend that would eventually populate even the most remote areas of Kentucky while the country's western border edged ever closer to the Mississippi River.

In late 1790 or the spring of 1791 when the Albins arrived in Kentucky, the Bruce clan headed by James Bruce Sr. was well established in Nelson County. The family had made a permanent home on farmland just south of the Ohio River having lived there for at least four to five years. More specifically, according to a brief February 1797 article in the *Kentucky Gazette* and the recollection of William Albin's second cousin, William Bruce Jr., James Bruce Sr. lived on Cox's Creek.[2] (By the time the Albins reached Kentucky, the James Bruce Jr. family had previously removed from Pennsylvania joining their relatives in Nelson County.)[3]

---

[1]Geni.com, The Account Book [of] Nicolaus Heinrich Crist as copied by Henry R. Selman, 1958,
accessed January 2, 2018, https://www.geni.com/people/Nicholas-Crist-Sr/6000000018811865690.
[2]*Kentucky Gazette,* Lexington, February 15, 1797, p.3, column 4, accessed January 5, 2018, http://nyx.uky.edu/dips/xt7t4b2x4b24/data/1358.pdf. The *Gazette*, first published in Lexington in August 1787 by John and Fielding Bradford, was the first newspaper in Kentucky. This article referenced a slave sale at the home of Bruce's brother-in-law David Cox of Nelson County. Bruce Sr. was offering to sell Caesar, his eleven or twelve year old Negro slave, on May 1, 1797.
[3]James Bruce Jr. arrived prior to October 27, 1786, as his daughter Elizabeth was born on that day in Nelson County.

Whereas in contrast to earlier Kentucky settlers who had first brought their families to some strong, fortified station for protection from Indian attack before constructing a home and clearing the land, the Albins were likely greeted and housed by their established Bruce relatives. The Bruces had endured the hardships of living their first winter and spring in the small village of Louisville upon their arrival in Kentucky. Garrisoned by U.S. troops, it provided a much-welcomed refuge for many newcomers. As a result of that experience, the Bruces were probably quite willing to help their Albin kinfolk during those difficult early years in Nelson County. Thus, it is very likely that the homeless Albin family remained with the Bruces during the time just after their arrival until their cabin was completed. From court documents we know that William and his family subsequently purchased a tract of land in1793.[4]

The choice of the Bruce family (and later perhaps that of the Albins) to resettle in Kentucky may have been related to the military service of William Bruce Sr. and his brother James. Captain William Bruce (1745-1818) of the 2nd Battalion 8th Company, Washington County, Pennsylvania Militia had served in Kentucky during the Revolutionary War. Stationed at Ft. Nelson in the area that is today downtown Louisville, Captain Bruce commanded a company under General George Rogers Clark in 1781.[5] Bruce's brother, James Bruce Jr., Piety Bruce's (later Piety Albin) father, made it a family affair and served with his brother also at Ft. Nelson.[6] During their Revolutionary War service in Kentucky, the Bruce brothers must have grown very familiar with the countryside in and around Ft. Nelson and Nelson County in general. Like William Albin's older brother John on his return from Pennsylvania during the French and Indian War, the Bruces, when they re-

---

[4]J.J. Marshall, Court Reporter, *Cases at Law and Equity Argued and Decided in the Court of Appeals of the Commonwealth of Kentucky*, (Frankfort: State of Kentucky, 1833), VI, 158-164, "Sprigg's Heirs vs Albin's Heirs."
[5]George Rogers Clark (1752-1818) was the brother of William Clark the explorer and one of the co-leaders of the Lewis and Clark expedition to the Pacific and back.
[6]Bruce, *Memoirs,* no page given. William Bruce's son later recalled that his father was absent from home in Pennsylvania some five or six months while serving in the army.

turned home to Pennsylvania, would have related impressive accounts to their family and friends of an enticing, but wild and sparsely populated Kentucky.

Thus, when the war officially concluded in 1783 opening the floodgates to Kentucky settlement, the Bruces soon made their way to Nelson County. Their arrival coincided with the influx of other settlers, particularly a large group of Virginia's Revolutionary War veterans who arrived in Kentucky to claim postwar land grants awarded them by the state of Virginia. Tax records confirm that during this postwar era James Bruce Sr. and his offspring indeed acquired land in Nelson County.[7] Later, perhaps as a result of both his Bruce kinfolk's favorable reports regarding Kentucky and perhaps equally enticing stories originating from returning visitors, William Albin and his family also decided to relocate to Nelson County.

Established in 1784 some seven years prior to the Albins' arrival, Nelson County was named after Thomas Nelson (1738-1789), a Virginia governor and signer of the Declaration of Independence. Known as Kentucky County in 1776, Nelson County had originally been a part of Virginia. Later, it became Jefferson County, and then in November 1784 Nelson County was formed with Bardstown as its county seat. The area had seen whites arrive some nine years before the Bruces had settled there.

Isaac Cox (1756-1788), a former resident of Frederick County, and later Hampshire County, Virginia, had preceded both the Bruces and Albins in Kentucky. In April 1775 Cox had traveled by boat down the Ohio River from Peters Creek, Redstone, Washington County, Pennsylvania, (the same area where the Bruce family had previously lived) to Nelson County. Joined by several other men including his brother David (whose wife Margaret was a Bruce), Isaac Cox settled on a 1,000-acre tract near the Cox's Creek (named for him) site where the Albins would reside nearly two decades later.[8]

Soon, Cox established the fabled Cox's Station (a fortified structure complete with cabins and a stockade) as protection

[7]No author, *Early Kentucky Tax Records*, (Baltimore: Genealogical Publishing Company Inc., 1987), "Taxable Property within District of Gabriel Cox," 217.
[8]Robert Rennick, *Kentucky Place Names*, (Lexington: The University Press of Kentucky, 1984), 70.

against Indian attack.[9] This outpost, located four and one half miles north of Bardstown (today at the junction of Highways 31 East and 509), served as a temporary safe haven for arriving settlers in the early '80s until they could construct permanent, secure homes.

Early Kentucky and Nelson County residents withstood a continuous Indian menace reminiscent of the hostile Indian threats and assaults citizens of frontier western Pennsylvania endured during the Revolutionary War years. A Congressional report titled "An Account of Indian Depredations in the District of Kentucky Since the First of May 1789" found that in Nelson County two men had been killed, two wounded and twenty horses stolen. Nearby Jefferson County reported four killed and three taken prisoner by marauding Indians.[10] According to a 1790 government report, 1,500 Kentucky settlers had been killed in Indian raids since the end of the Revolutionary War in 1783. Consequently, settlers maintained a constant state of vigilance as they went about their lives.

Decades later William Bruce Jr. recalled those early days in Kentucky just after his family made the journey from Pennsylvania in 1784. His description of a wild and sparsely settled Nelson County would have been somewhat similar to its appearance at the time of the Albins' arrival seven years later:

> Louisville was a small village and there was a garrison [Ft. Nelson] with some United States troops kept there. We lived there that winter [1784] and in the spring of 1785 moved on the waters of Coxes Creek named after my uncle David Cox [it was actually named after Isaac Cox] that [sic] had settled there a few years previous. My father bought 200 acres of land and commenced making a farm. The first settlers had just ventured from their forts. I recol-

---

[9]As time passed Cox's wealth increased with his land holdings in Nelson County.
[10]Blaine Guthrie Jr., "Captain Richard Chenowith, A Founding Father of Louisville," *The Filson Club History Quarterly*, Volume 46, #2, April, 1972, no page given, accessed May 16, 2014, http://www.chenowethsite.com/chfilson.htm.
In 1794, Indian resistance in Kentucky ended with General Anthony Wayne's (of Revolutionary War fame) victory over several tribes at Fallen Timbers (near present day Toledo, Ohio).

lect having to stand and watch while my father was at work with his rifle well braced against a tree close at hand. About this time [1788], Colonel Isaac Cox was killed by the Indians while out surveying…about four miles from where my father lived. This made quite a stir in the neighborhood and men were stationed at different places along the frontier settlements.

That was the last murder committed by the Indians between Salt River and Bardstown. From that time on until the close of the Indian War [1794], after General Wayne [the grandson of John Hunter's friend Anthony Wayne Sr.] gave them a scourging, times gradually became more safe [sic] and settlements were pushed on to the Ohio River.[11]

Though the Indian threat still existed, it had subsided significantly by the time the Albins arrived in 1790 or 1791. Nonetheless, Albin may have chosen the location for his homestead because of its proximity to both the Bruces and to Cox's Station and the security it afforded.

The Albins were among the last pioneers of this general migration across the Appalachians into Kentucky numbering more than 70,000 settlers between 1775 and 1792.[12] Prior to their arrival, William and Magdalina were probably aware of the remoteness of Nelson County and may have even compared it to that of early Westmoreland County. However, the degree of isolation may have surprised them. The Albins and their Nelson County neighbors remained utterly separated from the East by miles of moun-

---

[11]Bruce, *Memoirs*. William Bruce Jr.'s memory matches the historical record. Written in 1851, Bruce's recollection that his father claimed 200 acres corresponds exactly with the Bruce acreage detailed in a Taxable Property document of 1792. The Bruce *Memoirs* is also the source for the reference to the Bruces' previous residence near the mouth of Peters Creek in Washington County, Pennsylvania.

[12]Dippel, *Race to the Frontier*, 77, fn. 2. The origin of the word Kentucky may be an Iroquoian word for "meadow" or "prairie", but other explanations exist as well. Perhaps it is derived from a Cherokee name for the area south of the Ohio River. The early pioneers spelled the name in many ways, including "Kaintuckee" and "Cantuckey."

tainous terrain, wild rivers, and dense forests. Roads were non-existent. News reaching Kentucky arrived via conversation or an occasional, usually months old newspaper. However, the hope of a better life and *land* acquisition proved to be temptations even the isolation could not suppress.

A typical, Kentucky fortified station (fort) of the late 1770s and 1780s. Note how the rear wall of each cabin is part of the common exterior defensive wall of the station.

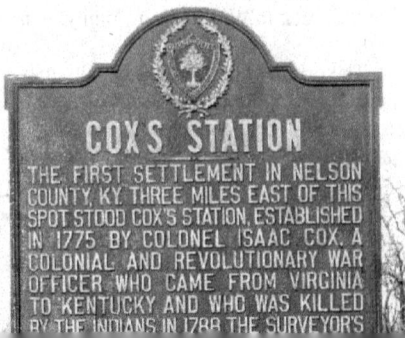

Historical marker commemorating Cox's Station close to the Albin and Bruce lands in Nelson County.

COX S STATION

THE FIRST SETTLEMENT IN NELSON
COUNTY, KY THREE MILES EAST OF THIS
SPOT STOOD COX'S STATION, ESTABLISHED
IN 1775 BY COLONEL ISAAC COX, A
COLONIAL AND REVOLUTIONARY WAR
OFFICER WHO CAME FROM VIRGINIA
TO KENTUCKY AND WHO WAS KILLED
BY THE INDIANS IN 1788 THE SURVEYOR'S

By June 1, 1792, Kentucky had become the fifteenth state, the first west of the Appalachian Mountains, and the third different state William Albin had lived in since his birth. With a flood of new pioneers, Kentucky's population increased so rapidly that by 1820 it was the sixth largest state in America. Kentucky's inaugural census of 1790 (taken shortly before the Albins arrival) showed 73,677 occupants out of a total United States population of slightly less than 4,000,000. Of Kentucky's inhabitants nearly 17% or 12,430 were slaves.

Nelson County recorded 11,315 people, considerably more people than one might expect for such a remote region. It reported 1,248 slaves (11% of the its total population) and just thirty-five free "colored".[13] By 1798 Bardstown, then ten years old and the county seat, counted 216 inhabitants, and was described by one writer as a "flourishing town."[14]

As the Albins adapted to their new setting, William's name began to appear in the Nelson County records, first on a local tax list. The county tithes (tax list) for 1791 shows William "Alban" assessed for two tithes (males over age 16), William and probably his oldest son William III.[15] Later, Albin's name is

---

[13]Charles Heinemann, compiler, *First Census of Kentucky 1790*, (Baltimore: Genealogical Publishing Company, 1965), 3. In 1790 Kentucky had not yet been granted statehood. It was therefore included as a *county* in the first census of Virginia. Unfortunately, the Kentucky Federal Census Schedules of 1790 and 1800 were destroyed in the British attack on Washington, D.C. during the War of 1812. Thus, Kentucky "census" records for 1790 relied on local 1791 or 1792 Tax Lists.

[14]William Perrin, *Kentucky – A History of the State, Embracing a Concise Account of the Origin and Development of the Virginia Colony*, (Louisville: F. A. Battey, 1888), 292.

[15]Tax list Nelson County Tithes 1785-1791, accessed May 15, 2014, http://files.usgwarchives.net/ky/nelson/taxlists/taxes/nelson2.txt. Below William's "Alban's" name on the same list are those of William's uncle, James Bruce, and his two sons (William Albin's cousins) James Jr. and William. Also appearing in the Nelson County tax records was a relative of William Albin, Isaiah Calvert. Calvert, a former Revolutionary War officer and the son of Richard Calvert, was a second cousin to William. Both these Calverts hailed from Frederick County and owned land near the Bruces and Albins on Opequon Creek. Isaiah paid taxes in Nelson County from 1793-1795 though he owned no land. Calvert's

shown on both a land purchase document and also in survey records.

In March or April 1794, William contracted with a relative, twenty-four year old James Cox, to survey 500 acres of land, a parcel more than triple the size of his Rostraver Township acreage. William had selected Cox, his second cousin and Isaac Cox's nephew, probably on the basis of familiarity and trust. Purchased in June 1793, the tract to be surveyed was situated on Murray's Run, a branch of the Caney Fork of Cox's Creek, just southeast of Cox's Station and roughly six miles northeast of present day Bardstown near William's Bruce relatives (Map 15).[16]

Oddly, William had contracted with Cox to undertake a survey a year *after* his land purchase had been completed. This atypical sequence - purchase, then survey - defied the established conventions of land transactions of the time. The tardy survey, combined with a glaring omission in William's contract, the lack of title transfer from the seller, would have stood as red flags to a savvy outside observer.[17] But, William's apparent trust of the seller may have eased any potential worries he might have had.

---

presence in Nelson County near the Bruces and Albins provides additional support for view that often these frontier settlers tended to collect near friends and family during times of resettlement.

[16]Ibid., and Albin, *Virginia Albins*, 239 and Chapter 6, fn. 4, i-iii. Cox, in a deposition given in August 1825, stated he had surveyed the land during April 1794.

[17]The property that William planned to have surveyed was no government gift, as he probably did not qualify for the generous land bounties provided to Revolutionary War Veterans. William's time in the Westmoreland County Rangers militia did not involve continuous service throughout the War and thus most likely precluded him from receiving any land bounty in Kentucky.

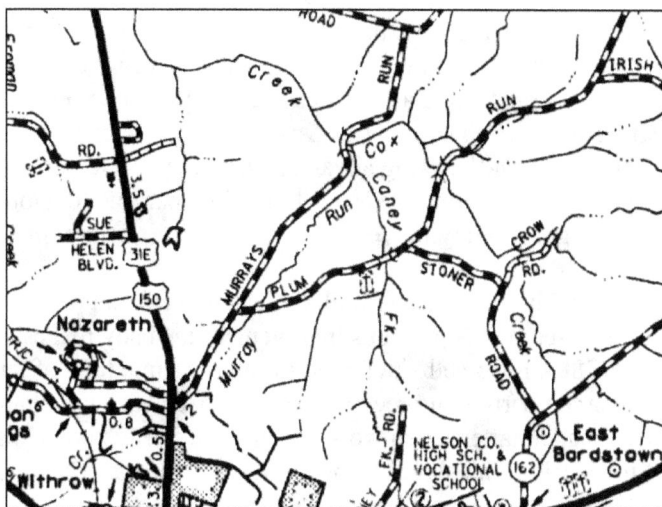

Map 15
A modern map showing the locale of William Albin's property on Cox (Cox's)
Creek and Murray's Run. Bardstown is to the lower left.[18]

A year *prior* to his survey, on June 3, 1793, William had
begun the process of land ownership, when he and Captain Richard Chenoweth executed a contract for the sale of the 500 acres.
The agreement specified that Chenoweth would provide a deed of
conveyance [transfer] to Albin within seven days or else Chenoweth would forfeit a fee he had previously paid to Albin:

> I Richard Chenowith [sp] of the County of Jefferson and
> State of Kentuck am held and firmly bound unto Wil-
> liam Albin of Nelson County...on the penal sum of three
> hundred eighty Pound[s] current money of the State of
> Kentuck....[19]

Subsequently, Albin never received a title to the land from
Chenoweth because Chenoweth claimed he never received a title

---

[18]General Highway Map, Nelson County Kentucky, 1999 Edition, *Kentucky Department of Highways*, accessed May 24, 2014,
http://ukcc.uky.edu/maps/ghm1999/nelson.gif.
[19]Albin, *Virginia Albins*, Chapter 6, ii, fn 4.

from the original owner, Osburn Sprigg.[20] Because of Kentucky's existing and chaotic land records system, such a scenario was entirely plausible. State land authorities had completed no preliminary land surveys, and boundaries were vague. As a result insecure titles were common.[21] Taking advantage of this imperfect system, Chenoweth failed to ever provide Albin's title, part of a devious pattern he began employing years before William's arrival in Kentucky.

Probably unknown to William, Chenoweth had a dubious reputation based on his previous involvement in shady real estate deals. In 1788 Chenoweth attempted to sell the same tract of land to two separate parties and receive payment from each simultaneously. To make matters even worse, he later offered to compensate one of the parties with slaves he never owned![22] On another occasion disclosed after Chenoweth's death, a court ruled his title to his own land (acquired in 1785) on Floyd's Fork "vague and uncertain" as he apparently had never obtained a patent for the land.[23] None of this boded well for Albin's current transaction with Chenoweth in 1793.

According to court documents filed years later, the truth was "Chenoweth could not have stipulated with Albin in good faith [regarding the deed]…because when he [Chenoweth] made that stipulation he had no conveyance from Sprigg and had paid no part of the [original] purchase money [to Sprigg]."[24] Furthermore, the court stated "there is not a particle of evidence…to show that he [Chenoweth] had, at the date of his contract [with Albin], any expectation of being able to procure the title in time to comply with it."[25] In other words Chenoweth had "sold" land to Albin that he had never owned. However, at the time of sale if William har-

---

[20]Ibid. See also, Marshall, *Cases at Law and Equity,* 158.

[21]William Bruce Jr. in his *Memoirs* reported that sometime after 1798 "I bought me a small tract of land on the waters of Coxes Creek, Nelson County… made a small farm when an older claim took it away from me [in the spring of 1805]."

[22]Guthrie, "Captain Richard Chenowith", accessed May 27, 2014, http://www.chenowethsite.com/chfilson.htm.

[23]Michael Cook, *Jefferson County, Kentucky Records,* (Evansville: Cook Publications, 1987), Vol. 5, 371.

[24]Marshall, *Cases at Law and Equity,* 158.

[25]Ibid.

bored suspicions about this man, he may have put them aside for a very good reason.

The seller, Richard Chenoweth (1734?-1802) "a large man of great strength", born in Maryland and now of Jefferson County, Kentucky, was no stranger to William Albin, but instead he was a distant relative and Virginia neighbor.[26] It appears that William and Richard Chenoweth were related through their common Calvert-Parrell line. Chenoweths had even resided in Frederick County, Virginia, since prior to approximately 1740, close to the time of William's birth. Richard's father John Chenoweth (wife Mary Smith) owned land on the drains of Mills Creek, and his name appears some twenty lines below William Albin Sr.'s on a list of Frederick County deed holders.[27] As a result, perhaps initially William did not worry unduly about the lack of title for his 500 acres. Given their kinship and history dating to Virginia, Albin probably trusted Chenoweth to provide the document at some future point.

Chenoweth's motive for selling land went back several years to the time of the founding of Louisville, Kentucky. By the time William Albin arrived in Nelson County in 1790-1791, Richard Chenoweth was very familiar to local inhabitants. He and his family had left Redstone, Pennsylvania, in Washington County in April 1778 and arrived on flatboats with an expedition led by Lt. Colonel George Rogers Clark on May 27, 1778. In October-

---

[26]Pirtle, *James Chenoweth*, 1. Part of Pirtle's book is the primary source reminiscences of Richard Chenoweth's son James (1777-post 1850). This description of Richard Chenoweth is from James's recollection related apparently in 1850. James also provides a chilling account of the so-called Chenoweth Massacre and the scalping of his mother Margaret McCarthy Chenoweth. As is true with the Albin surname, there are different spellings for Chenoweth in the historical record.

[27]It is very probable that William Bruce Sr. knew Chenoweth as well. Both men had been stationed at Redstone, Pennsylvania, and had served at Ft. Nelson under General Clark at the same time during the Revolutionary War. Also, Bruce's father, James Bruce, had lived near the Chenoweths in Frederick County. In addition, Richard Chenoweth's nephew, Jonathan Chenoweth (1757-1834) of Frederick County, had served with William Albin Jr.'s brother George Albin in Berry's company of the 8th Virginia Regiment in 1777 and as a member of George Washington's Lifeguard briefly until discharged on August 11, 1777, probably before George's arrival. "The Muster Roll Project", *Valley Forge Legacy*, http://valleyforgemusterroll.org, s.v., "John Chenoweth". In short Albin links to Chenoweths existed everywhere.

November 1783, he had served briefly in a battalion of the local Nelson County militia under Colonel Isaac Cox. By 1785 Chenoweth claimed 2,000 acres on Floyd's Fork in Jefferson County, Kentucky.[28]

In early 1781 Lt. Colonel Clark charged Captain Chenoweth with the responsibility for both the layout and the construction of Fort Nelson, on the Ohio River in the area of what is now downtown Louisville, Kentucky. "My father, being more experienced than anyone else in the party was selected to direct the building of this little fortification", 200 feet by 100 feet.[29] Considered one of the city's founders, Chenoweth may have learned that early planners had considered naming Louisville "Margaretville" after his wife, but they had apparently reconsidered. Later, "Mr. Chenoweth at his own expense (which was very considerable) completed the Fortification [Fort Nelson] in March 1781 in a proper manner".[30]

---

[28]Chenoweth's neighbor to the east in Jefferson County (north of Bardstown) was another former Virginian living on nearby Long Run Creek, Abraham Lincoln Sr., the grandfather of the sixteenth President. The two men most likely knew each other. Lincoln had moved there in 1785. In May 1786 while putting in his corn crop, Lincoln Sr. died in an Indian ambush attack. His son Mordecai Lincoln, still in his teens at the time, grabbed a rifle from the house and killed the Indian who was attempting to scalp his deceased father. Later, Mordecai and the remainder of the Lincoln family (along with a young Thomas Lincoln, Abe's father) moved to Nelson County, Kentucky, residing there for a time. Thomas Lincoln's name appears several lines below that of William Albin on the Nelson County Tithes List for the years 1785-1791. Years later Abraham Lincoln still recalled the family story of his Uncle Mordecai's killing of the Indian who had killed his grandfather Abe Sr. Coincidentally, Abraham Lincoln's family roots seem to extend back to Chester County, Pennsylvania. His ancestors Mordecai and Abraham Lincoln Sr. appeared on the 1725 tax roll at the same time John Hunter and the Albin orphans were living there.

[29]James Chenoweth in Pirtle, *James Chenoweth*, 14.

[30]Colonel George Slaughter in John E. Kleber, *The Encyclopedia of Louisville*, (Lexington: University Press of Kentucky, 2001), 175. Captain Richard Chenoweth is also famous in the early annals of Kentucky history for being a near victim of the Chenoweth Massacre. On July 17, 1789, a large party of Indians attacked his station in Jefferson County at Floyd's Fork killing three of his children and wounding Chenoweth and his son James. Chenoweth's wife, Margaret, was shot between the shoulder blades with an arrow and feigned death as an Indian scalped her. Rescued the next day, she survived, bore two more children, and lived approximately another thirty-six years, compelled to wear a skullcap for the remainder of her life. Kleber, *Encyclopedia of Louisville*, 175-176. This episode

Under an agreement with the state of Virginia (of which Nelson County was then a part) Chenoweth was to be reimbursed £30,725 in paper currency for his expenditures.[31] Virginia, however, failed to pay, and as a result he had to sell much of his property to pay debts owed for the construction of the fort.

On November 22, 1787, Chenoweth petitioned the Jefferson County Court in an effort to recover the money owed him. In his petition he claimed to have paid the hundreds of workmen while he was financially able, but that law suits brought by these same men for the balance owed them "have rendered him almost to beggary together with a small hapless family. He asks for relief."[32] On December 7, 1787, the court "allowed [Chenoweth] 768 [pounds] specie with interest."[33]

By the time of William Albin's purchase some six years later, Chenoweth still remained in a financial predicament. He continued his dubious sales of land parcels while fighting in the courts to win the money due him. At the same time, he was fending off lawsuits from angry creditors.[34] An examination of Jefferson County records reveals that in an effort to clear other debts in the 1780s and into the 1790s, Chenoweth secured land purchases and sales in the thousands of acres. Apparently his efforts to erase the debts continued for the remainder of his life, but nonetheless he died insolvent in 1802.[35] Chenoweth's son later wrote, "After I became old enough to know about such things, I learned that the contract my father had with Colonel Clark and the state of Virginia had been the cause of his making a financial failure."[36]

---

occurred not more than twenty-five miles from Nelson County and approximately eighteen months or less before the Albin's arrival.

[31]No author, "Certificate Book of the Virginia Land Commission 1779-1780" *The Register of the Kentucky Historical Society*, 1923, Vol. 21, 328. Sources differ on the amount owed Chenoweth.

[32]Ibid.

[33]Ibid. Specie is coined money.

[34]Guthrie, "Captain Richard Chenowith", no page given. In 1784 alone Chenoweth appeared in Jefferson County court fourteen times regarding complaints from creditors. He lost ten of those cases.

[35]Chenoweth is buried in the family graveyard (perhaps now renamed the Porter family cemetery) in Jefferson County, near Middletown, Kentucky.

[36]Pirtle, *James Chenoweth*, 23.

Unfortunately, William Albin had been one of the many ensnared in Chenoweth's web of real estate fraud. It must have been particularly difficult for William and his family to learn that a trusted relative had betrayed them. The disputed sale was not finally resolved until years later. Long after William Albin's death, due to an adverse ruling in a lawsuit involving Osborn Sprigg, the legitimate owner of the Albin's land, the Albins had vacated the property by 1815 or earlier.[37]

This calamitous turn of events resembled in many ways the circumstances and the outcome of the Fairfax land case that William Albin Sr. experienced in the 1740s. Though the events in question occurred many decades apart, both William Sr. and Jr. had lost land to which they honestly believed they held a legitimate legal claim.

In 1793, prior to his subsequent title troubles and with his land purchase seemingly secure, William Albin would have begun clearing his recently acquired acreage with the intent to plant tobacco, destined to be one of his primary cash crops. For at least several years prior to William's arrival, his Bruce relatives and other Nelson County residents had been cultivating the broad, leafy plant for profit. In demand worldwide, tobacco grew well in Kentucky, but transporting it to distant markets in New Orleans or the East proved very difficult.

On October 24, 1789, less than two years before William's arrival, his cousin William Bruce, along with more than 250 other Nelson County residents (all males), had created and signed a "Petition of Inhabitants of Nelson County." Revealing the significance of tobacco to the county's economy, the petition called for

---

[37]The complicated court case heard in the stone courthouse in Bardstown's town square involving the Albin land in Nelson County and Albin's and Sprigg's heirs stemmed from the fact that William had never received the title to the land from Chenoweth because Chenoweth had never received title from Sprigg, the original owner as mentioned above. Later, the Albins sold the land to Samuel Anderson (October 1821). Anderson paid each of four groups of Albin's heirs just $10 in the transaction according to court documents. The case had passed in and out of the local courts from 1813 until the final judgment by an Appeals Court in 1831. See Albin, *Virginia Albins*, Chapter 6, fns, ii-v and vii for transcripts of the depositions and court rulings. See also Marshall, *Cases at Law and Equity* 158-164, for the appellate ruling.

the local government to place a tobacco warehouse station at a more convenient location. It explained "residents are subjected to many inconveniences for want of a warehouse and inspection of tobacco at or near the mouth of Stewart's Creek on the North Side of Beech Fork."[38] Apparently the petition's tobacco-growing signees favored the Stewart's Creek site as it was navigable for large boats and was situated conveniently within one mile of Bardstown.

From Bardstown the tobacco (probably along with home-made Kentucky whiskey) could be floated on a flatboat to the Ohio River, then west to the Mississippi River. However, the last legs of the transport, down the Mississippi and arrival in Spanish-held New Orleans, would be problematic as such a conveyance violated Spanish law. Nevertheless, tobacco shipments, undertaken by profiteers willing to take the risks involved, continued illegally until 1795.[39]

On that same October day in 1789, another group of Nelson County residents signed a similar petition "to establish a warehouse and inspection point for produce" (near the proposed tobacco warehouse mentioned above) on the land of Richard Parker at Beech Fork at the mouth of Cartwright's Creek just south of Bardstown and southeast of Cox's Creek. The signatories cited the rationale for their request: "badness of roads" and "inconveniences in carrying their produce to market."[40] Whether the two petitions actually resulted in the construction of the desired warehouses is unknown. Nevertheless, active support for each petition forecast that dedicated commitments championing similar future projects

---

[38]"Certificate Book of the Virginia Land Commission 1779-1780", 357. The list of signatories, accessed May 23, 2014, http://archiver.rootsweb.ancestry.com/th/read/ELDRIDGE/2001-01/0978830951.

[39]In the absence of sufficient roads, boats were the trucks and waterways the highways of nineteenth century rural America. Farmers in Kentucky and other parts of the country relied on water transportation to carry their crops to Eastern markets. Until October 1795 American trade traffic bound for New Orleans on the Mississippi had to pass through territory then held by the Spanish and was therefore illegal. Charles Pinckney's famous treaty negotiated with Spain that year proved invaluable, as it allowed Americans (with their trade goods) free navigation on the Mississippi and the right of deposit in New Orleans. In 1803 this right was forever assured under the terms of the Louisiana Purchase.

[40] "Nelson County" Petition to Establish a Warehouse, accessed January 7, 2016, *http://kykinfolk.com/nelson/petition.htm.*

by members of Nelson County's agricultural community would play a central role in the county's expansion.

While tobacco must have provided a great portion of William Albin's farm income, he may have also grown corn, one of Nelson County's other main cash crops. At that time the cultivation of corn was immensely popular among county farmers because of its use in the production of corn whiskey. Part of the reason being it was easier to distill corn than to transport it to the distant markets by boat or packhorse. (A packhorse could probably only carry four bushels of grain, whereas it could transport the *whiskey* distilled from twenty-four bushels.)

If William indeed cultivated corn in the 1790s, he had no trouble selling it, as whiskey distillers proliferated in Kentucky during that period. As early as 1776 and on into the 1790s, John Ritchie produced whiskey near the same Cox's Creek area where William resided. Today Bardstown is known as the Bourbon Capital of the World.[41]

Most importantly, by 1793, no matter what crops William had chosen to cultivate, he had attained a position that only about slightly more than one third of all Kentuckians had realized, membership in the landowner class.[42]

While in Kentucky, William Albin continued his Baptist affiliation. On August 5, 1794, the last of William's ten children was born, but the first in their new Kentucky home. On that date Magdalina gave birth to her eighth son, Joshua Carmen Albin. William and Magdalina had named him after a local Baptist preacher and family member, Reverend Joshua Carmen, husband of William's cousin Sally Bruce. Some nineteen months earlier, perhaps in his Rolling Fork Baptist Church, the same Reverend Carmen had conducted the marriage ceremony when William's oldest son William III wed Genny Inlow (or Jane Enlow) on Janu-

---

[41]Perhaps William even operated his own still on Cox's Creek with his experience gained in another significant whiskey producing area, southwest Pennsylvania.

[42]Michael McDonnell, *The Politics of War: Race, Class, and Conflict in Revolutionary Virginia*, (Chapel Hill: UNC Press Books, 2012), 483.

ary 10, 1793.[43] These two events reveal the extent to which William and Magdalina must have admired and respected Reverend Carmen.

Though no documentation exists to support this supposition, a compelling factor involved in the Albins' connection with Reverend Carmen, in addition to the family relationship, may have had its origin in the time William had spent in Reverend Speers' church in Pennsylvania. When he arrived in Nelson County, William may have desired a change after belonging to a Westmoreland County congregation led by a slaveholder. (Speers it will be remembered claimed twenty slaves.) His pro-slavery stance may have given William added incentive to connect with someone whose views on slavery were more in line with his own - the anti-slavery and pro-emancipationist Carmen.

Joshua Carmen's affiliation with the Bruces and perhaps the Albins dated back to their Pennsylvania days and continued in Kentucky. Carmen had wed Sally Bruce in 1778 at Ft. Pitt during the Revolutionary War. He served initially as a private under Captain William Bruce in the 2nd Battalion 8th Company in the local Washington County militia. Carmen not only served with his brother-in-law, but he also lived in close proximity to both James and Capt. William Bruce in Washington County. Likewise, Car-

---

[43]Marriages, Record of Joshua Corman , 1792-1793, Nelson Co., Kentucky, accessed December 11, 2013,
http://files.usgwarchives.net/ky/nelson/vitals/marr/c6550001.txt.
Even though the name Corman differs from Carmen, I believe it to be a transcription error made from the original. The record also erroneously shows Jane's name as Jinny Denbro, which sounds like Genny Inlow. Other family members and relatives shared William's Baptist affiliation. An index to a Baptist publication produced in 1813 shows the names of Nelson County subscribers George Albin (William's son), James Bruce, and William Sands, the widower of William Albin's daughter Elizabeth. David Benedict, *General History of the Baptist Denomination in America, and Other Parts of the World*, (Boston: Manning and Lori, 1813), Vol. 2, Index, Nelson County Subscribers. Names are listed under the name of the state and county. Benedict lists George "Atbin" and William "Sonds" in his index. Accessed December 7, 2009,
http://books.google.com/books?id=cXoRAAAAIAAJ&dq=A+General+History+of+the+Baptist+Denomination+in+America,++and+other+parts+of+the+World,+1813.&printsec=frontcover&source=bn&hl=en&ei=vaUdS_-0MZTQsgOjsNH9CQ&sa=X&oi=book_result&ct=result&resnum=7&ved=0CB8Q6AEwBg#v=onepage&q=&f=false.

men appeared on the same 1781 tax roster as his two brothers-in-law.[44]

Later, Carmen may have shared the journey to Kentucky with his Bruce in laws in 1783 or 1784, and then resided near them in Nelson County. Records from 1791 reveal that he lived close to William Albin as both men appear on the 1791 Nelson County Tax List of Thomas Morton reporting for North Central Nelson County. Significantly, it was there in the Cox's Creek area in the fall of 1788, three years before the Albins' arrival, that Carmen had found his true calling, organizing the Rolling Fork Baptist Church with seventeen members. Historian J. Spencer wrote that

> ...for a number of years he [Carmen] was an active minister in the bounds of Salem Association, and was several times appointed to preach the introductory sermon before that body. He was regarded [as] a man of good ability, and was much beloved by the brethren.[45]

However, as Reverend Carmen eventually became a strong, "irreconcilable" advocate for the emancipation of slaves, his relationship with the Association soured.[46] He and another Rolling Fork preacher, Josiah Dodge, disturbed the local Nelson County Salem Baptist Association with their radical emancipation views (they were some years ahead of their time in this regard, especially in a slaveholding state like Kentucky) to such an extent that at the Salem Baptist Association Meeting at Cox's Creek on October 3, 1789, it was declared "the association judge it improper to enter into so important and critical a matter, [emancipation] at present."[47] Carmen and other preachers who spoke openly against

---

[44]Egle, *Return of Taxables for the Counties of Bedford (1773-1784), Huntington (1788), Westmoreland (1783,1786), Fayette (1785-1786), Allegheny (1791),Washington (1786), And Census of Bedford (1784) and Westmoreland (1783)*, 750, 767.

[45]J. H. Spencer, *A History of Kentucky Baptists 1769-1885*, (No publisher provided, 1886), Vol. 1, 162-163.

[46]Ibid.,Vol. II, 47.

[47]Ibid. In the 1840s James G. Birney and Cassius M. Clay led the Kentucky anti-slavery movement, the early seeds of which had been sown by Carmen and other Kentucky preachers in the 1790s. Ironically, Kentucky as a border state was

slavery "were bitterly assailed, since it was maintained that the promulgation of such doctrines [emancipation] would tend to cause insubordination among the slaves...."[48]

Carmen, Dodge, and Thomas Whitman preached against slavery so long and so often that the Salem Association was threatened with dissolution. By 1796 all except three members of Carmen's Rolling Fork Church had withdrawn from the Association over the slavery issue.[49] The Association had continued to tolerate slavery, and to Carmen and the other pro emancipationists such a stance was unconscionable. In turn, members of the Mill Creek Baptist church in Jefferson County backed Carmen and the other Rolling Fork supporters, and withdrew for the same reason. Working tirelessly, Reverend Carmen, along with Dodge, founded an antislavery, emancipation church supposed to be the first such institution in Kentucky. Located six miles northwest of Bardstown (near Albin's property) at Cox's Station in 1796, it failed to survive despite its noble intentions.[50]

William and Magdalina's admiration for and association with the abolitionist Reverend Carmen positioned them in a unique position as residents in an eighteenth century slaveholding Southern state. Traditionally, Albins in Virginia and in Pennsylvania had never owned slaves. Nonetheless, opposition or indifference to slavery was one thing, but to favor emancipation was quite another. For William and Magdalina to openly associate with an emancipationist (even though he was family), for them to allow him to preside at young William III's wedding, and then bestowing his name on their newborn son perhaps placed them if not in deed, then in perception, in both the anti-slavery and pro emancipation camps, each a glaring minority in slaveholding Nelson County. The Albins' slaveholding neighbors must have questioned that by embracing Carmen, weren't the Albins in effect endorsing his opposition to slavery?

---

among the last to free its slaves, in 1865, under the terms of the Thirteenth Amendment.
[48]Asa Earl Martin, *The Anti-Slavery Movement in Kentucky, Prior to 1850*, (Louisville: The Standard Printing Company, 1918), 20.
[49]Spencer, *A History of Kentucky Baptists*, II, 48.
[50]Ibid, Vol. I, 163.

In Kentucky some of William's neighbors and relatives held slaves. William's uncle, James Bruce Sr. (Sally Bruce Carmen's father), and his son William Bruce Sr. (William Albin's cousin and Joshua Carmen's brother-in-law) claimed slaves as shown in the Nelson County tax rolls. In 1786 James Sr. owned a slave, "Lib", and his son William Sr. kept an unnamed Negro boy in 1787 and 1788, and in 1791 a Negro female, "Rose."[51] These differing stances within the family regarding slaveholding must have made things very awkward for the Albins, Carmens, and Bruces. Though no record exists of any family strife being generated over the slavery issue, with an outspoken critic like Carmen railing forcefully against slavery from his pulpit, he may have caused some displeasure in the slaveholding Bruce family. Furthermore, his relationship with slaveholders James and William Bruce Sr. may have become even more fragile when, in 1796, Carmen encouraged Rolling Fork church members along with several members of Cox's Creek, Cedar Creek, and Lick Creek Baptist Churches to declare non-fellowship with all slaveholders![52]

It appears Carmen and the Bruces may have put aside any differing views on the slavery issue long enough to agree that

---

[51]William Bruce Jr., however, was not a slaveholder. In 1844 he hosted a young, anti slavery Whig, Abraham Lincoln, in his Bruceville, Indiana, home. Holding unpaid labor in the James Bruce Sr. household dated back at least four decades, to the time his family resided in Frederick County. James had inherited a white servant maid, Elizabeth King, on a transfer of indenture when he married Margaret McMahon. Elizabeth, who had witnessed the will of John Bruce (James' father) in 1747, sued James Bruce in August 1752, contending that Bruce by then held her illegally as a servant. She had conceived between one and three children (the record is unclear) out of wedlock since 1744 and each time years were added to her indenture for fines and for "upkeep of the child." In one instance churchwardens had ordered the sheriff to apply twenty-five lashes to her bare back for her inability to pay a fine levied on her for her illegitimate child. See Morton, *The Story of Winchester*, 54. On August 5, 1752, the court set Elizabeth free. See Albin, *Virginia Albins*, 5-6. The author, Ethel Albin, had meticulously researched this episode, admittedly using the Frederick County court order minutes as a source. But, she omitted (in an effort to cleanse family history?) a final significant detail in her retelling - this time the name (stated in the court records) of Elizabeth King's master, James Bruce Sr. She instead uses the phrase "she filed a complaint against her master", while citing the *Frederick County, Virginia Court Orders*, Book 4, page 223.
[52]Spencer, *A History of Kentucky Baptists* I, 163 and John B. Boles, *Religion in Antebellum Kentucky*, (Lexington: University of Kentucky Press, 1995), 114.

Carmen would preside at a Bruce family marriage service. On December 1, 1799, Carmen officiated at the wedding of a Bruce, this time James Bruce, the grandson of James Bruce Sr., and son of William Bruce Sr.[53]

Soon afterward the rift between the county's pro slavery elements and Carmen's anti-slavery stance had become irreversible. Carmen, with his wife, felt compelled to leave not only Kentucky but also the Bruce family with whom he had been associated for more than seventeen years dating back to Ft. Pitt.[54] Unable to bring large numbers of anti-slavery Baptists to his side, Carmen first resettled in Louisville then, in 1801, he moved to Ohio, a free state, settling in Warren County near Waynesville where he continued to preach.

Sally Bruce Carmen passed away in 1839, and Joshua died five years later in 1844. He was buried in Baptist Cemetery, Bellbrook, Greene County, Ohio, never having returned to Kentucky. Many decades later Sally's nephew, William Bruce Jr., a Baptist preacher in his own right, whose father had owned at least one slave, still remembered Carmen as "a man of excellent character and a considerable speaker."[55]

---

[53]The younger Bruce had married Mary Froman whose family had lived in Rostraver Township. She was the granddaughter of Joist Hite of Frederick County, Virginia. Hite's sons may have assisted John Bruce, the great grandfather of Mary Froman's husband, in his move to Frederick County back in the late 1730s. It should also be noted that when William Albin Jr.'s son, George Henry Albin, married just twenty days later on December 21, 1799, William Taylor, not Carmen, presided at the wedding. Perhaps this indicates that Carmen had left Nelson County by then.

[54]The Bruces remained in Nelson County past the census of 1800. James Sr., his sons James Jr. and William, his grandson William Jr., and a George Bruce appear in the Kentucky state census. See Glen Clift, *Second Census of Kentucky 1800*, (Baltimore: Genealogical Publishing Company, 1966), 37. The Bruce family soon dispersed to Corydon, Harrison County, Indiana, and various Kentucky counties. See also Bruce, *Memoirs*.

[55]Bruce, *Memoirs*. As late as ten years after Carmen's anti-slavery initiatives, at least one member of the Bruce family continued to deal in human bondage. In 1806 (the same year the Lewis and Clark expedition returned from its epic journey to the Pacific) James Bruce Jr., Piety Albin's father and Joshua Carmen's brother-in-law, had purchased 144 acres on the waters of the east fork of Cox's Creek (for 229 pounds of tobacco) from Thomas Elder Jr. As part of the sale agreement, Elder had agreed to convey an unnamed Negro woman between fourteen and twenty years of age to James Bruce. See Nelson County, Kentucky

If a family rupture had occurred (a strong possibility as the Carmens left their Bruce relatives behind when they moved to Ohio) it would only be a precursor of things to come for many Kentucky families. For in the next five decades, more and more Kentuckians would split over the slavery issue. Finally, in 1861 with the onset of the Civil War, many families would suffer the ultimate division, as some would side with the North while others aligned with the slaveholding South.

In 1796, in the midst of Joshua Carmen's anti-slavery crusade, William Albin passed away, a young man still at age forty-eight.[56] He had spent his life on the frontier, first in Virginia, then western Pennsylvania, and finally in Kentucky. A husband, father, frontiersman and farmer, the independent William eschewed slaveholding because he opposed its repression and the concept of reaping the rewards of someone else's unpaid labor. All the while he strove to provide the best for his large family. He never possessed a great deal of money, but in Kentucky he had acquired 500 acres of land. William was the embodiment of the American pioneer, an energetic worker, a devoted family man, a loyal parishioner, and one who willingly took risks. He took up arms against his King in defense of both his country and family in times of crisis and later faced the challenges of resettling in the untamed West.

Following her husband's death, Magdalina remained in Nelson County. Her children would probably have helped her manage the family farm until the mid 1810s. In the Federal Census for 1800, Magdalina is not mentioned as a head of any household, so she probably lived with one of her two sons - both George and John "Alban" are listed as separate heads of households in the

---

1803-1818, *Deed Book Abstract Book 6*, 459, accessed September 10, 2015, at http://archiver.rootsweb.ancestry.com/th/read/MDSTMARY/2008-04/1208032721. This James Bruce had to be James Jr., as James Sr. had died in approximately 1799. Perhaps, back in 1796 Reverend Carmen had realized the futility of advocating for emancipation in Nelson County when even his in-laws held slaves. Now ten years later, a Bruce still owned slaves, but Carmen had departed.

[56]Some sources erroneously report that William Albin is buried in Indiana, but I believe that is William III's gravesite. The two are often confused and are further confused in the court documents cited below.

census. But, in the 1810 Federal Census, Delina "Allen's" (Albin's) name appears as a head of household living with one female under sixteen, another under twenty-six, and one male sixteen or under, probably her youngest son, Joshua Carmen. (Delina's age should have appeared in the column "free white females over forty-five", but perhaps due to an enumerator's error it was omitted.) One year later, on a Nelson County tax list, "Linna" (Magdalina) Albin appeared. She declared no titheables, but she still owned 350 acres on Cox's Creek.[57]

On March 5, 1813, "Lenny" Albin made her mark on a document assigning "all my right title interest and Clame [sic] to the within Bond [from Chenoweth] to [her oldest son] William Albin [III]...."[58] Earlier, on April 4, 1811, William III had purchased a ninety-two and one-half acre parcel of land "on both sides of Cox's Creek". That purchase might have been located near this parcel his mother had ceded to him.[59] Following Magdalina's transfer in 1813 of the family farm to William III, she is not found in any additional Nelson County records. It seems, though, that according to court documents the Albins had vacated the original family property on Cox's Creek during 1813 as a result of the litigation in the Sprigg matter.

By approximately 1813 of the Albin children, only William Albin III remained in Nelson County. Nelson County Court records and the 1820 Federal Census show that in 1821-22 his brothers John, George, and Philip Albin were all living in Harrison County, Indiana.[60] James and Isaac Albin (with his wife) resided

---

[57]Bullitt County, Kentucky GenWeb, *"Quick Notes on Early Central KY Families"*, Surnames beginning with the letter A, accessed May 25, 2014, http://www.rootsweb.ancestry.com/~kybullit/bcqna.htm.

[58]Albin, *Virginia Albins*, Chapter 6, fn. 4, ii. Magdalina, too, had never learned to read and write.

[59]A copy of the bill of sale for William Albin III's purchase is in the author's possession, provided by the Nelson County Courthouse staff in Bardstown, Kentucky on November 7, 2009. See also Bullitt County, Kentucky GenWeb, *"Quick Notes on early Central KY Families"*, accessed May 25, 2014, http://www.rootsweb.ancestry.com/~kybullit/bcqna.htm.

[60]James Bruce Jr. and Mary, according to the historical marker mentioned below, previously had moved to Harrison County in 1808. James had likely not transported the slave he possessed, as Indiana was a free state. At the Bruce Cemetery there, approximately four miles east of Corydon on State Route 62 according to *Harrison County Cemeteries*, a marker provides the following brief biography of

in Gallatin County, Illinois, while his sister Sarah Albin Johnson remained in Shelby County, Kentucky. Mary Elizabeth Albin Sands had died just after 1800, several years following her father's death.[61] Young Joshua Carmen enlisted in June 1815 at age twenty-one as a private in the United States Mounted Rangers in the war against the Delaware Indians. In January 1816 three weeks after his discharge, he married Drucilla Abney in Shawneetown, Gallatin County, Illinois, where brothers James and Isaac lived. He later moved to Mississippi, then to Louisiana.[62]

It is not clear what became of Magdalina Albin. She probably passed away in Nelson County a short time after conveying the bond to William III in 1813. A true woman of the frontier, Magdalina had experienced a unique, but unheralded life in Vir-

---

James Bruce Jr.: "The James Bruce Homestead. James Bruce, Jr. & his wife, Mary "Polly" Runyan, filed on this land at the Vincennes Land office 20 Oct. 1807 & permanently settled here in 1808. James, son of James Sr. & his wife Margaret McMahon Bruce, was born in Frederick Co., VA in 1760. In 1770 the Bruce family settled in Washington Co., Pennsylvania, where James & Mary were married in 1779. During the Revolution, he served in the forces of Gen. George Rogers Clark. In 1784-5, the Bruces moved westward, settling in Nelson Co., KY where they remained until coming to Indiana Territory. This cemetery, a part of the original Bruce homestead, holds the remains of James & Mary & a number of their descendants." See *Images Find a Grave -* ttps://images.findagrave.com/photos/2006/242/CEM46809955_115704497638.jp g, accessed January 5, 2018.

The date of the Bruce's arrival in Indiana is questionable. See Chapter 5 below. It seems that James and Mary did not sell their Nelson County property until four years later, in 1812: No author, *Deed Book Abstracts Books 8-11 Nelson County, KY 1803-1818*, (Bardstown: Nelson County Genealogical Roundtable Inc., 200?), 59, accessed May 27, 2013, http://archiver.rootsweb.ancestry.com/th/read/KYNELSON/2009-03/1236282639. Though this excerpt is part of an online post, the source listing is correct: "pg 404 Feb 24, 1812: James Bruce, JR and wife Mary to Thos. Higdon, Jr. of Nelson Co for £255, 100 ac[res] in Nelson Co on the waters of Cox's Creek, including the plantation where James Bruce now lives and adjoining John Glasscock's line and that of William Bruce. Also selling a tract of 50 ac[res] to Thos Higdon, Jr. part of 200 ac[res] formerly property of William Bruce Sr. and now in possession of David Cox."

[61]Albin, *Virginia Albins*, Chapter 6, fn. 4, ii, iii, and vi-vii. By March 1813 Magdalina's youngest child would have been Joshua Carmen at age eighteen and a half.

[62]Ibid., 274. In either 1819 or 1820, Isaac received a license to operate a tavern in Gallatin County.

ginia, Pennsylvania, and Kentucky. She raised ten children, lived in log cabins on the outer edges of civilization, while experiencing the threat of a sudden, violent Indian attack. The daughter of German parents, Magdalina is responsible for introducing the unique German bloodline to successive generations of her Albin descendants through the ten children she and William Jr. raised. As a result, no longer were Albins exclusive products of a Scottish and English heritage.

Absalom Albin, the other remaining son, and one of the author's nine ancestral grandfathers in this line of the Albin family remains the topic of the next chapter.

CHAPTER VI

Absalom Albin (1778 - after 1850)

Wm Albin [III] and wife Jane, Benj. Johnson and his wife Sarah [Albin], Absalom Albin and Piety his wife, Isaac Albin and his wife for the sum of $10 each...paid by said Anderson [for the] tract of land lying and being in Nelson County, Murray run waters of Cox Creek it being the land [of] our father William Albin...[1]

> From a legal settlement concluded by the heirs of William Albin II for the sale of the family's land in Nelson County, August 15, 1822

Nelson and Ohio Counties, Kentucky

Absalom was born in Westmoreland County, Pennsylvania, at the height of the Revolutionary War in 1778 at the same time his father was serving in the County Rangers. Because Absalom was born after the thirteen colonies had declared their independence from Great Britain in July 1776, he was the first Albin in this family born in the United States of America. He also appears to have been the family's first male to attain literacy.[2] At age thirteen Absalom made the memorable flatboat journey with his family down the Ohio River to Kentucky. For a teenage Absalom, the trip must have been the adventure of a lifetime considering he had spent his entire childhood essentially isolated on the family's farm in rural Westmoreland County.

Since Absalom's father had most likely relied on tobacco as his primary cash crop, Absalom and his brothers would have been counted on to help provide much of the labor. Just eighteen when his father died in 1796, Absalom, along with his unmarried siblings, likely remained with their forty-four year old mother Magdalina on the farm. As the children grew older, all with the exception of William III left Nelson County.

---

[1] Albin, *Virginia Albins*, Chapter Six, vii.
[2] The 1850 census shows that all persons above twenty years of age in Absalom's family were literate.

On January 1, 1802, twenty-four year old Absalom married his cousin Piety Bruce. With Reverend William Taylor presiding, it seems the ceremonies took place in Bardstown. If this location is accurate, it might indicate theirs was a church wedding instead of a less formal celebration at the Bruce home. Absalom and
Piety's marriage, in conjunction with that of Absalom's brother
George to Piety's sister Margaret in 1799, further strengthened the
familial bond initiated nearly seventy years earlier on the banks of
Red Bud Run where the Albin and Bruce clans had lived side by
side. Later, these close family ties had continued, extending to
western Pennsylvania. Now, with this most recent union, the connection had spread to Kentucky.

The signed wedding agreement/obligation between the groom, Absalom Albin,
and the bride's father James Bruce. Piety's signature does not appear on the
document.[3]

---

[3]Kentucky, County Marriages, 1797-1954, *Family Search,* accessed March 17,
2015, https://familysearch.org/ark:/61903/3:1:939K-Y63H-
W2?mode=g&i=59&wc=S9CM-
YWG%3A148165601%3Fcc%3D1804888&cc=1804888: Albin and Piety Bruce,
01 Jan 1802; Nelson County, Kentucky, Madison County, Ky Courthouse, Rich-

Marriage bond of Absalom Albin and Piety Bruce. Listed several names below the Albins is that of Piety's sister Mary (Betsy) Bruce and Cornelius Westerfield. The Westerfields would eventually make their home next to the Albins in Ohio County.[4]

mond; FHL microfilm 000009665. By 1802 the Reverend Carmen had been living apart from his Bruce relatives and therefore did not preside at the wedding.
[4]Ibid., accessed January 13, 2016, https://familysearch.org/ark:/61903/3:1:939K-YX9N-BL?mode=g&i=9&wc=S9C9-W38%3A148216001%3Fcc%3D1804888&cc=1804888.

Piety, the daughter of James Bruce II and Mary "Polly"
Runyan Bruce, was born March 30, 1784, in Elizabeth, Allegheny
County, Pennsylvania.[5] Piety and Absalom had known each other
for years dating back to the time when their families had lived near
each other in Rostraver Township. John Bruce of Frederick County, Virginia, was the great grandfather of both newlyweds.

Though Piety and Absalom remained in Nelson County
for several years after their wedding, records indicate they eventually moved. By 1810 or before (1805?), they had settled seventy
miles west in Ohio County, Kentucky. According to information
developed by one Albin researcher, Piety's parents had moved to
Ohio County in 1805, so it would make sense that the Albins had
joined them that year. Contrary to the date given on the Indiana
historical marker for the Bruce's 1808 arrival in Indiana (Chapter
V footnote), Ohio County tax records of 1811 show that the
Bruces, Piety's parents James and Mary, lived then in Ohio County.[6] Evidence also suggests Piety's sister, Mary Bruce Westerfield
(1782-1842), wife of Cornelius Westerfield, moved with her husband to Ohio County perhaps in 1805.[7]

This relocation seems to have been another group endeav-
or, this time for the Albins, Bruces, and Westerfields. Earlier, it
will be remembered, both William Albin I and II had joined with
family, friends, and neighbors in relocating from Chester County
to Frederick County and from Frederick County to Westmoreland
County respectively.

As a result, in relocating to Ohio County perhaps simultaneously with Piety's parents, Absalom and Piety maintained the
historic Albin-Bruce link. On the other hand, it appears that living
in Ohio County meant Absalom Albin had separated from his siblings, as some remained in Nelson County while others had dispersed settling in Illinois or Indiana.

---

[5]Piety's grandfather, James Bruce Sr., the son of John Bruce and Sarah Parrell,
may have died in 1799 in Bardstown.

[6]Jerry Long, *Early Settlers of Ohio County* (Owensboro, Ky: McDowell Publications, 1983), 40.

[7]Roots and All, A Genealogy Blog, *The Westerfield Family*, July 11, 2014, accessed August 25, 2014, http://rootsandall.blogspot.com/2014/07/the-westerfield-
family.html. Without citing a source, the author states that the Westerfields arrived in Ohio County "around" 1805.

Absalom's shift to Ohio County marked the last in his family's series of westward progressions that had begun with his grandfather William Albin Sr.'s departure from Chester County in 1735. Absalom's son Benjamin Tolbert and later both a grandson and great grandson remained in Kentucky for another 125 years. Westward movement would not occur again in his narrow line of Albin descendants until 1957 when Absalom's great, great grandson moved from Michigan to Fresno, California.

Perhaps Absalom (and the Bruces) had been compelled to relocate to Ohio County for a reason then familiar to planters in Kentucky, Virginia, and other states where tobacco was a primary cash crop. The soil on their Nelson County farms may have finally succumbed to repeated tobacco plantings over the years. Certainly, after nearly two decades in Nelson County, Absalom and his tobacco-growing neighbors in the absence of any knowledge of the benefits of crop rotation or allowing fields to go fallow for a season, may have seen their yields steadily decline as the tobacco plants slowly consumed the soil's nutrients. While this scenario must remain speculative in Absalom's case, generations of Southern cotton and tobacco farmers particularly in the Deep South and Virginia had experienced the same problem. Soil exhaustion on their plantations had compelled them to move westward, as Absalom had done, seeking fertile and untilled land.[8]

Established in 1799 and named for the Ohio River that originally formed its northern boundary, Ohio County was particularly well suited to agriculture with its virgin soil and lush meadows. The county's population shown in the census of August 1810 during President James Madison's administration consisted of only 1,722 males, 1,537 females, and 533 slaves. While the census record shows no occupations, an agricultural based economy provided income for many of the local families. One of the nearest towns to Absalom's land was Hartford, just five miles away. It counted only seventy-four white citizens and thirty-six slaves, evidence that yet another Albin descendant resided in a decidedly rural, slaveholding area.

---

[8]As late as 1849, Kentucky ranked second to Virginia in United States tobacco production.

In 1810, at age thirty-two, Absalom, along with Piety, approximately twenty-seven years old, had three daughters and a son, all less than ten years old.[9] The couple eventually produced seven children (birth years are approximate): Rebecca 1804, Mary 1806, Joseph 1809, Malinda 1810, Benjamin Tolbert 1818, Eleanor 1823 or 1824, and Parthenia 1825.

But, Piety and Absalom may have lost two sons. In the 1820 census, four Albin males under age sixteen are tallied, and again in the 1830 census four males, excluding Absalom, are shown.[10] Two of these would of course be Joseph and Benjamin, but who were the other two? Searches of the census returns of 1840, 1850, and 1860 reveal no Albin males other than Joseph and Benjamin in Absalom's family. Therefore, it is possible that Piety gave birth to *four* sons, two of which died after the 1830 but before the 1840 census. An unusual eight-year gap between the births of Malinda (1810) and Benjamin (1818) exists during which time Absalom and Piety could have produced these two unaccounted for and short-lived male offspring, increasing the their number of children temporarily to nine.[11]

In naming their children, Absalom and Piety deviated from the normal pattern previously seen in the Albin family. Absent were the given names of William (Absalom's father and grandfather), James, George, and John often observed in past generations. Perhaps Absalom sought to demonstrate his individuality in breaking such a family tradition. However, in one respect, Absalom conformed to a notion instituted years earlier by his father William.

Just as William had named his son Joshua Carmen after the distinguished Baptist reverend of the same name, Absalom and Piety called their second son Benjamin Tolbert after one of the

---

[9]1810 United States Census, Ohio County, Kentucky, s.v. "Absolem [sic] Albion [sic]", accessed April 10, 2013, http://ftp.us-census.org/pub/usgenweb/census/ky/ohio/1810/pg00068.txt. Scroll to #103. Copy of transcribed page in author's possession. The United States' population then numbered 7,239,881.

[10]Ibid.1820 United States Census Ohio County, Kentucky, s.v. Absolam Albin, accessed May 27, 2013, http://us-census.org/pub/usgenweb/census/ky/ohio/1820/pg0003a.txt, 6 line 47.

[11]The 1830 census indicates one of the "missing' Albin males was between 10- and under 15 years old, and the other was between ages 15 and under 20.

most respected Baptist preachers in that part of Kentucky. Benjamin Albin's namesake, Benjamin Tolbert (c1760-1834), an itinerant Baptist clergyman, was credited with establishing several Baptist Churches in the Ohio County area including the Beaver Dam Baptist Church (located near Hartford) in 1798. (Reverend Tolbert preached there for twenty-eight years). Another, the Pond Run Baptist Church opened in 1820. He also organized the Nelson Creek Baptist Church in Muhlenburg County and may have been associated earlier with the Cox's Creek Baptist Church of the Salem Baptist Association in Nelson County where Absalom may have first encountered him.[12] Benjamin Tolbert Albin's name thus conveyed the family's close religious ties to the Baptist church and its clergy.

Absalom apparently had followed the Baptist faith beginning in Westmoreland County, and now in 1818, as an adult, he had named a son after a preacher both he and Piety must have greatly admired. Piety, too, most likely had adopted the Baptist religion as had her father James Bruce Jr. This strong religious tradition would continue late into the century as Benjamin's son James B. Albin, emerged as a devoutly religious man in his own right.

In Ohio County Absalom purchased a plot of unknown size on Pond Fork or Wolf Fork of Muddy Creek and farmed there for decades. His name appears in county road order records beginning in June 1811 where he was mentioned as part of a group tasked with opening a road from Hartford to Elizabeth, Kentucky.[13] Thirty-nine years later in 1850, seventy-two year old, Absalom still declared himself a farmer.

Though Piety's parents had left Kentucky several years earlier, the Albins still retained close ties with their relatives, Cornelius Westerfield and Piety's sister Elizabeth Bruce Westerfield. The Westerfields lived on the farm next to the Albins.[14] Wester-

[12]Wendell H. Rone, *A History of the Daviess-McLean Baptist Association in Kentucky, 1844-1943,* (Owensboro, Kentucky: Messenger Job Printing Co. Inc.,1944), 280-283.
[13]Order Books, Ohio County, KY, Volumes 1-3, 1799-1817, Book 3, Family History Library, Salt Lake City, Utah, microfilm roll 1912998, p. 90.
[14]1820 United States Census, Ohio County, Kentucky, s.v. "Absolom Albin."

field became a renowned commercial distiller of his own corn whiskey beginning in 1810 in what would become a thriving local bourbon whiskey industry. Absalom, during the next several decades, might well have sold a portion of his corn crop to support his brother-in-law Cornelius's whiskey distillery business.

Perhaps in need of cash, Absalom and Piety sometime after 1830 sold an unspecified portion of their land near Hall's Creek. A deed shows that a Maryland family, headed by slaveholder Bartemus Acton, purchased acreage on February 26, 1831, from the Albins for $280.[15]

Oddly, some fifty-seven years later in 1907, Absalom's (by then he was long since deceased) name appeared in the *Hartford Herald* in relation to his property. A legal dispute between two citizens resulted in the sale of land that the *Herald* reported bordered Absalom's property on Hall's Creek.[16] Whether or not the Hall's Creek property Absalom claimed in 1850 remained in the Albin family's hands in 1907 is unclear, but a document in the early twentieth century referencing the land still bore his name.

Raising a large family and working a farm of perhaps 150 acres or more must have made life difficult for the Albins in rural Ohio County. The fact that Absalom worked the same land for over forty years shows that the farmland's production was able to sustain he, Piety, and their seven children. Absalom worked mostly on his own, probably getting help with the farm's countless and often difficult manual labor tasks from his sons Joseph and Benjamin when they were old enough. After his two sons married, Joseph in 1835 and Benjamin in 1842, Absalom, was left to singlehandedly carry out the day to day outdoor labor on the farm, no easy task for a man in his late fifties. Despite the workload Absalom appears not to have resorted to the use of slave labor.

By the time a youthful Absalom arrived in Kentucky with his family in 1790, slavery had been legal there for three years. Under the terms of the Northwest Ordnance of 1787, the territory above the Ohio River was closed to slavery. Kentucky, located

---

[15] Ohio County History, *Susannah Caroline (Acton) Mitchell, April 8, 1826 - September 8, 1878*, accessed June 30, 2014, http://ohiocountykentuckyhistory.blogspot.com/2013/06/susannah-caroline-acton-mitchell.html.
[16] *Hartford Herald*, May 1, 1907, 3.

south of the Ohio and its defining boundary between slave and free states, was therefore open to slavery and became a slave state upon entering the Union in 1792. It was, however, very atypical of slaveholding states.

In the first half of the nineteenth century, Kentucky's small farms rather than large plantations so common in the Deep South dominated the countryside. Small-scale landowners like Absalom Albin simply could not make use of large slave gangs on their limited acreages. In fact, the average Kentucky slaveholder owned fewer than five slaves. Curiously in Ohio County, though its white population showed a dramatic increase in the 1820 census to 3,392 from 1,374 ten years earlier, the slave population declined. In 1820 records showed 468 slaves, down from 533 in 1810.[17] Thereafter, however, both the slave and white populations *increased* steadily so that by 1860 there were more than 1,300 slaves countywide.

Statewide, anti-slavery forces were at work. In an effort to placate the state's antislavery movement, Kentucky had banned the purchase and importation of slaves in 1833, an unprecedented act for a slave state. But, in 1849 the Kentucky legislature repealed the non-importation ban.[18] Up to this point, the Albins had claimed neither indentured servants nor slaves in Virginia, Pennsylvania, or Kentucky. By 1830, however, that would change ever so slightly.

The 1830 Federal census data for Ohio County reveals that Absalom Albin claimed a female slave between the ages of ten and under twenty-four years old.[19] Like any commodity in the marketplace, a slave's value fluctuated with the times. Whites had learned that many factors determined the value of slaves during the more than two centuries since they were introduced into Jame-

---

[17]1820 United States Census, Ohio County, Kentucky, Totals of Population, accessed May 27, 2013,
http://www.rootsweb.ancestry.com/~cenfiles/ky/ohio/1820/pg0003a.txt. Totals are found at the bottom of the census sheet tallied by the enumerator.
[18]Harold D. Tallant and Kathleen Smith, *Evil Necessity: Slavery and Political Culture in Antebellum Kentucky*, (Lexington: University Press of Kentucky, 2003), 141.
[19]1830 United States Census, Ohio County, Kentucky, s.v. Absolam Albin, accessed May 27, 2013, *Family Search*, 234, line 6, images 13 and 14, https://familysearch.org/pal:/MM9.3.1/TH-1951-25125-24183-64?cc=1803958.

stown, Virginia. Age, gender, health, strength, and possession of a skill all contributed to a slave's worth. The young female slave Absalom reported in the 1830 census might have represented an investment of $450 or more. Since she was female, we can assume she more than likely worked indoors and not in the fields, for if Absalom required a field hand he would have utilized a male.

Could Absalom in 1830 have afforded the $450 to purchase a slave? It appears unlikely for two reasons. First, he was already supporting a large family of eleven counting both himself and Piety. Second, as a fifty-two year old farmer still working his fields in rural Kentucky, Albin's income was probably very limited. Even twenty years later he reported the cash value of his farm as a mere $200, less than half of the price of a female slave in 1830. To support his family and maintain a farm with the limited means available to him would have precluded anything as extravagant as the purchase of a slave. On the other hand, a more plausible explanation is that Absalom had not purchased this slave at all. Instead, he had merely hired her temporarily from her master (a common practice) to fill an immediate need with her wages going to her owner of course. There is no evidence Absalom claimed this or any slave, male or female, in any of the two subsequent censuses to which he responded, so perhaps this explanation is valid. And, since the young girl probably worked in the house, perhaps she was brought in only to help Piety during her time of illness or physical impairment.

In 1840 Piety and Absalom "Alion" (in the census), perhaps acting as good relatives or neighbors, seem to have taken in five young girls under ten and a woman between thirty and forty years old (their mother?). Because Absalom's name is the only one recorded in the 1840 census, their identities remain a mystery. Perhaps they were Albin or Bruce relatives or boarders, but they could not have belonged to Absalom and Piety's son Joseph, as he is listed elsewhere in the enumeration.[20]

By 1850 Absalom still farmed but on a lesser scale probably due to his advanced age (seventy-two). He and Piety did not

---

[20]Appearing in the Ohio County census for 1840 were Walter and Nicholas Earp, the grandfather and father of Wyatt Earp, the legendary marshal of Dodge City and Tombstone. Two of Wyatt's brothers, James and Virgil were born in Hartford only miles from the Albin property. Wyatt was born in 1848 in Illinois.

realize much profit from the farm they had worked since approximately 1810. Claiming just 100 acres by then, only twenty of which were under cultivation, Absalom owned one of the smaller farms in his area probably because he had previously transferred or sold fifty acres to his son-in-law John Watson. Absalom raised primarily tobacco (1,030 pounds) and Indian corn (300 bushels). His few livestock were valued at $130 while the cash value of his farm amounted to $200.[21]

Only one of the Albin's children, the unmarried twenty-six year old Eleanor, lived with them in 1850. Mary "Polly" had married John Wilson on April 5, 1823, Malinda married Robert Beasley on September 28, 1828, Rebecca, the oldest daughter, had wed Thomas Marlowe on November 25, 1837, and Parthenia had married John Watson on April 30, 1843. The youngest son, Joseph Runyan (he bore the maiden name of Piety's mother Mary Polly Runyan), married Mary Cox on March 11, 1835. In all but Joseph's marriage, Absalom had served as bondsman.

At mid-century Absalom and Piety not only had two married daughters living near them, but also five grandchildren. Daughter Parthenia Watson (she is listed as Bartena in the census), her husband John, and their three-year old daughter Martha lived on a farm adjoining that of Absalom and Piety. The Albin's older daughter, Mathilda Malinda Anderson (formerly Beasley), and her four children lived either next to or with the Albins.[22]

This 1850 census would be the last in which Piety and Absalom would appear, as both passed away sometime during the decade. Their childhood years spent on the frontier in Pennsylvania and their subsequent courtship and marriage in Nelson County helped maintain the historic Albin-Bruce family connection forged in Frederick County more than a century earlier. Married for at least forty-eight years, they maintained a simple life, and died pre-

---

[21]The Agricultural Census for Kentucky 1850, Ohio County, reel 35, Production of Agriculture. Absalom is respondent #17. In Ohio County the census for agriculture was enumerated on September 4, 1850, and the data compiled represented totals as of June 1, 1850.

[22]1850 United States Census, Ohio County, Kentucky, District No. 1, Microfilm Reel number: M432-215, page 25b, Lines 27-37. Malinda's second husband, Henry Anderson, is not listed in the enumeration. Copy of page in author's possession.

sumably on their Ohio County farm near some of their children
and grandchildren.

CHAPTER VII

Benjamin Tolbert Albin (1818 - February 20, 1889)

Ohio County, Kentucky

Benjamin Tolbert Albin, the second son of Absalom and Piety Albin, was born in 1818. He and his other siblings, with the exception of his sister Rebecca (born in Nelson County), were born in Ohio County. He would live there until his death most likely spending his early years on the family farm working alongside his father and older brother Joseph. Given the rural nature of Ohio County at that time, it is unlikely that he had much schooling, but Benjamin did learn to read and write.

On April 4, 1842, Benjamin, twenty-four, married twenty-year old Cynthia Faught, also a native of Ohio County. A daughter of the Albin's neighbors William and Polly (Autry) Faught, Cynthia likewise was raised in a farming family.[1] The Faughts had lived near the Albins for decades, as William Faught's name had appeared in the Ohio County census since 1820.

Not long after Benjamin and Cynthia married their first son James B. Albin was born on September 22, 1843. In approximately 1847 daughter Betsey M. arrived. One year later, in 1848 a second son, Zachariah, was born. Then in 1849 tragedy struck as Cynthia, just twenty-seven years old, died of unrecorded causes.

Given that the Albin's second daughter Kitty Ann was born the same year as her mother's death, it is possible Cynthia died of complications related to childbirth. In the 1840s the lack of immediate access to a physician in such remote areas as Ohio County combined with an absence of quality medical care sometimes resulted in medical tragedies that otherwise might have been avoided. Often, the most "medically skilled" family member or neighbor performed treatment until a physician arrived. While this scenario regarding the circumstances of Cynthia's death remains speculative, the fact remains that Cynthia had passed away at a

---

[1]None of the early records for Ohio County point to William and Polly Faught as Cynthia's parents. However, in the 1870 Ohio County census Kitty Albin, the second daughter of Cynthia and Benjamin, is listed as a cook for her grandparents William and Polly Faught.

young age. With Cynthia's death, Benjamin must have experienced mixed emotions, the heartbreak of losing a wife contrasted with his elation accompanying the birth of his daughter during that same year.

Benjamin now confronted a difficult and unexpected situation. He not only had to cope with the loss of his wife, but also as a single parent he assumed sole responsibility for managing the household and farm while caring for his four children, including the infant Kitty, all under eight years old. Prior to their deaths, the aged Absalom and Piety may have been able to help care for the youngsters, but they could not be expected to perform farm labor. However, soon after Cynthia's passing Benjamin remarried.

Though Benjamin's name does not appear in the 1850 census, records show he married Clarissa Watson on March 4, 1850, in Ohio County. Born in 1822, the same year as the deceased Cynthia, Clarissa was the sister of John Watson, Benjamin's brother-in-law (his sister Parthenia's husband). Thus, Benjamin and Clarissa must have been acquainted at least from the time of Parthenia's marriage or before.

Soon, Benjamin and Clarissa began to raise a family of their own. Clarissa appears to have been a kind-hearted person, as the couple named their first child after the deceased Cynthia. Such an act conveys a great deal about Clarissa's character and security in her relationship with Benjamin. She also seems to have been accepted by her stepson Zachariah, because years later he named his daughter Clarissa.[2] Four years later on December 28, 1856, Benjamin and Clarissa had their last child, Joseph Runyan Albin, named after Benjamin's older brother.[3]

Just after marrying, Benjamin and Clarissa may have lived briefly in Illinois. Their first daughter, Cynthia, in both the 1870 and 1880 Ohio County censuses (under her married name Morris) is shown with an Illinois birthplace. (However, the 1860 census lists her birthplace as Kentucky and also reveals that she was illiterate.)

[2]Albin, *Virginia Albins*, 272.
[3]Joseph Albin later married Arzina Embry in November 1874 and thereby established a lasting link between the Albin and Embry families (chapter 7). On December 19, 1853, Clarissa had delivered an unnamed stillborn female. *Ancestry.com*, Death Certificates, Ohio County Kentucky, accessed July 11, 2014.

By 1856 or before, the Albins returned to Ohio County, most likely occupying the family property near Hall's Creek. Benjamin apparently had inherited a portion of the 100 acres originally owned by his parents. On February 14, 1860, Benjamin purchased an additional forty-two acres from his brother-in-law John Watson for $200. (Perhaps this acreage represented a portion of the fifty acres Watson had acquired from Absalom earlier.) Since the Watsons lived nearby, this land likely adjoined Benjamin's existing acreage. On his modest farm, Benjamin raised primarily tobacco. In 1860 he produced 4,400 pounds, making him one of the leading producers in the county's Cromwell district.[4]

Later that year Benjamin's real property was valued at $500 and his personal property at $434.[5] Though Ohio County counted more than 1,100 slaves in 1850 and more than 1,300 in 1860, Benjamin, like many of his Albin ancestors, chose to work his land himself avoiding the use of slave labor despite its presence among his neighbors.

While life seemed to be improving slightly for the Albins in Ohio County, during the fourth and final year of James Buchanan's ineffectual Presidency, war clouds were gathering over an America that had become increasingly divided over the twin issues of slavery and state's rights.

For the past seven decades, the slavery controversy continued to bore an ever-widening hole in the social, political and legal fabric of a young America. Beginning at the Constitutional Convention in 1787, the North and South began a decades-long series of slavery-related compromises in an effort to maintain the uneasy balance between slave and free states. The give and take had continued into the new century with the Missouri Compromise in 1820 and the Compromise of 1850. Simply put, both sides,

---

[4]The Agricultural Census for Kentucky 1860 Ohio County, reel 41, Production of Agriculture, 33, "Talbott" Albin, enumerated on July 14, 1860. The thirty-nine other respondents on the same census page all produced less than Albin's 4,400 pounds.
[5]Ibid., and 1860 United States Census, Ohio County, Kentucky, s.v. Tabbott Albin, accessed May 27, 2013, 116, line 1. At some point Benjamin may have moved eastward in Ohio County to a farm near Cromwell and Baizetown, but the evidence is unclear.

slave and free, attempted to forestall what some believed was an inevitable civil war by agreeing to mutual concessions regarding slavery, new states entering the Union, and the acquisition of new territories. In the years following the Compromise of 1850, the polarization continued in a country still half slave and half free.

A decade later, during the 1860 Presidential campaign, Kentucky's own Abraham Lincoln ran on a Republican platform that would allow slavery to exist where it stood. But, he opposed its expansion into the new western territories, a combustible principle that would soon ignite the Southern states.

In December 1860, with Lincoln's Presidential victory and the limitation on slavery's expansion assured, South Carolina seceded from the Union, the first of eleven Southern slaveholding states to do so. Border slave states Maryland, Delaware, Missouri, and Kentucky suddenly found themselves in unique positions as slaveholding states that remained in the Union. Four months later in April 1861, with the Confederate attack on the Union outpost at Ft. Sumter in Charleston Harbor, the Civil War that so many had feared finally erupted.

The conflict over the slavery issue and states' right had now ruptured the Union. Torn by the opposing factions of its radical antislavery group and an equally aggressive proslavery element, Kentucky at the outbreak of the Civil War attempted the impossible and chose to remain neutral. The governor warned both the Union and Confederacy not to invade. The threat fell on deaf ears. Confederate forces soon entered, occupying Bowling Green in nearby (to Ohio County) Warren County and other parts of southern Kentucky. In September 1861 with the tide of its public opinion turning, the Kentucky state legislature formally declared its allegiance to the Union. As a result, Kentucky did not experience the severe impact of the fighting and destruction during the war as did her neighbors Virginia and Tennessee. Nevertheless, guerilla warfare remained constant, and occasionally Confederate cavalry made daring raids into different parts of the state.

For Kentucky it truly was a civil war. Neighbors, friends, and families became bitterly divided in their allegiances. Estimates show that 64,000 Kentuckians served in the Union Army while just less than half that, approximately 30,000, sided with the Confederacy. The duality of Kentucky's position in the Civil War is further illustrated by the fact that Union President Lincoln and Jefferson Davis, the President of the Confederacy, were both born in south central Kentucky.

During the War parts of Ohio County and the surrounding countryside became scenes of intense guerrilla activity. In July 1864 in Daviess County just north of Ohio County, Confederates ambushed a Union element at Rough River Creek, killing four. On February 20, 1865, Grayson County Home Guards attacked a Confederate guerrilla camp near Hartford, Ohio County, close to the Albin's land. The Home Guards killed four and wounded four others. For Ohio County residents, though, the most damaging Confederate incursion of the war occurred on December 20, 1864, when 800 Rebel troops under the command of General Hylan B. Lyon captured the Hartford county seat and burned the courthouse there. One of the Confederate raiders reported the scene as he re-membered it:

> We entered the town of Hartford, garrisoned by a battalion of Federal troops who, on our approach, took shelter in the Courthouse. They were speedily surrounded, captured, and paroled and the courthouse burned.[6]

It is quite likely that the Albins and their neighbors witnessed the fire's billowing plumes of smoke sure to have filled the air west of their farm. It would seem that the attack on Hartford might have been as close as the Albin family came to the war's impact. Logically, Benjamin Tolbert Albin would have been too old (forty-three at the beginning of the war) to take up arms.

Yet, the historical record belies this assumption. Surprisingly, on June 15, 1861, Benjamin Albin enlisted as a private in the pro Union Cromwell Kentucky Home Guards of Ohio County. His name appears as B.T. Albin, one of 140 privates shown on the unit roster.[7] Available records indicate the Home Guard saw very

---

[6]Colonel James Q. Chenoweth in Otto Rothert, *History of Muhlenberg County*, (Louisville, Kentucky: J.P. Morton, 1913), fn. 3, 280. Chenoweth may have been a member of Richard Chenoweth's (the builder of Ft. Nelson) family.

[7]Kentucky, Military, Report of the Adjutant General State of Kentucky, Union Kentucky Volunteers, Volume 2, Schedule C Militia Regiments and Components, "Roll of the Cromwell Home Guards of Ohio County", *Ancestry.com*, 859.

limited action, participating only in a single skirmish on December 31, 1861-January 1, 1862, at Borah's Ferry on the Green River near today's Cromwell. According to a Cromwell Home Guards report of privates, the Guards suffered one man killed, a local, John A. James, and three captured in the engagement.[8] Any casualties among the Guard's officers and non-commissioned officers as well as those of Confederate force remain undiscovered.

Whether Benjamin participated in this encounter is unknown. However, the fact that at age forty-three and with a family to support he had volunteered for the Guard is reason for amazement. His desire to serve and protect and perhaps his aversion to slavery had been the motivating factors in his decision. Moreover, in volunteering for the Home Guards, Benjamin continued the Albin tradition of military service dating back to his ancestors in Frederick County, Virginia, during the French and Indian War and later in the Revolutionary War.

Benjamin's oldest son James, age seventeen when the war erupted in 1861, would have been eligible to serve when he turned twenty in September 1863. In that same year in an effort to bolster the strength of the Union Army, the United States Congress passed a conscription act that eventually resulted in the first wartime draft of citizens in American history. The act called for the registration of all males between the ages of twenty and forty-five by April 1, 1863. Consequently, in June 1864, James Albin complied.[9] No record, though, has been found showing any military service for James. Perhaps his marriage in April 1864 had allowed him to avoid the draft, as married men were not required to serve until all unmarried men had been drafted. (Years later, Benjamin Tolbert Albin's granddaughter in her published reminiscences never mentioned any Civil War military service for her father James Albin.)

See also, Cromwell Home Guards, *Ancestry.com*, accessed July 20, 2014, http://ohiocountykentuckyhistory.blogspot.com/2012/08/cromwell-home-guards.html.
[8]John James' wife and mother were both Borahs after whom the ferry was named.
[9]"United States, Civil War Draft Registration Records, 1861-1865", Enrollment List of Persons Subject to Military Duty in the Second District of Kentucky, Ohio County, p. 400, *Ancestry.com*, accessed September, 18, 2017.

Thus, during the country's four-year long conflict with itself, Benjamin's family was spared the heartbreak of losing a loved one in the fighting. However, in this, the bloodiest of all America's wars, thousands of other grieving families on both sides were not as fortunate. During the war Benjamin became the first Albin to pay the recently enacted Federal Income Tax on individuals. Because of the Union's enormous expenditures incurred as a result of the continually escalating hostilities, the American government required additional sources of revenue. Consequently, Congress enacted the first income tax on individuals in July of 1862. Benjamin Albin had first entered Ohio County's local tax list as a twenty-one year old in 1839, but in 1864 this new Federal income tax applied to citizens throughout all Union States.[10] That year Albin owed the United States government a modest $6.75 tax assessed at a rate of five percent of his equally modest income of $135. Albin also owed as of March 1864 a hog tax as part of the Federal government's excise tax law. For the four hogs he slaughtered which were valued at $10 per hog, Benjamin owed twenty-four cents.[11]

With the Union victory in April 1865, life in Ohio County returned to normal unlike that of many other counties in a war ravaged South. The county and Kentucky as a whole had been spared the catastrophic destruction suffered by those slave states siding with the Confederacy during the war. By the end of the year, the county's slaves were freed. Benjamin and his family still remained on their farm, as they adjusted to an America attempting to heal itself after four years of bitter fighting.

The first postwar census in 1870 shows just Benjamin, fifty-two, and "Clerica", forty-eight, living with fourteen-year old Joseph Runyan, their only child remaining in the home. Benjamin farmed while Clarissa was "keeping house". They valued their real property at $800 and personal property at $500. (A mystery person also resided with the Albins at this time, thirty-five year old Sally

[10]Long, *Early Settlers of Ohio County*, 135.
[11]U.S. IRS Tax Assessment Lists, 1862-1918, *Ancestry.com*, s.v. B. T. Albin, accessed July 11, 2010.

Albin. Born in 1835, Sally is merely listed as "at home" but without a child or husband. She is not one of Benjamin's sisters because none were named Sally, and she is too old to be a daughter.)
Living next to the Albins was their nineteen-year old daughter
Cynthia, now grown and married to Presley Morris, a farmer.
James B. Albin also lived nearby in Ohio County. In March 1868
the Albin's other son, Zachariah, who lived in Daviess County,
had married Margaret Morris, most likely Presley's sister.

Benjamin and Clarissa continued to reside in Ohio County
well into the late 1880s. However, on February 20, 1889, just a
week after his grandson James Presley Albin (son of Zachariah
Albin) had visited him in the hospital, Benjamin Albin passed
away during a measles epidemic then sweeping through the Hartford area. Infected also, but not fatally, was Parthenia Watson,
Benjamin Tolbert's younger sister, and her husband John. Benjamin's obituary appeared in the *Hartford Herald* and referred to
him as "Uncle" Tolbert Albin. On the following day, he was laid
to rest at Fairview Church Cemetery."[12] Benjamin's final resting
place at Fairview lies just southeast of Hartford and east of Beaver
Dam near where he had lived for most of his life.

Benjamin's will bears testimony to his and Clarissa's
modest life of thirty-nine years spent together. Among the possessions listed in his property inventory are those implements and
household goods one would expect to find on a late nineteenth
century Kentucky farm – farm tools, a wagon, and a spinning
wheel. Benjamin's livestock included a yoke of oxen, two hogs,
two cows, and his most costly possessions, two horses, valued at
$150. In addition Benjamin's tobacco crop, projected to yield
3,500 pounds, appeared in the inventory. Many of these items sold
at an auction to his sons James B. and Joseph and his son in law
'Press' Morris.[13]

Some nine years later, on September 22, 1899, "the aged
widow of Mr. Tolbert Albin" passed away of "old age and paraly-

[12]*Hartford Herald*, February 20, 1889, 3, column 5 and February 27, 1889, 3,
column 5.

[13]Kentucky Probate Records, 1727-1990," Ohio County Inventories, Index, 1888-
1898, Vol. L, images 39-41, *Family Search*, accessed July 29, 2014,
https://familysearch.org/pal:/MM9.3.1/TH-1951-20787-22313-
86?cc=1875188&wc=M9WR-NSV:1150064168.

sis in her seventy-seventh year."[14] Clarissa was not buried in the
same cemetery as Benjamin, but instead she was laid to rest in
Baizetown Cemetery on Highway 505 just over one mile south of
Benjamin's gravesite at Fairview Cemetery.

An 1894 photograph showing Benjamin Tolbert Albin's second wife in the front
row, from left Clarice (Clarissa) Watson Albin, an infant Homer Albin, and
Joseph R. Albin (Clarissa and Benjamin Tolbert Albin's son). At the far
right is a relative Tom James.[15]

---

[14]*Hartford Herald*, September 27, 1899, 3, column 5.
[15]Reprinted in the *Ohio County Times News* (Hartford) July 8, 2004, p. 3C.

CHAPTER VIII

James B. Albin (September 22, 1843 - June 7, 1927)

> *"A Christian man, he took pride in trying to teach us the
> Bible and honesty in every respect."*
>> Daughter Lola Albin Embry in a remi-
>> niscence of her father, James B. Albin
>> December 2, 1977

> *"The Grand Jury returned the following indictments....*
> *James Albin, adultery."*
>> *Hartford Herald*, December 12, 1883[1]

Ohio County, Kentucky

James B. Albin was the first son born to Benjamin and
Cynthia (Faught) Albin. His parents may have attempted to retain
the historic Bruce surname in the family as James' middle name
may have been Bruce. Unlike many of his Albin ancestors, he apparently attended school and learned to read and write.[2] As noted
above James spent his early years on the Albin farm in Ohio
County in the 1850s and early 1860s. His name appears in the
1860 census as a teenager of sixteen living on the farm with his

---

[1] Page 3, column 6.

[2] Some of the information concerning James B. Albin originates from the published recollections of one of his daughters, Lola Albin Embry (1885-1977). Recorded first in 1966 and later republished on December 2, 1977, the remembrances
appeared in the Beaver Dam, Kentucky *Messenger* on page 4. They provide a
detailed and fascinating first person account of what Lola recalled of her early
life, her Albin family, and the area near Beaver Dam, Kentucky, where she and
her siblings grew up. Titled "From Oxcart to Atom Bomb" these reminiscences
occupy one entire standard size newspaper page. The only known copy is in the
author's possession, provided by my aunt, Joann Albin Bombelis, the niece of
Lola Albin Embry. The information regarding James B. Albin's literacy is derived from the article where Lola recalls her father reading the Bible to the children at night.

father, stepmother Clarissa, and four brothers and sisters.[3] More than likely he was of the Baptist faith. Unfortunately, little else is known about James' early life.

In April 1864, five months shy of his twenty-first birthday and one year before the end of the Civil War, James married Elizabeth A. (Wall) Baize, a young widow. Elizabeth Ann was born on January 16, 1847, in Henderson County, Kentucky, into the farming family of Miles and Betsy Sandefur Wall.[4] By 1860 it appears that Elizabeth and her two younger siblings had been orphaned. A search of the 1860 Ohio County census revealed neither of her parents, but in that same record Elizabeth was counted twice.

Elizabeth was living, as of the July 13,1860, census, with her sister Isabel Wall Ezell and her husband Russell Ezell. Yet, Elizabeth's name appears again on a July 26 census sheet, this time with the Shoultz family, also of Ohio County. This location with the Shoultzes may have been her primary residence as both of her siblings were counted there as well. It appears the Albins and Shoultz (Shultz) families were also acquainted, as the Shoultzes lived next to James B. Albin's aunt, Parthenia Albin Watson, the daughter of Absalom and Piety Albin.

Prior to marrying James, Elizabeth, then just fourteen, had wed William R. Baize in June 1861, two months after the outbreak of the Civil War.[5] The twenty-three year old Baize soon enlisted in the Union Army in October of that same year. In February 1862, while serving with Company D of the 17th Regiment, Kentucky Infantry, Baize suffered a gunshot wound at the Battle of Ft. Donelson, Tennessee. His thigh wound worsened, and later that evening he passed away. The widowed Elizabeth subsequently applied to the United States government and was granted a monthly pension of $8.

---

[3]Transcribed copy of the 1860 United States Census, Ohio County, file 695, p. 116, sheet 702, accessed April 11, 2014, http://www.usgwcensus.org/cenfiles/ky/ohio/1860/.

[4]Ancestry.com, "Death Certificates in Ohio County", s.v. Elizabeth Albin. In the 1900 census Elizabeth gave her middle initial as "A" but stated she was only fifty years old, instead of fifty-three.

[5]Ancestry.com, "Kentucky Marriages Ohio County 1851-1900", s.v. Elizabeth A. Wall.

A little more than two years later, on April 12, 1864, Elizabeth married James Albin. The ceremony occurred in the home of Elizabeth's guardians, the Shoultzes.

The intent to marry document for James Albin and Elizabeth Baize

The marriage bond for James and Elizabeth attested to by James' father Benjamin T. Albin[6]

The newlyweds' family grew quickly. On February 9, 1865, approximately ten months after their marriage, James and Elizabeth welcomed their first child Tolbert Albin, named after his grandfather, Benjamin Tolbert. Martha Ann Albin soon followed

---

[6]"Kentucky, County Marriages, 1797-1954," *Family Search*, accessed January 25, 2016, https://familysearch.org/ark:/61903/3:1:33S7-91GK-9BPF.

on October 18, 1867, and in February 1870 Benjamin Albin (later shown as John W. in the 1880 census) was born.

Six years after their marriage, the Albins resided in the Cromwell District of Ohio County. At that time James (he is shown as James Allen in the census) valued his real property at a modest $500 and his personal property at a mere $200. James farmed, as did most of his neighbors, while Elizabeth was "keeping house". James' parents, Benjamin Tolbert and Clarissa, resided, just several farms away.[7] In addition Joseph B. Carter Jr., a twenty-two year old from Tennessee and presumably the son of the Albin's neighbors, lived with James and Elizabeth perhaps as a boarder.

On Saturday, March 18, 1876, the twelve-year marriage between James Albin and his wife Elizabeth came to a sudden, permanent and, undoubtedly for Elizabeth and the three young children, unexpected conclusion. That day James and Lenileoti James, the daughter of Joseph F. (Frank) and Melissa James, the Albin's Ohio County neighbors in the Cromwell area, ran off accompanied by the girl's brother. The trio reportedly "crossed Rough Creek [near Green River] at Hines' mill [today's Dundee] on Sunday, and said they were bound for Evansville, Indiana."[8]

Lenileoti, the object of James' affection and the cause of his life altering decision to abandon his family, was born in Ohio County not far from the Albins. Various sources note her birth month as February, but the year varies from 1858 to 1860. (In the 1860 census record she is one year old but is misidentified as Lenitoli).[9] The youngest of the James family's eight children Leni, as she was called, grew up and attended school in Cromwell. Whether or not her parents knew beforehand of Leni's intent to

---

[7]1870 United States Census, Ohio County, Kentucky, s.v. James 'Allen', *Family Search*, accessed July 20, 2014,
https://familysearch.org/pal:/MM9.3.1/TH-266-11769-105647-52?cc=1438024.
[8]*Hartford Herald*, March 22, 1876, 3, column 2. The *Herald* concluded its report of the "Elopement" with the following: "This thing of married men running off with young girls is getting to be very common." The *Herald* reported that Lenileoti was no more than fifteen years old.
[9]1860 United States Census, Ohio County, Kentucky, s.v. Lenitoli James, *Family Search*, accessed July 20, 2014, https://familysearch.org/ark:/61903/3:1:33SQ-GB9V-9S9K?i=163&cc=1473181. In some searches her file is misplaced. See census page 88, Ohio County, Hartford District, for the accurate location.

elope is unknown. If they had somehow become previously aware, did they approve or did they attempt to dissuade her from taking such a drastic step with a married man seventeen years her senior and the father of several children?

The reaction of Elizabeth Albin and her three children to James' selfish action must have been a combination of surprise, hurt, betrayal, anger, and worry. Though she apparently retained the house, Elizabeth faced multiple daunting and immediate problems, the first of which was how to support the three children and herself. Moreover, several creditors would soon be seeking debt payments. Because of her illiteracy, she lacked any marketable skills.[10] Consequently, Elizabeth was compelled to perform "day work" (menial jobs) in an effort to care for her family.[11] The fact that the oldest child, eleven-year old Tolbert, realistically could not be expected to seek employment only intensified the family's difficulties. Additionally, upon her marriage to James twelve years earlier, Elizabeth had been legally compelled to forfeit her widow's pension of $8 monthly. As a result, in her time of hardship she could not even rely on that income source. (Much later, she would spend a great amount of time, effort, and possibly legal fees, in an effort to have the pension reinstated.)

James' sudden departure appears to have been premeditated. In a statement made years later, Elizabeth declared that prior to deserting her James had sold everything.[12] She never described what she meant by everything, but Elizabeth may have been referring to household furnishings and perhaps farm equipment. James' sale of these possessions could only have served to worsen his wife's already dire predicament.

Furthermore, once James had left he offered no financial support for Elizabeth and his three children. His half-brother, Joseph R. Albin, *thought* James may have provided some money for Elizabeth, but he was unsure. In contrast, Jordan Pearson, the husband of one of the Shultz daughters (it was the Shultz family who

---

[10]*Fold 3*, "Civil War Widow's Pensions", Kentucky, Infantry, 17th Regiment, Company D, s.v. William R. Baize, 83. At the bottom of Elizabeth's personal statement dated February 7, 1902, submitted with the hope of reinstating her widow's pension, Elizabeth signed with an X.
[11]Ibid., 38.
[12]Ibid., 85.

had acted as Elizabeth's guardian when she was younger), swore James had never contributed any funds to support his abandoned family.[13]

When James Albin deserted Elizabeth and his three children, he intended to leave Ohio County permanently in favor of Daviess County, Kentucky, located approximately thirty-five miles north. According to the 1880 census, James B. Albin resided one residence away from his brother Zachariah Albin (not exactly a role model himself) and his family in Yelvington.[14] Leni shared the home with James *as his wife* along with their son, Ben Franklin Albin, born in December 1879.[15]

Furthermore, though Leni had described herself as James' wife in the 1880 census, other documentation shows this to be untrue. Despite their claim that they had married, Lenileoti James and James B. Albin did not marry until November 1884, some eight years after they eloped. Thus, the birth of not only Ben Franklin Albin in 1879 but also Minnie Albin (later Green) in 1881, and James O. Albin in 1883 occurred out of wedlock.[16]

Four years after James abandoned her, Elizabeth still lived in her Ohio County home with her children Tolbert, Martha, and John W. (Benjamin). Because Benjamin Tolbert Albin had previously allotted forty-five of his 100 acres to his son James B., Elizabeth had been able to continue living on that same plot with her children, evidence that James at least had not sold the family farm

---

[13]Ibid., 71, 72. The Pearsons had named their first daughter Elizabeth.

[14]1880 Daviess County, Kentucky, s.v. James Albin, accessed July 31, 2014, https://familysearch.org/pal:/MM9.1.1/MCC6-MFK. Zach Albin died on May 8, 1933, in Muhlenberg, Kentucky. On his death certificate appears the name Clarissa Watson, shown as Zach's mother. In fact Zach's birth mother was Cynthia Faught, but since she died when Zach was just one, Clarissa was the only mother he ever knew. According to the *Hartford Herald,* July 28, 1875, 3, column 3, Zach and another man were arrested "on Saturday last" for having committed adultery on Mahala Moore. On that same day Zach had been tried and fined for whipping the little son of Charles Baize. Unable to pay the eight-dollar fine, Zach Albin spent four days in jail. Later, in 1883 and again in 1884, Zach's name appeared on a list of Ohio County's delinquent taxpayers. *Hartford Herald,* January 17, 1883, 1, column 5 and January 30, 1884, 1, column 7.

[15]Ben Franklin Albin apparently died in September 1880 in Daviess County, Kentucky. He appears in the 1880 census as a nine-month old.

[16]In the 1900 census, Minnie Albin Green and her husband lived next to Leni and James B. Albin.

before he eloped with Leni.[17] Perhaps too embarrassed to admit to the census taker that she and James were separated, Elizabeth had chosen to describe her marital status as "widowed" (technically she was the widow of her first husband William Baize). She would continue to cling to that widowed classification through the remaining years of her life while never remarrying. In the years after James' departure, Elizabeth would probably have maintained contact with James' family, as she and her three children lived next to James' half-sister Cynthia Albin Morris and James' parents, Benjamin Tolbert and "Carisa".[18]

In approximately August 1883, James and Leni, along with their two children Minnie and James O. (Benjamin Franklin Albin had died in September 1880) returned to Ohio County. James had spent more than seven years apart from Elizabeth, his three children and his parents. He had reappeared seeking a divorce.

On November 27, 1884, a judge granted James's wish. According to the documents available, the same court inexplicably dismissed Elizabeth's petition for alimony payments.[19] Elizabeth later stated that she never filed for divorce during the time James lived in Daviess County because she couldn't afford the cost.[20] Following these proceedings James and Leni married the next day.

After spending more than eight years together and with the births of three children during that time, James and Leni were legally wed at the bride's house. It seems the couple may have finally chosen to marry for yet another reason. Earlier, in December 1883, seven years after they had eloped, both were indicted by the Ohio County grand jury. James faced charges of adultery while Leni stood accused of fornication, or sexual intercourse between an unmarried woman and a man.[21] Subsequent to those charges,

---

[17]The Agricultural Census for Kentucky 1880, Ohio County, reel 58, Production of Agriculture, p. 4. B.T. Albin is shown with 55 acres while Elizabeth claimed 45.

[18]1880 United States Census, Ohio County, Kentucky, s.v. *Elisabeth* (sic) Albin, *Family Search*, accessed July 31, 2014, https://familysearch.org/pal:/MM9.1.1/MCZ2-WMP.

[19]"Civil War Widow's Pensions", 73-74.

[20]Ibid., 41.

[21]*Hartford Herald*, December 12, 1883, 3, column 6.

James and Lena were ordered to appear in court twice, once on June 3, 1884, and the second time on November 28, 1884.[22] While the outcome of these separate hearings is unknown, it should be noted they scheduled the wedding the same day as their November court appearance. Perhaps the two hoped for a favorable ruling from the judge on the 28th when they announced to him that they were now legally married and that James had obtained a divorce the day before.

Given the small town atmosphere of Hartford and Cromwell where everyone seemingly knew everyone else, the continuing drama of James and Leni's extramarital elopement and court appearances as covered in the local newspapers must have provided ample fodder for local gossips over the years. As a result, all of James' children, the three he fathered with Elizabeth and the eleven he eventually fathered with Leni may have experienced a certain amount of ridicule and embarrassment while growing up because of the scandal surrounding James and Leni.[23]

If a post separation relationship existed between James B. and the three children he had fathered with Elizabeth, it remains unknown. Later, in 1900, James and Leni with their children lived close, just five residences away, to James's oldest son Tolbert Albin and his family. Making matters even more awkward for all concerned was the fact that Elizabeth also resided with Tolbert. Any interaction that may have occurred between father and son because of that proximity is unknown. Perhaps, with Tolbert's death in November 1900, James drew closer to Martha Ann and

---

[22]Ibid., November 19, 1884, 2, column 5. A minor curiosity spanning the four decades of James and Leni's relationship concerns the actual length of their marriage. In 1900 in the Ohio County census, both declared they had been married for twenty-three years, which would place their wedding date in 1877 (the year after they eloped) instead of 1884. Ten years later in 1910, both reported incorrectly they had been married for *twenty-four* years (in 1886) instead of actually twenty-six years (1884).

[23]Ironically, nearly ninety years later in 1964, a grandson of James and Leni repeated his grandfather's indiscretions. In California he abandoned his wife and teenage son and began an adulterous relationship with a waitress employed at his restaurant. They soon married, and in 1965 the couple, accompanied by her children, left California and settled in Detroit, Michigan, having left his first wife and son behind to fend for themselves.

James W., the two surviving children he had fathered with Elizabeth.[24]

The marriage certificate for James and Leni dated November
1884.

---

[24]The relationship between James and his aging and widowed stepmother Clarissa may have soured following his father Benjamin's death in 1889. An apparent disagreement between James and Clarissa over a land parcel reached the Ohio County court in 1894. On March 30 of that year, the judge rendered a judgment for sale in Clarissa's favor. *Hartford Republican*, March 30, 1894, 3, column 4.

The marriage bond[25]

---

[25]"Kentucky, County Marriages, 1797-1954," *FamilySearch*, accessed May 20, 2018, https://familysearch.org/ark:/61903/3:1:3QS7-89SS-S57S?cc=1804888&wc=QD3Q-WJ5%3A1300476566.

Ohio County Kentucky Census of 1880 showing part of the Albin clan. First, the abandoned Elizabeth Albin and her children, second, Cynthia Morris, James Albin's sister, and last, James' parents Benjamin Tolbert (B.T.) and "Carissa" Albin all living in proximity to each other.

Residing with Tolbert, his wife Mary Autry Albin, and their three children must have brought Elizabeth a small measure of security and happiness until Tolbert's death.[26] Soon afterward she experienced additional financial problems. To raise money she sold her only cow for twenty-five dollars. Later, pursuant to a court case in which F.E. Keown had won a judgment against her, Elizabeth apparently had been forced to sell the 100 acres she

---

[26]1900 United States Census, Ohio County, Kentucky, s.v. James Albin, accessed July 31, 2014, at *Heritage Quest Online.*

owned on Indian Camp Creek in June 1906. In September she offered thirty more acres for sale.[27]

During the next several decades Elizabeth found herself living with other relatives or friends due to her ongoing money struggles. In 1910 she resided (still in Ohio County) near James B. and Leni. At sixty-two, she was living with an older cousin, Sarah Parson and another cousin, sixty-seven year Mary J. A. Albin.[28] Ten years later she resided with a Jakes family but in nearby Daviess County, Kentucky.[29] There, she was misreported in the 1920 census. She is listed as an eighty-year old, an obvious error by the census taker, as she would have been no more than seventy-three then.

Furthermore, intermittently for nearly the final twenty years of her life, Elizabeth attempted without success to have her Civil War widow's pension reinstated though it had been nullified by her 1864 marriage to James. (Her first claim had been rejected in 1891). Numerous references in her pension applications describe her as reputable, of good character, and virtuous. Sadly, at one point and out of apparent desperation, Elizabeth had written to President Warren Harding requesting that he personally "get her back on the pension list" while suggesting perhaps a special act of Congress would help resolve her pension request.

In a final determination dated March 13, 1925, the pension bureau again rejected her request on the same basis as before, her previous marriage to James Albin had nullified her eligibility. Fifteen months later Elizabeth passed away virtually penniless and enduring until the end the undeserved consequences of the abandonment that had befallen her nearly fifty years earlier.

After returning to Ohio County in 1883 that then counted a population of more than 19,600, James and Leni settled on several hundred acres on Sixes Creek, a tributary of Indian Camp Creek.[30] Their house or log cabin, located near the foot of a hill

---

[27]*Hartford Herald*, June 13, 1906, 4 and September 1, 1906, 4, accessed June 10, 2014, http://chroniclingamerica.loc.gov/lccn/sn84037890/issues/.

[28]1910 United States Census, Ohio County, Kentucky, s.v. *"Elezethabeth"* Albin, accessed July 30, 2014, at *Heritage Quest Online.*

[29]Ibid., 1920 United States Census, Daviess County, Kentucky, s.v. Elizabeth Albin.

[30]Embry, 4.

overlooking the Sixes Creek bottoms, stood in the center of the
Albin property approximately one mile from Baizetown. Daughter
Lola Albin Embry describes that home in which she grew up:

> In the beginning it was a large, well-built *log cabin*
> [emphasis mine].... As the family grew, the house was
> enlarged. First a large kitchen was built, and then another
> story and half log house was constructed, with a weather-
> boarded room connecting the two log buildings, finally
> making an L arrangement of the whole house with a total
> of five large rooms. There was a split level arrangement to
> the floor, going thru [sic] the room that connected the two
> log buildings, this being long before the time that anyone
> decided to call them "split levels."[31]

Despite the cabin's improvement, the Albins at that time
lived without running water, electricity, indoor plumbing, and later
a telephone. Lola, however, defended the idea of being born in a
log cabin. She wrote that

> A similar experience seemed to have been helpful to
> Abraham Lincoln and there was no stigma to having been
> born in a log cabin in 1885. The same was happening to
> about all my neighbors who were being born about that
> time.[32]

Because of the responses she gave in the newspaper interview, an Albin family member for the first time in this narrative is
documented describing another family member. In this case the
question posed to Lola Albin in 1977 - "What kind of man was
James B. Albin?" - tested Lola's remembrance of times seven decades earlier. According to Lola's somewhat sanitized memories of
her father, James was a very accommodating man to his neighbors
when they were in need. Lola added that, "If he ever had an enemy

---

[31]Ibid. Lola recalled that her uncle, Frank James, also "lived in a double log
house in Baizetown."

[32]Ibid. Indicative of the county's continued rural nature is the fact that fifteen
years shy of the twentieth century inhabitants of the Hartford/Cromwell area still
resided in log cabins.

on Earth, I never heard of it." Taking in orphan children and reading the Bible to his own children almost every night were two of the things she most remembered about her father. Lola also recalled that James was

> one of the finest men of his time. A Christian man, he took pride in trying to teach us the Bible and honesty in every respect. He never turned away an orphan child. He would take them into the home and they fared just like the rest of us.[33]

It is extremely difficult to read Lola's description of her father James as one who opened his home to orphaned children without thinking of his own three children by Elizabeth whom he had *abandoned* in 1876. Likewise, her phrase, "a Christian man, he [James] took pride in trying to teach us the Bible and honesty in every respect," rings hollow in light of his elopement with Leni and the subsequent adultery charges brought against him. And, Lola, in her lengthy reminiscences mentioned above, never referred to a divorce, Elizabeth Baize Albin, or the three children (Lola's half brothers and sisters) James had fathered with Elizabeth. Perhaps the subject of her father's previous "life" was a forbidden subject within James' new family. Or, perhaps, she was too ashamed of his actions to admit to them in an interview. For Lola, ignorance could not be an excuse. In the small towns of Beaver Dam and Baizetown where the scandalous articles regarding both James and Leni had been printed in the local papers, Lola, and other family members had to have learned of the circumstances surrounding her parents' previous infidelities and their subsequent court appearances.

In further describing her father, Lola also explained James worked extremely hard on the farm and "took great pride in his land." Using his yoke of large oxen, he would break the land for the crop, and "when the crops were to be tended, he would plow with one of them." James used the oxen to haul timber, building materials, and firewood, tasks related to a late nineteenth century American farmer's survival. Probably out of necessity, James was

---

[33]Embry, 4.

a "fair carpenter and a blacksmith." He had even constructed a shop to repair his and his neighbor's tools.

In politics James supported the Republicans having joined the local Party chapter sometime prior to 1900. His name appears in the December 7, 1900, edition of the local newspaper among those Republicans of the small town of Select who were endorsing a local Republican for County Court Clerk.[34]

Additionally, James B. Albin's name appeared often in the Hartford newspapers over the years in connection with pay due him for community work on the county's roads and bridges. In January 1903, he earned $1.50 for "plowing on the road", in 1907, $5.00, in 1908, $6.00 for a "team [of mules?] on the road, and in 1910, $2.25 for the same.[35]

Locally, the Albins were linked with a distinctive geographic feature found on their property. On or near James' land was Albin's Cliff, a precipitous, deadly ledge noted in the *Hartford Herald*. In reporting an incident regarding local resident Luther Daugherty, the *Herald* noted that apparently Daugherty had been hunting at night and mistakenly ran off the cliff to his death while chasing a raccoon.[36]

In the family James raised with Leni, there were five boys and six girls. According to daughter Lola, they all referred to James as "Pap" and Leni as "Ma". The oldest was Minnie Albin (born September 1881), followed by James Oscar, (February 4, 1883), Lola (May 1885), Mary Lillie (1887), Thomas Alva (1889), Earlis (1892), Joseph B. (1894), Mauncy (1896), Arvilla (1898), Stella (1901), and Golda (1902). Combining these eleven with the three children from his marriage to Elizabeth, James fathered a total of fourteen children who survived and one additional child who died as a youngster.

School in 1891 for Lola and probably the other Albin children meant attending classes in a log church. Belonging to the Church of Christ, the building/school stood in a field on the east side of a road about a quarter of a mile north of where the Baptist

---

[34]*Hartford Republican*, December 7, 1900, 2.
[35]*Hartford Herald,* January 28, 1903, 4, and *Hartford Republican*, April 17, 1908, 7, October 30, 1908, 2, and January 7, 1910, 3.
[36]*Hartford Herald*, October 9, 1912, 5.

Church stood then.[37] In the most rudimentary fashion, the children sat on rough log benches, and as Lola describes it "studied our lessons while a teacher and an assistant heard recitations at each end of the building." The "assistant teacher", one of the more advanced pupils, helped without pay during a school year that lasted just five months then.[38] Presumably, all age levels were taught in the same class, which made for a less than ideal learning environment.

As with most families, sooner or later the older children began to marry and move away while the younger ones were growing up. A twenty-one year gap existed between the birth of the oldest child, Minnie, in 1881 and the youngest, Golda, born in 1902, which resulted in frequent visitations by the older, married children and their families. Lola recalled that when the children and grandchildren would gather at James and Leni's house for a holiday or a visit sleeping arrangements were never a problem. "There were two large beds in each of the rooms [of the Albin house] except the kitchen, making a total of eight double beds." Four or five of the smaller children would sleep crossways on the bed or on pallets on the floor. The older boys rejoiced in being able to sleep in the barn loft. Lola left unexplained what accommodations were made later in the 1920s when all eleven of the Albin children with their spouses and grandchildren in tow reunited at the Albin farm.

Transportation for the Albins and their neighbors to nearby Cromwell, Beaver Dam, or Rosine meant using the family ox-cart. Lola recalled the time the family made a trip to Cromwell for some sort of "big event" dressed in their Sunday "go to meeting" clothes. On the hot, dusty road, the oxen slowly trudged pulling the cart with the children riding inside and James walking along-

---

[37]Embry, 4. I include this imprecise description as provided by Lola Albin Embry for its value to the story as well as a reference point for any future researcher hoping to pinpoint locations in the Sixes Creek area. The newspaper cited here is unavailable elsewhere unless a copy exists in the Beaver Dam *Messenger's* archives.

[38]Lola also reported that her husband, Reverend Marion A. Embry, earned $30 a month from his first teaching job in 1896, half of which went for room and board. She added that he taught for forty-four years and the highest salary he earned during that time never reached $100 per month.

side prodding the team to move at a faster pace. Suddenly, the thirsty oxen smelled water. Lola described what happened next:

The original James B. Albin "log cabin" built in the early 1880s on Sixes Creek as it looked when modernized in the 1960s. The photo was taken from the *Beaver Dam Messenger* December 2, 1977. It was here the James B. Albin family lived into the 1920s. It is likely the couple standing on the porch is James B. Albin's daughter Arvilla Albin Cook (1898-1973) and her husband, Stonewall W. Cook.

> When we approached a creek between Select and Cromwell, the ox team being thirsty, picked up speed and headed over the embankment for a water hole in spite of all of Pap's frantic efforts to keep them from doing so. Fortunately no one was hurt, only mussed up a little.[39]

---

[39]Embry, 4.

Afterward, James said, "I will never start out with the family again to any place too far to walk until we have a better way to travel." That better way to travel would not occur until the next century with inventions of the automobile and later commercial passenger aircraft.

Years later, Lola put the travel aspect of the episode into perspective when she stated that the air travel time from Baizetown to New York City in the 1960s equaled the time spent in the family oxcart journeying from Baizetown to nearby Cromwell in 1890, a distance of about six miles.[40]

In the *Beaver Dam Messenger* article, Lola provided details about some of her relatives she remembered while growing up in the Beaver Dam-Cromwell-Baizetown area of Ohio County. Her uncle (her father's half-brother) Joseph Runyan (she calls him Jose) Albin lived on the farm just below James and Leni. Lola's brother "Buddy" Albin ran a store in Baizetown at the top of the hill, long since bypassed by a blacktop road. Nearby, her Uncle Tom James operated a blacksmith shop, where he also sold hardware and... caskets. (Tom is pictured in the photograph at the end of Chapter VII.) According to Lola, Silas Baize administered the post office in his small grocery store while one of James Albin's contemporaries, John Henry Baize, also established a store in Baizetown in 1880.[41] Lola referred to others Baizes as "Uncles", but the connection to the Albins is unclear.

---

[40]Ironically, the construction of a superhighway in 1967 bypassing Baizetown caused the demise of that city according to Embry.

[41]Embry, 4. See also Rennick, *Kentucky Place Names*, 12, where he writes that in 1893 John D. Oliver (a person Lola also mentions) established the Baizetown post office. Oliver stated the post office was named after the Baize family or John Henry Baize. In the newspaper article, Lola also speculated on the origin of the name Baizetown. Though she admitted the story was "not entirely clear in my mind" and that the source was sketchy I repeat it here for its value to future researchers. She recalled, "Baizetown got its name from the Baize family. Ozna Schultz, who was County School Superintendent shortly after the turn of the century, frequently told the story that a young boy was found in this area, his parents probably having been killed by Indians. From the child's speech, it was believed that he was of German extraction and that his name was 'Baize, or something that sounded very much like that.' As I recall it, Mr. Schultz claimed that the boy was taken in by a Schultz family and possibly married a Schultz." Note that Elizabeth Wall Baize Albin had lived with a Schultz (Shoultz) family prior to her marriage to James Albin.

Gradually, James and his family saw the population near Baizetown decline. By the 1960s Lola recalled that the young folks in and around the area where she grew up had "moved away to find better opportunities", in the areas near the "blacktop" where the conveniences of electricity, good roads, and telephones became more commonplace. Despite the advances of the twentieth century that came to Ohio County, Lola declared, "the countryside is the same and is eternal."

From 1900 through 1910, James B. Albin still farmed the land on Sixes Creek. James and Leni lived with their six remaining unwed children. But, by the end of that decade their daughter (Mary) Lillie Taylor and her three young children had moved in with them. The Albins owned their home, but the record reveals they still maintained a mortgage on the property.[42]

During the next ten years, most of James and Leni's children had moved away leaving only Golda and Earlis at home. Earlis worked and lived with his parents helping his seventy-six year old father who, by then, was too old to perform the daily tasks associated with farming. Draft registration cards show that in 1917 both Thomas and Mauncey worked on their parents' farm with their brother Earlis, but they apparently did not reside there.

In addition, a great granddaughter, Magdelene, age seven, lived with the Albins. This child was more than likely the daughter of William Ray Albin, the late Tolbert Albin's son. (William Ray had indicated on his 1917 draft registration card that he was a single parent with one child and that he worked for J. B. Albin.)

The two decades that passed since the turn of the century had brought awe-inspiring changes to residents in not only Ohio County, but also to others across the nation. Americans had witnessed the inventions of the telephone, motorcar, and airplane. They closely followed reports of the catastrophic destruction and appalling loss of life during the four-years the Great War had gripped Europe. Additionally, a new phenomenon, the radio set, was just beginning to make an appearance. And, somehow, the Albin family had escaped the devastating effects of the horrific killer influenza of 1918-1919. The very rural nature of the area in

---

[42]1920 United States Census, Ohio County, Kentucky, s.v. James Albin, accessed July 30, 2014, at *Heritage Quest Online.*

which the Albins lived perhaps had isolated them from this worldwide scourge.

Beginning with Elizabeth Albin's death from pneumonia on July 25, 1926, in Owensboro, Davies County, (widow and housekeeper were shown on her death certificate), the next three years would bring the deaths of James and Leni also. Having never remarried, Elizabeth lies buried in the Baize Cemetery, Ohio County, next to her son Tolbert and his wife Maggie or Mary (Autry). Not far from Elizabeth's plot is that of James Albin, who died on June 7, 1927, near to her in death, but nearer as always to Leni who is buried *next* to him. Leni had passed away on March 15, 1928, just nine months after James.[43]

After James and Leni passed away, Lola Albin Embry's sister Arvilla Albin Cook and her husband Stonewall eventually occupied the home on Sixes Creek. They modernized it with the use of plasterboard and floor coverings, included electricity and a telephone, and thus created "an attractive and livable home."[44] As of approximately 1966, it was still standing.

---

[43]In the same Baizetown Cemetery, rests Clarissa Albin, James Albin's stepmother.

[44]Embry, 4. Though Lola's remembrances of the family are fascinating, they are not without error. Lola, perhaps based on information from her father or some other family member, erroneously recalled that, "My grandfather Albin [Benjamin Tolbert Albin] was born in Ireland and moved with his family to Illinois from where he came to Ohio County." Here Lola erred significantly in that it was her great, great, great grandfather, William Albin Sr., who arrived from Ireland, not Benjamin Tolbert. Benjamin Tolbert had lived in Illinois for a time and then returned from there to Kentucky, but he certainly was not born in Ireland.

The headstone of Leni and James B. Albin[45]

---

[45]Leni's headstone shows a birth year of 1858 and not 1860 continuing the vari-
ance referenced earlier regarding the year of her birth.

CHAPTER IX

James Oscar Albin (February 4, 1883-January 17, 1931)

Ohio County, Kentucky

James Oscar Albin Jr. was the first surviving son born to James B. and Leni. Some records indicate that James was born in Butler County, Indiana, but they are in error. His son Ray's birth certificate indicates James O. was born in Butler County, Kentucky, in 1883. Likewise, the 1900 census confirms Kentucky as the birthplace of James Jr.

James grew up on the family farm on Sixes Creek with his ten other siblings. He probably attended the same schools as Lola, his younger sister. As his father and Albin grandfathers before him had done, James worked on the farm undoubtedly under the guidance of James Sr. As an adult James O. would continue to farm in Ohio County for his entire life, cultivating corn and most likely prized Kentucky tobacco.

On May 27, 1905, James O. Albin wed young Annie (Anna) Cook, born on June 9, 1888. Their wedding announcement appeared in the *Hartford Republican* on Friday, June 2: "J. O. Albin of Baizetown, age 22, to Miss Annie Cook of Arnold [just northeast of Baizetown], age 17."[1] Anna Cook was the second oldest daughter of Ohio County Judge McClellan (Mack) Cook and his wife Nancy who lived just over the hill (on Pea Ridge) from the Albin property on a branch of Indian Camp Creek.[2]

---

[1]*Hartford Republican*, June 2, 1905, 5, column 3.

[2]McClellan (Mack) Cook, the author's great grandfather, was born on May 18, 1866, near Dexterville, Butler County, Kentucky. He was one of eight children born to John McHenry Cook and Paulina Jean Daughtery Cook. Cook attended Butler County Schools and later enrolled at the Morgantown Seminary for three years. He began teaching at age seventeen at Oak Ridge (Butler County) for $12.50 per month. On September 30, 1885, he married Nancy Elizabeth Evans born also in 1866. (She was the daughter of Moses and Lucy Evans.) The Cooks had eight children including Anna. After Nancy's death Mack married Anna Carter, one of Ohio County's more popular teachers, on December 9, 1921. They had one son, Mack Jr., who went on to teach mathematics at the University of Louisville. Mack Sr. spent fifty-three years on the farm and the last twenty-seven living in Hartford, Kentucky. In addition to teaching and farming, Mack served as Ohio County Magistrate from 1909-1913 and as a county Judge from 1918-1922. He was a member of the Mount Vernon (Green Brier) Baptist Church. He pur-

Though the Cooks and Albins were separated geographically, marriages between various members of each family soon brought the two families closer together.

Several of Anna's siblings and relatives had also married into the Albin family. Her brother Stonewall Cook married Arvilla Albin, James O.'s younger sister, while her other brother Monroe Cook married another of James' sisters, Stella. In addition, Anna's cousin Flora Cook married Mauncy Birch Albin, one of James' younger brothers.

By 1910 Anna and James were living next to his father and mother along with their first child, four-month old daughter Edrie born in December 1909. James farmed an unknown amount of acreage next to the Sixes Creek property while Anna managed the house. Later that year the Albins moved from Baizetown to the small town of Arnold where Anna had lived prior to her marriage.[3]

During the early years of his marriage, James attempted to augment his modest farm income by working as one of Arnold's election officers. Beginning in 1906 James filled the role of officer, then in 1907 he performed clerk duties. The following year he is listed as a judge (not a court magistrate), and in 1912 he worked again as an election clerk, this time with his father-in-law Mack Cook. Though the pay was minimal, James and Anna undoubtedly welcomed the additional income.[4]

James had not followed the political example of his father. Instead of supporting the Republican Party as James Albin Sr. had done, the younger James aligned with the rival Democrats. Late in March 1905, James O. and a group of other Democratic supporters publically urged a local Democrat to run for office.[5]

In 1914, the Great War broke out in Europe. Subsequently, in 1917, the United States committed a large contingent of

---

sued his hobbies of reading and gardening. Information for this brief biography was derived from a scrap of paper cut from the April 17, 1947, edition of the *Hartford Republican*, copy in author's possession. Cook died shortly after the article was printed.
[3] *Hartford Republican*, December 16, 1910, 8, column 4.
[4] Ibid., June 8, 1906, 2, September 20, 1907, 4, November 27, 1908, 2, and *Hartford Herald*, September 25, 1912, 6.
[5] *Hartford Herald*, March 29, 1905, 2, column 4.

troops to assist the Allied cause. With the United States' entry into World War I in 1917, the government ordered eligible draft age young men to register. A year later James Albin, on September 12, 1918, just two months prior to the Armistice, registered for the draft. As a thirty-five year old James, with a wife and several young children, never had to serve, but nonetheless James complied with the government directive. The registration card shows that James was "tall", of "stout' build with blue eyes and light hair. He described himself as a self-employed farmer living near Baizetown, Kentucky, probably in the area near Sixes Creek. James' younger brothers Thomas, Joseph, Earlis, and Monsey (Mauncy) all had registered fifteen months earlier on June 5, 1917, not long after the United States had declared war on Germany in April.[6] An armistice agreed to in November 1918 ended the war after four ruinous years of deadly fighting.

At that time James and Anna still resided in their home on Sixes Creek. In the span of five years three additional children had been born, probably in Beaver Dam: Nell Patsy (1912), Thelma (1914), and Thurman (1917). In addition, James O. claimed and farmed at least twenty-seven acres of land that his father had generously gifted to him with "love and affection."[7]

---

[6]"United States World War I Draft Registration Cards, 1917-1918, "*Family Search*, accessed February 13, 2016, https://familysearch.org/ark:/61903/1:1:K78N-J9Y: James Oscar Albin, 1917-1918. For future researchers the following personal descriptions are gleaned from draft registrations cards. Notice the propensity among this group for blue eyes, a trait in the Albin family dating to at least 1794 with the blue-eyed Joshua Carman Albin (Absalom Albin's son). James O. Albin's youngest son, James Glendon Albin (see below) was also blue-eyed. The author examined ten draft registration cards for Albin males in Ohio County. The cards revealed that all ten had blue eyes. (Some of these Albins are omitted below as they were not part of this Albin lineage):
Thomas Avery (Alva?) Albin: blue eyes, brown hair, medium build, medium height
Joseph Albin: blue eyes, brown hair, tall, stout
Earlis Albin: blue eyes, brown hair, tall, slender build
Monsey (Mauncy) Birch Albin: blue eyes, brown hair, tall, medium build. Mauncy was wounded in action during the fighting.
William Ray Albin (J.B. Albin's grandson): blue eyes
[7]*Hartford Herald*, May 16, 1917, 4, col.3. The Herald noted each man was "of Baizetown."

Beaver Dam, where most if not all of James and Anna's children were born, is located at the junction of US Highways 62 and 231 less than one and a half miles southeast of Hartford. A German immigrant, Martin Kohlmann (Coleman) first settled Beaver Dam in approximately 1795 (near the time that William Albin Jr.'s family lived in Nelson County). Coleman is said to have named the local stream Beaver Dam Creek for obvious reasons as beaver then thrived in the area. The first settlers arrived in 1798 and founded the first Baptist Church there, under the guidance of Baptist Elder Benjamin Tolbert, Benjamin Tolbert Albin's namesake. Within a few years, the small settlement grew around the Baptist Church and Tolbert preached there for nearly three decades. In early times the area was covered by canebrakes and teemed with bear, deer, and buffalo. Over the years Beaver Dam never achieved a large population. Instead, it remained perennially eclipsed in size and importance by Hartford, the Ohio County seat.

By 1910 though it claimed only 1,000 people, downtown Beaver Dam possessed a tobacco rehandling warehouse, two liveries, a combination harness shop and jewelry store, a corncrib, a feed store along with an array of banks, grocery and drug stores, and a combination undertaker-grocery-hardware-paints store. On the corner of Madison and Second Streets stood both a Christian Church and a Methodist Episcopal Church. Main Street was "macadamized, but the town lacked a fire department. Water facilities were "not good". In addition, there were no streetlights.[8] Seventy years later in 1980 during a visit by the author, Beaver Dam still retained its quiet, small town atmosphere. By 2000 its population numbered only 3,033.

On September 10, 1922, a second son, Ray, was born to James and Anna in Beaver Dam. Several curiosities concerning both Ray's birthdate and his various names endure. First, he always maintained his birth occurred on September 8. However, an examination of his birth certificate and Army discharge papers by the author (Ray's son), confirmed Ray's actual birth date was in-

---

[8]The information regarding Beaver Dam was taken from a map produced by the Sanborn Map Company in 1910 for local insurance companies. Accessed September 19, 2014,
http://kdl.kyvl.org/catalog/xt7t4b2x4036_1.

deed September 10.[9] Likewise, his birth certificate shows Ray as his given name without any middle name. Somehow, he was also referred to as James Glendon, and when he returned to Beaver Dam in 1980 his aunt greeted him at her door and referred to him as "Glendon." In fact, in several internet sources and the 1930 census, his name appears as Glendon Albin. Yet, Ray is the name he used his entire adult life. His mother, Anna, affectionately referred to him even in his later years as Jabe, short for Jay Boy, a childhood nickname. Few people, if any, ever called him James. Yet, in a January 1938 school picture taken in Detroit, Michigan, he is referred to J. Albin.

Five years later in August 1927, Joann, the last of the six children of Anna and James Albin, was born.

The Albin children all attended school. Their education levels, with the exception of the oldest daughter Edrie, are unknown. Edrie became the first Albin in this history to not only attend college but to also earn a college degree! She later became a successful social worker in Detroit, Michigan. Ray never graduated, having left school sometime after either the eighth or tenth grade.[10] Later, in January 1938 with the Albin family residing then in Detroit and the nation in the midst of the Great Depression, Ray dropped out of school to pursue full time employment.

Further evidence of the rural and somewhat impoverished side of Beaver Dam can be seen in a 1927 school photo (below.) Two of James Albin's school-age children attended the Union Grove School. They, with their classmates of varying ages, were all grouped and taught together apparently in the same classroom by the same teacher. In the photo a young Thurman Albin is seen seated in front of his older sister Thelma Albin (the author's uncle and aunt respectively). Near Thelma, is her cousin the lanky Theron Cook. (Most likely, Ray attended this same school beginning in 1928 when he turned six.) At least three of the young boys pic-

---

[9]Ray's birth certificate incorrectly shows he was his mother's ninth child when in fact he was her fifth.

[10]The 1940 census indicates Ray's highest grade attained was eight. On the other hand, in his school picture taken in January 1938 when he was just over fifteen years old, the caption reads "9A graduates". To further confuse matters, Ray's Army discharge papers reveal he completed eight years of grammar school and two years of high school.

tured in the front row have come to school barefoot, an indicator perhaps that even in 1927 shoes remained a luxury for some of the county's underprivileged families.

Ray told the story of how his modest family lived on their small farm near Beaver Dam. He recalled that his father James owned a horse to help plow the field to grow the corn to feed the horse. Though the anecdote was meant in jest, there existed in it an element of truth. James and Anna were not well off by any means, but none of their children ever went hungry.

As a boy Ray raised rabbits then sold them at the train station in Beaver Dam to help raise money for the family. The other children likely worked on the farm or in the town of Beaver Dam during their youth to help make ends meet. However, by 1930 James and Anna saw the inevitable occur when the first of their children married and left home.

In 1930 James and Anna resided with their five of their six children in a home they owned along State Highway 71, a north south route that passed through Hartford and Beaver Dam. A year earlier James and Anna's second oldest daughter Patsy married "Frenchie" French. Of those children still living at home, Edrie taught in the local public school while her siblings Thelma, Thurman, Glendon (Ray), (minus three-year old Joann) all attended classes. The working class locale in which the Albins resided is evidenced by the employment information included in the 1930 census that reveals all of their closest male neighbors were either farmers like James or coal miners.

Another indication of the Albin's limited financial status in the late 1920s is revealed by a unique question that appeared in the 1930 census. The Albins (and all of their neighbors) responded "no" when asked if they owned a radio. Apparently, none could afford one of the more coveted inventions of the day. The advent of the radio in the 1920s provided both city dwellers and country folks with an inexpensive form of entertainment and a reliable source of news and information. As America approached the eve of radio's Golden Age, the government desired an indication as to how many American households owned such a device. Perhaps James and Anna regarded it a radio as a luxury item, something they could do without during the onset of hard economic times that later developed into a worldwide economic downturn, the Great Depression.

At 1 p.m. on January 17, 1931, during the second year of the Depression that was then gripping America, tragedy struck Anna and the children. James died at age forty-seven just weeks shy of his forty-eighth birthday. Ironically, Dr. Willis, the same family doctor who had delivered Ray nine years earlier, treated James' illness, beginning on December 27, 1930. Ray later recalled that his father died of pneumonia. James' death certificate indicates that indeed pneumonia had played a part in his death, but as a secondary factor. Dr. Willis reported that an abscess of the liver actually was the primary cause of death. The family buried James the following day.[11] According to his grandson James (Jim) Albin, James O. lies buried behind the Methodist Church in Beaver Dam.

Ray, age nine at the time of his father's death, may never have had a close relationship with his father. I cannot remember him mentioning anything the two of them did together, nor do I recall Ray relating any father-son type stories. Perhaps James was so occupied with the farm work and raising the six children that he had little time for leisure activities.

How Anna and the children managed after James' death is anyone's guess. The Albins owned their home in Beaver Dam, but according to the 1930 census they were still paying on the mortgage. Faced with a house payment and raising four children seventeen or younger on a rural farm without a husband in the midst of the worst economic crisis ever seen in this country, Anna must have been distraught. Daughter Edrie, twenty-two, probably became the main breadwinner helping support the family on her modest teacher's salary. With James's passing the majority of the farm work probably was left to fourteen-year old Thurman. Undoubtedly, times were extremely difficult for the children and their mother. Soon, though, the decision was made to leave the farm and Ohio County.

---

[11]"Death Certificates in Ohio Co. Ky", *Ancestry.com,* s.v. under James O. Albin., accessed April 11, 2011.

nion Grove School – 1927

is picture of Union Grove School was made in 1927. It
is brought to the TIMES office by Mrs. Una Ward of
oute 3, Hartford.

the front row, left to right, are John Ray Bratcher,
harles Johnson, Glendon Sandefur, Buel Bennett
glesby, Kermit Cook, Delmar Bennett, Talmage Ben-
tt, and Willard Harris.

In the second row are Otto Bratcher, Thurman Albin,
Una Plummer, Grace Haycraft, Minnie Haycraft, Ina
Barrett, Mary Frances Brown, Mattie Oglesby, Lillian
Haycraft, Glanna Shultz.
In the back row are Anna Plummer, Flora Plummer,
Thelma Albin, Lillian Bratcher, Theron Cook, Mary
Belle Barrett, Ruby Sandefur, Myrtle Embry and Miss
Annie Shultz (teacher).

The Albin children at school, 1927[12]

---

[12]*Ohio County Times*, January 9, 1969, 3. Kermit Cook, a cousin to the children
of James O. Albin, sits in the front row fifth from the left. He was a pallbearer at
the funeral of his aunt Lola Albin Embry in 1977. (Picture cropped in the original.)

A young James O. Albin and Anna Cook Albin circa 1905. Perhaps a wedding photo? This is the first known photograph of any male member of this Albin family line.[13]

Not long after the death of James and prior to 1934, the Albins left behind the farm life of Kentucky in favor of the industrial giant to the north, Detroit, Michigan. Why Michigan? Why the city? Why Detroit? Perhaps the answer was that even though the Depression was continuing, there were more jobs there than in Kentucky.

The family remained for decades in Detroit. Life there during the Depression was challenging, but even though the family unit itself became separated out of economic necessity, eventually all would prosper.

With the link to Kentucky and farming now broken because of the move to Michigan, a centuries-old way of life had ended. In the long history of the Albins both in America and dating back centuries to Ireland and England, this was the first time any family members had forsaken the farm for city life. (Of the six

---

[13]Thanks to my cousins Jim Albin and Al Sim, the grandsons of James and Anna, for their help with the identification of the people in this picture.

children, only Thurman eventually returned to Kentucky and the farm.) In all probability neither Anna nor any of her children were aware of the unique and prolonged extent of the family's bond to the land. Adding to this historical perspective is the fact that young Ray would become the first in this long line of Albin males to reject farming as a career. Instead, he turned to sales.

Anna would not remarry until the late 1940s. At that time she married Bob Hancock, and they lived in Inkster, Michigan. In the late fifties, Anna was widowed again, but she eventually wed a retired postal worker, Walter Schad. The two remained married until Anna's death at age eighty-three on August 26, 1971, in Highland Park, Michigan, a suburb of Detroit.

The James O. Albin Family circa 1918.
From left, Anna Albin, Edrie (in back), Thurman (in father's right arm), James O. Albin, Thelma (in father's left arm) and Nell (Patsy) in front. Ray and Joann were not yet born.

The gravestone of James O. Albin near Beaver Dam

A graduation picture of Ray Albin Sr. age 15,
Jackson Intermediate School, January 1938, Detroit, Michigan.

Map 16
Map of Ohio County, Kentucky, showing Hartford, Beave[r] Dam, and at the
point of the arrow the site of Baizetown

CHAPTER X

Ray Albin Sr. (September 10, 1922 – May 21, 1996)

Ohio County, Kentucky, Wayne County, Michigan, and California

Ray or James Glendon Albin was born in Beaver Dam, Kentucky, in 1922, the fifth child and second son of James and Anna Albin. He may have been nicknamed after his uncle Ray Cook. As a young man, he had taken on the build typical of his immediate family, a tall, slender frame with wiry arms and legs. As an adult he had grown to six feet two inches, shorter though than his older brother Thurman. At the time of his separation from the military in 1946 he weighed 155 pounds. The combination of Ray's blond hair, light blue eyes, and exceptional height created a striking appearance.

Ray grew up in Beaver Dam, living near the sites of his Albin grandfathers dating back nearly seventy-five years to Absalom Albin. Following the death of Ray's father James, Anna and the children moved to Detroit probably when Ray was ten or twelve. There he attended school, but he never graduated. However, he attempted to make up for this lack of education by remaining an avid reader for the rest of his life. For a time he delivered false teeth in Detroit for a local dentist. During this time he discovered golf, which soon became one of his great passions.

Ray often proclaimed that some of his happiest hours were those he spent as a youth in Detroit at first caddying to earn extra money for the family or later playing golf. One of the courses where he caddied most often was Chandler Park in East Detroit not far from his home on Hurlbut. All his life he played well and was always known for his booming tees shots. Following the war he thought about turning pro, but someone stole his clubs, and Ray could not afford the replacement cost. In addition, he had a family to support and simply could not meet the additional start up expenditures associated with professional golf. Through the years Ray always enjoyed the camaraderie and competition a round of golf would bring and never passed up a chance to play for money.

In the 1930s during the family's first difficult few years in
Detroit, the Albin children remained scattered due to marriages
and economic necessity. Ray lived with relatives because Anna,
minus any significant source of income following James' death,
remained unable to afford a home of her own. By 1940 Ray lived
with his sister Pat French and her husband at 12143 Longview
Ave. on Detroit's East Side. He had left school in approximately
1938 at age sixteen to take a job in one of Detroit's many machine
shops. Ray worked roughly thirty-two hours a week as a jigsaw
operator and a surface grinder. Just down the street from the
Frenchs at 11830 Longview lived Edrie, Ray's older sister, and her
husband Asa (Howard) Wright. They had generously taken in Anna and Ray's younger sister Joann. Though economic hardship had
compelled the family to separate, all managed to stay connected
with one another.

Pat had been the first of Anna and James' children to marry (in 1929), but Ray's other three siblings also wed soon thereafter. Edrie married in 1933, followed by Thelma in 1936, and
brother Thurman in 1937. Life in Detroit during the Great Depression could not have been easy for the widowed Anna and her two
younger children Ray and Joann. In truth, however, I never heard
Ray utter a single complaint about those Depression years.

One of President Franklin Roosevelt's social programs
inaugurated during the Great Depression was a system of social
security that sought to provide retirement income for American
workers by deducting a small amount of money from each pay-
check. Ray applied for and received a Social Security card on September 26, 1940, shortly after his eighteenth birthday. Later, following his retirement Ray became part of the first generation to
receive these Social Security benefits. Soon after enrolling in this
new social program, Ray found the United States government
would become involved in his life in a much different way.

Following the Japanese attack on Pearl Harbor in December 1941, which thrust America into World War II, Ray realized it
would only be a matter of time until he was drafted. Consequently,
a little more than two years later he received his induction notice,
on March 2, 1943. One week later on March 9, Ray, not yet twenty-one, entered into active service in the U.S. Army joining thou-

sands of other young American men who had also received their draft notices or enlisted.

Inducted at Ft. Custer, Michigan, Pvt. Ray Albin, serial number 36578662, trained as an engineer, later serving in 1504th Engineers Water Purification Company. Part of his training occurred in the dry, eastern parts of Oregon, near Bend. He was later assigned to Ft. Lewis, Washington, before being deployed overseas. Apparently, he also spent time at one of America's largest training centers, Camp Howze, Texas, near Gainesville, for it was there that he married Geraldine Elizabeth Abt of Detroit, Michigan, on St. Patrick's Day, March 17, 1944, a little more than one year after entering the army.

Geraldine, (Gerry), a petite brunette about five feet six inches tall, weighed perhaps 115 pounds. A kind and gentle person who always wanted to do the right thing, she rarely lost her temper. She had attended school in Detroit and graduated in 1935.

Gerry was the second daughter of German and Swiss parents. Her father Edward Abt's roots extended, like Magdalena Shepler Albin's, to Germany's Rhenish Palatinate. Her mother, Katharine Tschudi, was of Swiss extraction, and like Edward she was raised in Detroit. Married on October 6, 1908, Edward and Katharine later had a daughter Katherine (Kay), and on May 27, 1917, Geraldine Elizabeth was born.

Following Edward's death, between 1916 and 1920, the widowed Katherine married a rather gruff and unpleasant man, Albert Kohler, a Lithuanian barber, in perhaps 1923. With Albert she had one additional child, Gerry's half sister Shirley Kohler (later Saunders) born in 1924. The family, with stepfather Albert now the breadwinner, resided on Hunt Ave. in East Detroit. Their home was very close to Cleveland St. where Gerry's grandparents the Tschudis had lived for decades. Nearby was St. Aubin Street where Gerry, her sister Kay, and their widowed mother had lived immediately following Edward's death.[1]

Geraldine had met Ray in Detroit. She later joined Ray in Texas for the wedding ceremony while Ray continued to serve in

---

[1]Today Cleveland Street no longer exists in that part of Detroit. The author was able to approximate its location by using the neighboring streets the census taker in 1930 listed as she made her rounds. Waterloo, Dubois, Gratiot, and St. Aubin Streets are all in the same locale, thus Cleveland Street must have been nearby.

the Army. The fact that Gerry was five years older than Ray made
little difference to each of them then or later in their marriage.

During their time in Texas, Ray recalled that there wasn't
much to do in Gainesville on a Saturday night and there wasn't
much money to do it with. So he and Gerry would walk up and
down the main street, often stopping to buy two Dr. Pepper soft
drinks for a nickel each. A big night on the town!

After they were married, Ray and Gerry lived in Texas,
perhaps on the base where he was stationed, always dreading
Ray's inevitable overseas deployment. Subsequently, after just
four months of marriage and sixteen months of active duty in the
stateside army, Ray received his orders. On July 12, 1944, Ray
shipped out for the PTO, Pacific Theater of Operations having
bade Gerry a sad farewell days earlier. He and the others aboard
the troop ship spent nineteen days sailing from the west coast (Seattle?) to his destination in the Pacific, probably New Guinea, arriving there on July 31, 1944.[2]

His discharge papers indicate he participated in the New
Guinea and Luzon (Philippines) campaigns, mostly likely as a
non-combatant, but nonetheless still in a combat zone. He remained overseas for eighteen months and three days, culminating
his tour of duty with American occupation forces in Japan following its surrender in September 1945. On New Year's Eve day December 31, 1945, after spending more than four months in Japan
Ray, along with hundreds of other returning GIs, eagerly boarded
a troop ship, this time for the long return voyage across the Pacific
to the United States.

Ray arrived, probably in San Francisco, two weeks later
on January 14, 1946. He was rapidly separated from the service.
He received an honorable discharge nine days later on January 23
at Fort Sheridan, Illinois, having spent thirty-four months and
twenty days in the Army. At the time of his discharge, Ray had

---

[2] During World War II, Ray's cousin, Jewel Creston Embry (1920-1992), the son
of Marion and Lola Albin Embry, served as a submariner aboard the *USS Grena-
dier* until he was captured by the Japanese in 1943. He was imprisoned, tortured,
and starved in various prison camps in Japan until the end of the war when he
was released. In 2016 Kentucky designated Kentucky Route 505 in Ohio County
in honor and memory of Jewell Creston Embry of Baizetown.

attained the rank of Technician 5th class much like a corporal to-day. He received $300 mustering out pay and $15.50 travel pay probably to cover the cost of train or bus fare from Ft. Sheridan to Detroit. Sometime later that January, Ray undoubtedly rejoined Gerry and his family in Detroit, perhaps at a joyous Welcome Home celebration. Ray soon became one of thousands of discharged veterans making the adjustment to civilian life in an energetic postwar America.

Curiously, on Ray's discharge papers line "17, No. Dep." (Number of Dependents) shows three. Since Gerry and Ray had no children by 1946 the three dependents would be Gerry, probably his widowed mother Anna, and his sister, eighteen-year old Joann. Army records revealed a Detroit residence address of 5745 Hurlbut Ave.

Not long after his discharge, Ray took a job as a salesman with Sears Roebuck and Company selling vacuum cleaners in its Gratiot and Van Dyke Avenue store in downtown Detroit. He would remain a successful salesman with Sears for the next seventeen years.

Following the war Americans were eager to buy those consumer goods that had been "off limits" or unavailable during the war years. Putting four years of warfare behind them, consumption-minded Americans with money in their pockets purchased autos, furniture, washers, dryers, and vacuums at a frenzied pace in the postwar years. Such a climate provided a great opportunity for energetic young sales people who quickly learned they could make a comfortable living selling what people wanted. Ray could smell a phony a mile away and his keen people-reading instincts served him well in his new job as a low-pressure salesman. He believed that in sales customers sold themselves, and if given enough time they would reveal everything he needed to know to help accommodate them.

On Friday, April 11, 1947, at 2:50 p.m. Gerry and Ray had their first child, Ray Robert Albin. Ray Jr. was born in East Side General Hospital in Detroit with Dr. Best the attending physician. He measured twenty-four inches long, weighed eight pounds two ounces, and like his mother he was left-handed with brown hair and eyes. (Some years after Ray Junior's birth, Gerry gave birth to a stillborn son. Ray Robert, as a result, grew up an only child.) By this time Ray and Gerry lived at 4245 Pacific Avenue in Detroit, located not far from where Ray Jr. would eventually work for General Motors Corporation on Grand Blvd. in 1965-1966. Later, the Albins moved to 20938 Dexter Ave., off Eight Mile Road near Gratiot Avenue and the White Castle hamburger stand there in Warren, Michigan, a Detroit suburb.

Geraldine Elizabeth Abt Albin and mother Katherine Tschudi Abt, later Kohler, circa 1940s Detroit, Michigan

The Albin house on Dexter with Ray's 1950 Ford, circa Christmas 1951

By the time Ray Jr. was five in 1952, the family had moved again, purchasing a slightly larger, newly constructed home at 28096 Hollywood, off Martin Ave. in the suburb of Roseville about twelve miles north of downtown Detroit.

From 1952 to 1956, the Albins lived in Roseville while Ray Sr. continued working at Sears, selling vacuums, then appliances. Each year the family took a vacation, usually driving long distances all across America, to Wyoming, Montana, Minnesota, Illinois, Kentucky (to visit Uncle Thurman), Colorado (to the summit of Pikes Peak), North and South Dakota (Mount Rushmore), but never east, so that by the time Ray Jr. was ten, he had visited 25 states. The postwar middle class prosperity the family enjoyed allowed Ray Sr. to purchase a new car every few years, a 1950 Ford, a 1954 Ford, a 1957 Ford Fairlane, and in 1960 yet another Ford.

The house on Hollywood in Roseville, Michigan, circa 1952. Ray Jr. is sitting on the porch.

Ironically, despite living in Detroit, the Motor City, Gerry never learned to drive. Once, during a practice session she ran onto the median near Martin and Gratiot Avenues, one of Roseville's busiest intersections. After that harrowing episode, Gerry remained reluctant to get behind the wheel of a car again.

Gerry was content to be a housewife, maintaining an immaculate, well-ordered home. Regularly, she placed clean clothes, pressed and neatly folded, in the bedroom dressers. Beds were always made, floors vacuumed, meals prepared (Gerry and Ray both were good cooks) and linoleum scrubbed. The Albins were a typical, middle class suburban American family. Living comfortably, Ray Sr. had time for golf and poker parties while Gerry read and stayed in touch with her family and friends.

By 1956 the same western wanderlust that had driven Ray's great, great, great grandfather William Albin Jr. and before him William Albin Sr. touched Ray Sr. as well. In April of 1956, after ruling out a move to Seattle, Washington, following a visit there, Ray, Gerry, Ray Jr., and Ray Jr.'s cousin eighteen year old Barbara Langlois, a recent high school graduate, loaded the family's 1954 Ford and drove to the Albin's new residence in Fresno, California. With this relocation, Ray Sr. became the first Albin male in this line to live west of the Mississippi River.

Fresno, in 1956, was Ray Sr.'s kind of town, a small, yet thriving farming community in the expansive and fertile San Joaquin Valley of central California. Very hot, dry, but humidity free summers and mild, snowless, though often foggy, winters contrasted greatly with Detroit's typical Midwestern weather. Springtime in Fresno brought assorted aromas of fruit blossoms that filled the night air. During the scorching summer months just outside of town, grapes, products of the region's thousands of acres of grapevines, dried in flat trays, placed in neat rows between the vines where they eventually developed into the raisins for which Fresno was then so famous. Figs grew on unusual looking, knobby trunked trees in different sections of the city and countryside.

On arrival, Ray began working at the new Sears store on Blackstone Avenue selling appliances. The family lived in a motel on the outskirts of town, also on Blackstone Ave., for 2 weeks while Ray canvassed the city for permanent housing. Finally, late in April, the family rented a duplex at 827 Shields, just off Blackstone Ave., near a noisy railroad track and close to a new hamburger stand called McDonalds, the first built in Fresno. By late summer cousin Barbara had returned to Detroit and the Albins had moved again. Ray and Gerry had purchased a new two-bedroom home at 2822 East Griffith Way, near the Starlite Drive-In theater in a newer section of a rapidly expanding Fresno. In this area of Fresno, unlike homes in Detroit, initially there were no fences between residences. As a result a person standing in his backyard had an unobstructed view in both directions of the entire block. A backyard cyclone fence did exist, however, to separate the homeowners' property from the narrow irrigation canal that ran parallel to Griffith Way.

Ray, Gerry, and Ray Jr., 1951, Detroit, Michigan. Ray Jr. is holding a replica of his father's 1950 Ford.

In July 1958 after two years in Fresno, the Albins moved again. Gerry, who had a mild heart condition due to a bout of strep throat that resulted in her contracting rheumatic fever as child, had great difficulty coping with the stifling 100 degrees daytime temperatures during Fresno's seemingly endless summer months. As a result, Gerry and Ray sold their Griffith Way home for $13,500 and moved to Menlo Park, California, a small, but quaint city some thirty miles south of San Francisco, near Palo Alto and Stanford University.[3] The climate there was much milder with temperatures seldom reaching above 85 in the summer.

The family rented a two-bedroom apartment in a beautiful, tree-lined neighborhood at 416 Waverley near Burgess Park. Ray continued to work for Sears, this time in the Mt. View store, selling furniture while Gerry remained a homemaker.

---

[3]Ray and Gerry's granddaughter, Lauren, would enroll at Stanford University forty-seven years later in 2005.

In the summer of 1959, the Albins bought a new home in San Jose, California, approximately twenty miles south of Menlo Park. Built in the middle of a vast uprooted cherry orchard on the west side of the fertile Santa Clara Valley, the new tract home had three bedrooms and one and a half baths. The selling price was approximately $14,000.

Then Santa Clara Valley was known primarily for agriculture, especially its abundant orchards, and a little-known (to the outside world) but thriving canning industry. In 1960 San Jose had only 204,196 people, but ten years later the population had exploded to more than 459,000. Ray continued to work as a salesman in Mt. View, driving the twenty-five miles round trip each day. With gas at thirty cents a gallon it was not a costly commute.

The Albins remained in San Jose for six additional years, living at first happily and comfortably in the home at 5258 Northlawn Drive. However, financial hardship caused by Ray's decision, with Gerry's somewhat hesitant approval, to quit Sears and open a restaurant along with marital troubles brought on by Ray's infidelity made their last three years in San Jose from 1963 to 1965 an extremely stressful and difficult time for all.

In 1963 Ray quit his job at Sears after seventeen years and withdrew his accumulated profit sharing totaling more than $50,000, a hefty sum in the early sixties. With that money and perhaps a bank loan and minus any experience in the restaurant business, Ray purchased land in a small, but upscale shopping center at the corner of Prospect Road and Saratoga-Sunnyvale Road in Saratoga. There he had built a beautifully appointed restaurant, The Coach House. It proved to be Ray's and the family's undoing. Ray's inexperience in all phases of the restaurant business led to his bankruptcy just two years later.

By 1964 after losing the restaurant, Ray left Gerry and quickly married one of his waitresses who had several children from previous marriages. In so doing he abandoned Gerry and Ray Jr. in San Jose and moved back to Detroit - a decision that closely resembled that of his grandfather James B. Albin in 1876 when he, too, had abandoned his family in favor of a younger woman. As a result of Ray's decision, both mother and son were left destitute. Ray Jr. landed a summer job from June through September working on a pear ranch off Highway 101 in San Jose. The $1.25 hour-

ly wage didn't go far, but it helped. However, by September Gerry, unable to make the mortgage payment on the family home of
six years, faced a bank foreclosure. Later that month, with financ-
es dwindling Gerry and Ray Jr. lost the home and were compelled
to move back to Detroit for survival.

In Detroit Gerry lived with her sister Katherine (Kay)
Langlois, while Ray Jr. lived on Detroit's East Side at 12733
Glenfield for several months with his cousin Les Langlois (his
Aunt Kay's son), Les's wife Shirley, and their infant daughter
Michelle. To this day Ray remains more than grateful for their
extreme generosity. Later, when the Langloises vacated, Ray Jr.
and Gerry rented the first floor for some ten months until October
1966. During this time Ray Sr. provided no support to either Gerry
or Ray, compelling Ray Jr. to forego any full-time college plans at
Detroit's Wayne State University and take an entry level job in
Public Relations (mail room) at General Motors Corporation on
Grand Blvd. in downtown Detroit. Ray attended night classes at
Wayne State while he worked for GM. Gerry, having no real marketable skills, did what she could even attempting door-to-door
sales at one point.

So unhappy was Ray Jr. in Detroit that after just thirteen
months there he quit his job at General Motors and enlisted in the
United States Army in November of 1966, at the beginning of the
long Vietnam War. Ironically Ray reported for induction at Ft.
Wayne, Michigan (in Wayne County), both named after the Revo-
lutionary War general Mad General Anthony Wayne.[4] It was
Wayne's grandfather who had been such a close friend to Captain
John Hunter the uncle of the four Albin orphans in 1722.

Regrettably, Gerry had experienced an extremely difficult
several years - the pain of Ray's infidelity, the divorce, the loss of
her home, and the forced return to Detroit. Ray Jr. had not helped
by enlisting and then volunteering for the infantry, a decision that
guaranteed he would be sent to Vietnam and thereby causing more
worry for his mother. Ray's Army salary plus combat pay and the
government benefits awarded to his dependent mother allowed

---

[4]Ft. Wayne is located very close to St. Aubin St. where Ray's mother Geraldine
(at age 3) was living when the 1920 census was taken.

Gerry to continue living in an upstairs rental in a quiet Detroit neighborhood near her relatives.

Following Ray's return and with no visible wounds from a one-year tour of infantry duty in Vietnam, he trained Vietnam replacements for eighteen months at Ft. Lewis, Washington. After Ray's Army discharge in 1969, he returned to San Jose to begin college. The plan was for Gerry to join him, but sadly she passed away after a six-month battle with cancer in October 1971. Gerry had never recovered from the divorce and lived out her last days near her sister in Detroit, unable to make the move to California. She will always be remembered as a fine person, great mother, and role model. She deserved better. She lies buried next to her mother Katherine Tschudy Abt Kohler in Gethsemane Cemetery near the small Detroit City Airport on Conner and Gratiot Ave., not far from where Ray Sr.'s family lived on Hurlbut Avenue during World War II.

Ray Sr. divorced his second wife in 1972. He attempted to reconcile with Ray Jr. after Gerry's death. To a certain extent the reconciliation did occur, but the damage had been done. He and Ray hunted and fished together, but they never achieved the close bond that had existed previously.

In 1974 Ray Sr. remarried. He and Dorothy Joy Albin moved to a new home on a golf course in a small, rural town, Hollister, California. Ray rejoined Sears working in San Jose's Eastridge Shopping Center and willingly making the long daily commute in exchange for the peace and quiet Hollister afforded. After retirement Ray continued to play golf regularly. He took great delight in his two grandchildren Lauren and Ryan, Ray and his wife Catherine's children. Ray Sr. died of cancer in 1996 and is buried in Santa Clara City Cemetery in Santa Clara, California.

Since this family history has focused primarily on the male line of the Albins, I offer a brief remembrance of my father Ray Sr. His sense of humor was keen and off the wall, very much similar to that of his younger sister Joann with whom he was very close. He was not a man to tout his own abilities or accomplishments always believing such things would "speak for themselves". Ray was very competitive especially playing golf, cards, or selling merchandise. He knew how to win and lose graciously. Significant errors in judgment and morals caused Ray and his family great pain. Excesses in smoking and drinking helped contribute to poor health in his later years. He seemed to want to break the generations old Albin farm boy image by reaching, often recklessly, for the stars, yet at the same time the 'farm' remained in him throughout his life.

While Ray Albin Sr.'s death signifies the culmination of this history, this family line continues through his son Ray Jr. (the author) and his children Lauren Albin Roller and Ryan Albin. Their stories remain to be told.

As of the date of this writing, nearly four centuries have elapsed since the Albins, somewhat sketchily at first, appeared in the historical records of Derbyshire, England. The circumstances surrounding this generational saga of a generally hard working, adventurous family as it evolved through the centuries in England, then Ireland, and finally across the Atlantic to the American colonies and eventually to several of the United States undoubtedly paralleled similar accounts of millions of other American immigrant families. Yet, at the same time, each of these immigrant histories, including that of the Albins, remains a unique experience intertwined though with the common thread of this great American adventure.

REFLECTIONS

During the eight plus years of research that culminated in the writing of this Albin family history, I began to gradually realize an unanticipated common link to many of the geographic locations where the Albins' story took place. During my travels from the 1960s through the 1990s, long before I had any hint of my broad family roots, I unknowingly had journeyed within miles of several of the locations where Albins had lived, worked, and raised their families in both Europe and the United States.

On a road trip to Scotland, I had passed through Derbyshire, England, where their story begins, never suspecting my English roots originated there. In Ireland I visited County Wicklow near Rathdrum, the seventeenth century home of John Hunter, and Dublin near where James Albin Sr. and Jr. had lived from the late 1660s to 1710. Later, on a trip to Germany, I spent a day in Heidelberg, near where the Sheplers, Magdalina Albin's parents, probably lived in the 1730s prior to their journey to America. During a visit to the East Coast, I stayed in Front Royal not far from Winchester, Virginia, where the Irish-born William Albin Sr. had settled in 1735. During these trips I had no idea of their significance to the Albin family story. In 1965 while living in Detroit, Michigan, in Wayne County, I attended Wayne State University, and in 1966 I was inducted into the Army at Ft. Wayne in Detroit, all named after General Anthony Wayne. Of course, I was completely unaware of any link Wayne's grandfather Anthony had in my family history. While stationed at Ft. Knox, Kentucky, in late 1966, I was also unaware that Absalom Albin and his father William Albin Jr. had farmed and lived for two decades in nearby Nelson County.

In retrospect, it appeared as though a genealogical magnet had drawn me to these divergent settings. As my research progressed in the years following these visits, "If only I had known when I was there" echoed repeatedly as this surprising array of geographic links to my previously unidentified Albin ancestors became more and more apparent.

On a different note, the connection between families, specifically the Albins, Bruces, and Sheplers, while casual at first developed to a remarkable degree as the decades progressed. In eighteenth century Frederick County records, these three families appeared first merely as neighbors, but more complex relationships emerged through their descendants' contacts with one another. During the nineteenth century, these bonds extended and tightened through intermarriage and the survival challenges they faced together in forging a future in the wilderness.

Today, if one journeys to the Shenandoah Valley and Winchester, Virginia, road signs point the way to two small, nearby communities. The first, Brucetown (originally Bruce's Mill), is named after my ggggg grandfather John Bruce (Mary Bruce Albin's father) and is situated near the site of John's old gristmill. The second is Albin, Virginia, named after the Irish-born William Albin (or the family), the progenitor of this Albin family in America (Map 17). Each community lies just off of today's Interstate 81 and Highway 11, known to both William Albin and John Bruce nearly three hundred years ago in 1745 as the *Great Wagon Road*.[1]

---

[1]The last gristmill on the Bruce site seems to have disappeared in the 1940s. Just south of Winchester in Stephens City, there is an Albin Estates subdivision on Albin Drive there. In the Winchester area, over the years there have been Albin and Brucetown voting precincts. Near Albin, Virginia, there is Albin's Run, a small stream meandering through the Virginia countryside. Albin descendants still reside in the Winchester area.

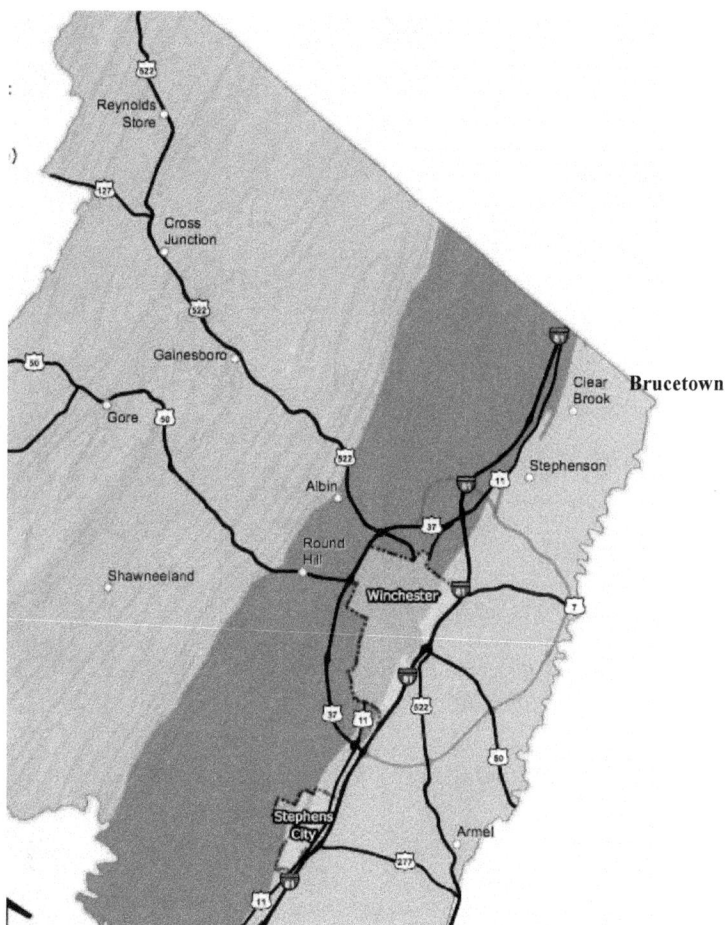

Map 17
Contemporary map of the Winchester, Virginia, area showing sites of Albin and
Brucetown

APPENDIX I

Three of the four Albin children who arrived in Pennsylvania in 1722 lived out the remainder of their lives in Chester County.

James Albin III purchased a house and twenty-one acres in Chester County on November 12, 1736. He married Jane Edge, the daughter of John Edge, a Quaker, without her mother's consent in approximately 1737 (she apparently had requested marriage by a priest). Both signed a marriage certificate for newlyweds Hannah Howard and John Yarnall at Newtown Quaker Meeting on September 7, 1739. It is unclear, however, if James was affiliated with the Quaker Church

On July 22, 1739, James purchased thirty-five acres of land next to Crum Creek and also the land of Henry Howard from Mary Edge, his widowed mother in law, paying £2 six schillings per acre. On October 14, 1740, James sold the land and a "messuage" (a dwelling house with its outbuildings) he had purchased in Newtown four years earlier for £80 to John Williamson.[1] Albin later sold another parcel to George Morgan on November 11, 1740.

In 1740 James Albin III settled in West Marlborough, Chester County, Pennsylvania, where he acquired various tracts of land there from different sellers.[2] He worked as a tailor. Eventually, he became a yeoman like his grandfather and perhaps his father. The Albins had no children. He died in Chester County on September 29, 1750, having named his cousin James Hunter (son of John Hunter) one of the executors of his will along with his brother-in-law James Bennett. James III is buried in St. John's Episcopal Courtyard, Concord Township next to his sister Elizabeth (Albin) Bennett per his will. His widow Jane is shown in the

[1]Gilbert Cope, *Genealogy of the Smedley Family,* (Lancaster, Pennsylvania: Wickersham Printing Company, 1901), 49, 63, 91, 94, accessed March 25, 2009, http://www.archive.org/details/genealogyofsmedl00cope.
[2]"Grantee Index A 1681-1802," *Chester County Archives*, accessed February 11, 2018, s.v. Albin or Alban, http://pa-chestercounty.civicplus.com/DocumentCenter/View/46791/1715-1764-Chester-County-Tax-Index-A-C.

West Marlborough Taxables list as late as 1753 having inherited one-third of James' personal property and one-half of the real estate. She later became a minister in 1756, married Thomas Downing Jr. that same year, and eventually died in January 1779. James did not mention William Albin, in his will. However, his brother John Albin appeared at the estate sale.

Elizabeth Albin, James' sister, married James Bennett, but she died at a young age, 36, on May 23, 1748, perhaps in Chester County. Elizabeth's children Mary, Hannah, and James, inherited part of her brother James' estate.

Of **John Albin** we know little other than the fact he appeared in the tax lists of Chester County as a freeman from 1758 into the 1760s.

APPENDIX II

John Bruce Last Will and Testament
Frederick County, Virginia

*In the name of God, Amen. The fourth day of November 1747.
I John Bruce of Frederick County in the Colony of Virginia
being sick and weak of body but of perfect mind and memory
thanks be to God calling to remembrance it is appointed for
all men once to die, do make, Constitute and ordaine this my
last will and testament as follows, viz.*

*Item- I give and bequeath to my son James Bruce ye
plantation I now live on with all ye improvements thereunto
belonging being 150 acres.*

*Item- I give and bequeath unto my son George Bruce
150 acres of ye remaining tract of land lying on the south side
of ye aforesaid plantation & in ye Licks with ye clear land & is
now and also that his brother, James Bruce, be one half in
building 1 house 24 foot X 16 foot with a shingle roof.*

*Item- I give and bequeath to my son George Bruce
and Ann Bruce all my movable estate to be equally divided
between them and the desertation [discretion?] of Wm
McMachen and Hugh Parrel after debts and funeral charges
are paid, except my carpenter tools which I give to my son
James Bruce and one yearling heifer to Richard Colbart [Cal-
vert?] & out of ye above perquists I do oblige my sons James
Bruce and George Bruce to maintain my loving wife Sarah
Bruce as long as she lives or remains a widow.*

*Item- It is my will and desire my son George Bruce
also out of ye above perquists give to my daughters Margaret
Carter & Mary Albin ten shillings of currency each to be paid
in grain.*

*Item- I give and bequeath to my son James Bruce my
new great coate and bever hat & to Richard Carter, my son-in-
law, my sute of woolin clothes and to my son-in-law William
Albin my sute of linnen clothes.*

*Item- I do constitute and ordain my sons James Bruce
and George Bruce Executors of this my last will and testament. I do utterly disannul other wills and testaments etc.,*

made here to fore by me & allowing this my last will and testament & no other. In witness whereof I have set my hand & seal this fourth day of November 1747.

Signed and Sealed and delivered in ye presence of
Edward Parrel
James McCoy
Elizabeth King
John Cusee
[Elizabeth King was an indentured servant.]

APPENDIX III

George, John, James, and Robert Albin
Brief Sketches, Including Revolutionary War Service

While William Albin was serving with the Westmoreland County Rangers his brother George, born in 1756 eight years before William, was also serving the American cause. On February 28, 1776, approximately ten months after the war broke out and just fourteen days past his eighteenth birthday, **George Albin** enlisted in the Virginia Continental Line at Winchester, Virginia. He began his two-year enlistment as a private in Captain Thomas Berry's company in the Eighth Virginia Rifle Regiment commanded by Colonel Peter Muhlenberg.[3] Possessing the same outdoor and weapons skills as his brother William, George probably made the transition from civilian to infantryman easily. There is evidence that George was also a skilled and experienced horseman.

Soon after George's enlistment Colonel Muhlenberg's regiment marched to Fredericksburg, Virginia, then to South Carolina. Having reached the coast at Charles Town (Charleston) the force then pushed on to Savannah, Georgia.[4] One of the 8th Regiment's first missions involved an advanced expedition to Sunbury, Georgia, south of Savannah. From there they were to proceed to attack the British in East Florida.

By March of 1776, less than one year into the war, General Washington realized that the nature of the war was changing. It was less and less a static affair and instead a highly mobile one with bands of Tory Loyalists and British moving about the countryside. A surprise raid on his headquarters became a real possibility. In response to such a threat, Washington, on March 11, 1776, issued an order from Cambridge, Massachusetts, for the formation of a personal guard:

---

[3] Albin, *Virginia Albins*, 303. The 8th Regiment was known as the German Regiment and was comprised of nearly equal numbers of German and English native speakers.

[4] Ibid. This differs from George's memory on his pension application. He stated that his regiment remained in Charleston during the summer of 1776.

Head-Quarters, Cambridge March 11, 1776
The General is desirous of selecting a particular number of men as a guard for himself and baggage. The Colonel or Commanding Officer of each of the established regiments, the artillery and riflemen excepted, will fur-
nish him with four, that the number of wanted may be
chosen out of them. His Excellency depends upon the
Colonels for good men, such as they can recommend for
their sobriety, honesty and good behavior. He wishes
them to be from five feet eight inches to five feet ten inches, handsomely and well made, and as there is
nothing in his eyes more desirable than cleanliness
in a soldier, he desires that particular attention be
made in the choice of such men as are clean and spruce.
They are to be at headquarters tomorrow precisely
at 12 o'clock at noon, when the number wanted will be
fixed upon. The General neither wants them with
uniforms, nor arms, nor does he desire any man to
be sent to him that is not perfectly willing or desirous
of being in this Guard. They should be drill'd men.[5]

Popularly called "The Life Guards" by the soldiers, they
were led by Captain Caleb Gibbs. Their mission as they moved
with the army was to protect Washington, his headquarters staff,
Washington's Continental Army records, and his personal papers.
As the group evolved, enlistments expired, and by April 1777,
Washington established a "new" lifeguard. For the new group,
Gibbs secured distinctive blue and buff uniforms, red vests, and
leather helmets with a bearskin crest, accompanied by a medium
blue and white plume worn on the left side. The guards were said
to be the best uniformed and best equipped of all the soldiers in
Washington's Continental Army.
On April 28, 1777, General Washington requested men
from several of the Virginia regiments to fill the open positions in
the "new" Lifeguard. He wanted men he could trust. On May 1,

---

[5]John Fitzpatrick, ed. *The Writings of George Washington from the Original
Manuscript Sources*, (Washington: United States Government Printing Office,
1931), Vol. 4. 388.

1777, George Albin, probably chosen by Colonel Muhlenburg himself or his company commander, Captain Berry, reported for duty, transferring from Muhlenburg's Regiment to Morristown, New Jersey and the Commander-in-Chief's Guard there.[6] Albin was probably well respected as a soldier and a person to have merited his selection to this, perhaps the most prestigious unit in the Continental Army. Just maybe Washington, while seated at his desk in his headquarters in Morristown reviewing the list of those new guards selected, paused and smiled when he read the uncommon Albin surname, recognizing it from his seventeen-year prewar association with Winchester, Virginia. This, he may have thought, was a man who could be trusted.

Several months later, on September 11, 1777, the Continental Army, with the Lifeguard accompanying General Washington, battled British forces at Brandywine, Delaware, and later at Germantown, Pennsylvania, on October 4, 1777. There is no record of the Guards sustaining any casualties in either of these clashes so perhaps they did not engage in any actual combat at either place.

The Guards, including George Albin, along with Washington's entire Army arrived at Valley Forge on December 19th, 1777, and set up winter quarters. General Washington selected the Isaac Potts House for his Headquarters and posted the Lifeguards behind it.[7] Within days of their arrival, the Schuylkill River was frozen over, and on the ground six inches of snow had fallen. Crude huts provided shelter, but the army suffered from constant shortages of food and clothing throughout the horrible winter months of 1777-78. By the time the ordeal had ended in the spring of 1778 nearly 2,000 of Washington's men had perished.

Battling the harsh conditions and struggling to help Washington maintain his army that winter at Valley Forge was the leg-

---

[6]Albin, *Virginia Albins,* 303 and Godfrey, *The Commander-in-Chief's Guard,* 113. According to the roster in Godfrey's work, there were but two other men in the Lifeguard from the 8th Virginia Regiment, Jonathan Chenoweth from Frederick County, Virginia, and Robert Wadsworth. Albin's height, between five feet eight and five feet ten, would have made him one of the taller men of his generation.

[7]Valley Forge Muster Roll Data Sheet, accessed July 22, 2015, s.v. George Albin, http://valleyforgemusterroll.org/.

endary General "Mad" Anthony Wayne. Wayne was raised approximately five miles east of Valley Forge in Easton Township, in Chester County, Pennsylvania, where George Albin's father as a young orphan had grown up in the 1720s following his arrival from Ireland. In one of the curiosities of history Wayne's grandfather Anthony Wayne, with his close comrade John Hunter, may have accompanied William Albin and his siblings on the ship from Ireland to America back in 1722. Now, in winter quarters at Valley Forge William Albin's son George, some fifty-five years later, shared the same hardships and bleakness with Anthony Wayne's grandson. Perhaps neither knew of this historical ancestral quirk or, if both did, were they aware of the other's presence there? And, if they met, did they converse? Would a general talk to a private about the personal relations their ancestors shared? I like to think so, even if the conversation lasted only briefly. In addition to possibly meeting with Anthony Wayne, George probably was aware of the presence of a relative from Winchester at Valley Forge.

Also on the muster roll lists for Valley Forge that winter was the name George Bruce of Virginia. This was George Albin's cousin, the son of James Bruce Sr., Mary Bruce Albin's brother. Private George Bruce had enlisted in September 1776 for three years.[8] He served in the 13th Virginia regiment.

As winter turned to spring, George Albin's luck had held, because for the second time in the past year he had survived extreme hardship, first in steamy, disease ridden Georgia the previous summer and now the cruel Pennsylvania winter. By February 28, 1778, George's two-year enlistment had expired. Three days later he reenlisted at Valley Forge, this time in Captain Jeremiah Dunn's company of express riders.[9] He would serve in that capacity until November 1778.

During the Revolutionary War, one of the more hazardous duties was that of these express riders. The riders were the essential "rapid" communication links of their day, carrying vital military information between commanders of the different units. Capturing express riders, because of the battle plans, orders, and gen-

---

[8] Valley Forge Legacy, http://valleyforgemusterroll.org/muster.asp, accessed October 31, 2017, s.v. George Bruce.
[9] Albin, *Virginia Albins*, 303. Godfrey, *The Commander in Chief's Guard*, 113.

eral information they carried, was of paramount importance to both sides in the war, hence the extreme danger. Only determined, fearless young men to whom horseback riding at the full gallop was second nature volunteered for this duty. George Albin was one of the few who met these qualifications. Though riders were a mounted detachment of the Guards, it is likely George still retained his Guards position temporarily. Records from Valley Forge show George Albin on the Life Guards muster roll from the time he joined in 1777 until the Army left camp in June 1778.[10]

On Friday, November 20, 1778, at Washington's Headquarters in Fredericksburg, Virginia, George Albin appeared before a general court martial. Presided over by Lieutenant Colonel Williams, "George Albin, Express Rider" stood accused of stealing $2,014 from Captain Dunn (his company commander).[11] Unfortunately, it appears the records of the trial were destroyed in a fire some 35 years later, so we do have not all the facts in the case. Probably, Capt. Dunn had entrusted George with a sum of money in George's capacity as an Express Rider. By the end of the trial, the court found Albin guilty as charged, but for stealing $1,294, a lesser sum. George was to "remain under confinement until he has refunded what Money is still deficient to Captain Dunn amounting to five hundred and seventy four dollars."[12] In addition, George was "to receive one hundred lashes on his bare back." On November 23, 1778, Washington approved the punishment and ordered "it to be put in execution; the stripes to be inflicted" the following morning.[13]

What had caused an apparently responsible and trustworthy George, who had been placed in such a prestigious position by people who knew him and his character, to steal this large sum? No answer appears in any of the documents available. Being only twenty years old and raised in cash-starved Frederick County at a time when funds in his own family were scarce, George may have considered the money entrusted to him as more than he might earn

---

[10]Valley Forge Muster Roll Data Sheet, accessed July 22, 2015, http://valleyforgemusterroll.org/.
[11]Fitzpatrick, *The Writings of George Washington*, Vol. 13, 314.
[12]Ibid.
[13]Ibid.

in ten years. George simply could not resist the temptation, and accordingly he acted extremely foolishly.

On Tuesday morning November 24, 1778, "at the Provost Guard [Military Police] in the presence of the old and new Guards" the sentence was carried out.[14] In *The Virginia Albins*, the author wrote that George was discharged on November 24, 1778, with "some indication he suffered from the effects of his sojourn [the whipping?] at Valley Forge."[15] George's humiliation at the court martial proceedings and the flogging surely tested his character. In addition, his ignominious return to Winchester and the reunion with family and friends must have been extremely trying.

George lived in Frederick County after his discharge as his name, along with that of his brother Robert, appears on the personal tax list of Frederick County in 1784.[16] In approximately 1783 George married Jane Green, and over the years they had ten children. He apparently moved from Frederick County to Brooke County, Virginia, and then in 1797 he moved again to Jefferson County, Ohio. The family settled on Mingo Bottom, later named Cross Creek.[17]

As the years passed, it seems that George tried to lead a respectable life, perhaps in some way attempting to atone for his moral lapse while in the army. In 1805, he assumed a civic duty in Jefferson County. He and four other citizens were appointed to "view a remonstrance [protest] against [a] road from Bezaleel Wells' sawmill to Cross Creek near where he lived" and presumably make a report for later evaluation on what they heard.[18] Later, he was among the charter members to join the first Methodist Episcopal Church in Jefferson County in 1814.[19] It seems that George had not been dishonorably discharged from the service in 1778, because on December 28, 1833, he received notice that his

---

[14]Ibid, 315.
[15]Albin, *Virginia Albins,* 303. Given the extent of Ethel Albin's research in her magnificent work, it is unusual that she did not discover this key piece of information in George's life, his court martial.
[16]Ibid.
[17]Ibid.
[18]W. H. Hunter, "The Pathfinders of Jefferson County", *Ohio History,* Volume 8, 1898(?), 251.
[19]Ibid., 157.

Revolutionary War pension application had been approved. He would receive $80 per year, including $200 in "arrears" pay. George Albin died near Steubenville, Ohio on January 29, 1840.[20]

George's brother **John Albin**, born in 1740, married Ann McNeil(l) of Scottish descent probably in 1768. John had served with a Captain McNeill in the Virginia Regiment during the French and Indian War in 1762, and he may have been Ann's father.

In Frederick County in August 1770, John appeared as a witness to the will of Richard Calvert, who was perhaps a nephew to John's great grandmother, Ann Calvert.[21] John and Ann continued to reside near Winchester as proved by a road order document dated November 6, 1771. However, on August 28 or 29, 1772, John sold the last of the Albin family land on Red Bud Run to George Purkett.[22]

John and Ann may have left Frederick County in the fall of 1773, but their whereabouts until 1776 is a mystery. Perhaps the land he had inherited on the Albin homestead had worn out due to extensive tobacco planting over the years. Or, perhaps the neighboring farms, which were being bought up by large landowners using extensive slave labor, became too competitive for small farmers like John.[23]

In 1776, John purchased 400 acres of land in Monongalia County, Virginia, later West Virginia. Located on the "Head of Peddlars Run, a branch of Simpsons Creek" and approximately 100 miles due west of Winchester in north central West Virginia, the land would later be incorporated into Harrison County in 1784.[24] Simpson's Creek runs through the village of Bridgeport, and John's land, east of the village near the Taylor County line,

---

[20]Albin, *Virginia Albins,* 314 (i) fn 1. In his application he, of course, made no reference to his court martial, merely stating "he had permission from Capt. Dunn to retire from the service."

[21]Albin, *Virginia Albins*, 21. "Sarah Colvert [Calvert] and Morgan Morgan named executors. Witnesses: John Albin, William Milburn, Andrew Milburn." Recorded in Winchester, Virginia, *Will Book* 4, 14.

[22]Ibid., 22 and Chapter 3, footnote 14, p.iii.

[23]Ibid., 22.

[24]Ibid., Chapter 3, footnote 17, p. iv.

was hilly but possessed rich soil.[25] Moreover, in April 1781 John
added another 1,000 acres adjoining his original purchase of 1776.
Since this land came with a preemption,[26] it may have been
awarded for his service in the Revolutionary War, not an uncommon veteran's benefit in those days.

John Albin, the oldest of William and Mary's sons, served
in the Revolutionary War, though the records relating to his military time are sparse compared to those of his brothers William Jr.
and George. John's status, as a veteran of the French and Indian
War, had made him a likely candidate to join in the war against
England. No dates revealing his length or location of service were
found, but it is known that John served in the Virginia Continental
Line as an infantry sergeant.

However, based on the birthdates of his nine children, we
can surmise the dates of his service in the Continental Army. John
and Ann's firstborn, Joseph, (circa 1771), was soon followed by
William in 1775 or 1776. Thereafter, no other children were born
until John Jr. on April 16, 1780. Perhaps during that approximately four-year span, 1776-1780, John served in the army. Later, between 1782 and 1794, his remaining six children were born, five
in newly formed Harrison County. John had already received a
land entitlement for his wartime service, but on August 23, 1783,
with the war officially ended, he also received a pay warrant issued by the Auditor's Office to " John Albin, Sgt. Inf." for fifty-
five pounds, six shillings and six pence as a final compensation.[27]
Apparently, John never applied for a pension.

From 1782 on John's name appears in various documents
in the public record. In the local census of Monongalia County for
1782, John "Abben" (Albin) reported seven whites in his household and no slaves.[28] Later, the countywide 1785 census of Harrison County shows seven Albin whites and one dwelling.[29] According to the Harrison County Court Minutes on April 19, 1791, John

---

[25]Ibid., 25.
[26]A preemption is a right to purchase something, in this case government owned
land, before others. In the records for John's preemption his last name is spelled
"Alban".
[27]Ibid., 24. A copy of the warrant found online is in the author's possession.
[28]Ibid.
[29]Ibid.

was appointed surveyor of the highway.[30] In the local census surveys for 1786, 1788, 1789, 1793, 1802, and 1805 John and Ann's family grew and then evolved as some of the older boys lived separately.[31] By 1810 most of his family, excluding John and Ann, had moved to Greene County, Ohio, (later Clark County in 1818). Between 1801 and 1811, records show John and Ann continued to reside in Harrison County. On October 19, 1801, they began to sell off certain land parcels. First, they "sold" fifty acres to son John Jr., now twenty-one years old, for one dollar.[32] Next, on that same day, they sold sixty acres to neighbor Daniel Davisson Jr. for $300, followed by a third sale of ninety acres to Benjamin Wilson Jr. for another $300.[33] All of these plots originated from John's land grant on Peddlar's Run. Nine years later on February 16, 1810, John and Ann sold an additional 200 acres on Peddlar's Run for $1,400. During almost the same time period, John's sons Joseph and William were either buying or selling land as well.[34]

By 1811, with most of their family residing in Ohio, it seems John and Ann, along with their remaining son George, prepared to join them. Before leaving Anne and John must have sold the remainder of their land, but no records of any sale exist after 1810.

From 1811 to his death on April 26, 1820, an apparently financially secure John remained in Clark County, Ohio, in Greene Township. He is buried in the Ebenezer Cemetery there. Ann died sometime after 1820, having been mentioned in John's will dated three weeks before his death.

---

[30]Harrison County, Virginia Court Minutes (transcribed), p. 339, accessed January 23, 2018, https://hackerscreek.com/cpage.php?pt=77.

[31]Albin, *Virginia Albins*, 24. The 1801 Harrison County Tax List shows John Albin with four titheables (males 16+ years of age including himself) and six horses. 1801 Tax List, Harrison County, accessed April 11, 2016, http://www.binnsgenealogy.com/VirginiaTaxListCensuses/Harrison/1801Persona lA/01.jpg. Joseph Albin, John and Ann's oldest son, is shown living separately on this tax list.

[32]Ibid., Albin, Chapter 3, p. v.

[33]Ibid. Wilson's father, Colonel Benjamin Wilson Sr., was born in Frederick County, Virginia, in 1747.

[34]Ibid.

Another of William Albin's sons to serve in the Revolutionary War was **James Albin**, born in 1753. In 1776, James enlisted in the 8th Virginia Regiment, the same unit as his brother George. He "served through the Revolutionary War."[35] No service records have been found for James.

In 1780 he married Ruth Shannon, and they subsequently had four children. With the death of Ruth in perhaps 1786 or 1787, James married Barbara Hoover in approximately 1788. They had eleven children. Apparently, James and his family soon left Frederick County, Virginia, as 1784 tax lists indicate he lived on the Capon River in Hampshire County (later Hardy County), Virginia. A Head of Families List indicates three white persons in his household and ownership of one "other building."[36] Later, Hardy County deeds show John and Barbara sold their 198 acres on September 9, 1805, to Philip Cline of Hampshire County for $430.[37] James could read and write as he signed his name to the deed, but Barbara simply made her mark.[38] Like his brother John, James later moved to Ohio, making the trip there in a covered wagon in 1806 with his wife and their two daughters, Rebecca Slater (Albin) and Sarah Slater (Albin) and their respective husbands.[39]

James and Barbara lived in Guernsey County, Ohio, (not far from his brother George in Jefferson County) for the next twenty-one years until James' death on April 26 or 27, 1827. A copy of his will appears in *The Virginia Albins*.[40]

Robert Albin, the second oldest son of William and Mary, was born in 1743. He probably served in the Revolutionary War, but no documentation has been uncovered to support this supposition. There is a Robert Albion listed as a prisoner of war on the infamous English prison ship "Jersey", anchored in New

---

[35]Albin, *Virginia Albins*, 281.
[36]Head of Families, Hampton County Virginia, 1784, accessed October 15, 2014, http://www.historichampshire.org/nrm/head1784.htm. See also, Albin, *Virginia Albins*,, Chapter 7, footnote 2, p. i.
[37]Ibid. Chapter 7, footnote 2, p. ii.
[38]Ibid.
[39]Ibid., 281 and Chapter 7, footnote 4, p. ii.
[40]Ibid., Chapter 7, footnote 4, p. ii.

York in the East River.[41] If Robert was indeed a prisoner aboard this ship, his survival was probably due to good fortune as these British POW ships were notorious death traps.

Robert was the only son to remain in Frederick County for his entire life. He resided east of Winchester, near Stephens City until his death. He married twice, Anne (?), then in 1791 Elizabeth (?), leaving a total of twelve children.[42] Ethel Albin in the *Virginia Albins* notes that

> Robert, like his older brother John, who lived in Harrison Co. VA/WV…was opening up his home to itinerant [Methodist] preachers. This leadership in establishing worship centers was repeated again and again down through the early generations of the Albin families. Several of them were to grant land for cemeteries and churches.[43]

Robert Albin died in Frederick County in April 1814, after making a will on March 13, 1814. In his will he named his son Elijah the sole executor, leaving his estate to his "beloved wife, Elizabeth Albin."[44] His "x" marked his signature on the document.

---

[41]See the online resource of 8,000 alphabetized names of American POWS held on these ships during the War, http://www.usmm.org/revdead.html, accessed April 11, 2015, s.v. "names of American pows on the prison ship Jersey in Revolutionary War." Unfortunately, only the names are provided without an indication of the prisoner's home state or if the prisoner lived or died.

[42]Albin, *Virginia Albins*, 203.

[43]Ibid., 205. Robert's younger brother, George, was among the first to join the first Methodist Episcopal Church in Jefferson County, Ohio, in 1814 (see above).

[44]Ibid., Chapter 5, no page number, "Will of Robert Albin."

APPENDIX IV

The Author's DNA Test Results

A DNA test completed by the Ancestry.com lab in 2015 provided insights into the author's ethnicity. According to the results, Ray Albin's Jr.'s ethnicity estimate reads as follows:

72% West European, 17% Ireland
and 11% trace regions - unverifiable links to various other European regions

The 72% West European designation is no surprise, as that area includes England (from the Albin line in Derbyshire), Germany and Switzerland, (the latter two are linked to my German Shepler ancestor and my mother's Swiss and German heritage). However, the Irish connection, as was indicated in the opening chapters, seems to be unproven with only a slight possible Irish link occurring early in this history. That is not to say the DNA indicator for Ireland is erroneous, *because the Irish designation also includes areas of England and Scotland.* Because of the proven historic Scottish connection beginning with William Albin's marriage to the Scottish Mary Bruce in the 1730s, it is assumed that this so-called Irish DNA link is actually a marker for Scotland.

BIBLIOGRAPHY

Order Books, Ohio County, KY, Volumes 1-3, 1799-1817. Microform. Family History Library, Salt Lake City, Utah.

Hartford Herald. Various dates, 1890-1927.

Hartford Republican. Various years 1889-1910.

Virginia Gazette (Williamsburg), June 20, 1771, Rind ed. Accessed April 11, 2014. http://research.history.org/DigitalLibrary/vagazettes/VGSinglePage.cfm?issueIDNo=71.R.16.

"Kentucky Probate Records, 1727-1990." Family Search. Accessed December 11, 2014. https://familysearch.org/pal:/MM9.3.1/TH-1951-20787-22313-86?cc=1875188&wc=M9WR-NSV:1150064168. Ohio County Inventories, Index, 1888-1898, Vol. L, images 39-41.

"Ohio County, Kentucky." 1820 United States Census. Accessed May 27, 2013. http://uscensus.org/pub/usgenweb/census/ky/ohio/1820/p g0003a.txt.

No Author. "1744 Frederick County Clerk Fees", " US Gen Web - VAGenWeb. Accessed February 16, 2014. http://www.genealogenie.net/vafreder/1744.shtml.

"1850-1930 United States Census, Ohio County, Kentucky, District No. 1." Microform.

No Author. *A New and General Map of the Middle Dominions Belonging to the United States of America,*. London: Laurie and Whittle, 1794. Accessed November 11, 2015. https://www.raremaps.com/gallery/enlarge/15675.

Albin, Ethel Winifred. *The Virginia Albins: The History of the Albin Family out of Old Frederick County: Immigrants, Mary Bruce and William Albin and Their Descendants Who Migrated Westward with the Opening of New Territories Carving a Civilization out of a Wilderness.* Decorah, IA: Anundsen Pub., 1989.

Bagshaw, Samuel. *History, Gazetteer and Directory of Derbyshire, with the Town of Burton-upon-Trent Comprising a General Survey of the County, with a Variety of Historical, Statistical, Topographical, Commercial, and Agricultural Information: Shewing the Situation, Extent, and Population of All the Towns, Parishes, Chapelries, Townships, Villages, Hamlets, and Extra-parochial Liberties, Their Agricultural and Mineral Productions, the Lords of the Manors and Owners of the Soil, Their Public Institutions, Charities, Magistrates, and Public Officers, and Their Seats of the Nobility and Gentry.* Sheffield: William Saxton, 1846.

Beers, J. H., comp. *Commemorative Biographical Record of Washington County, Pennsylvania, Containing Biographical Sketches of Prominent and Representative Citizens, and of Many of the Early Settled Families.* Chicago: J.H. Beers, 1893.

Benedict, David. *A General History of the Baptist Denomination in America, and Other Parts of the World.* Vol. 2. Boston: Manning and Lori, 1813.

Berkin, Carol. *First Generations: Women in Colonial America.* New York: Hill and Wang, 1996.

Boles, John B. *Religion in Antebellum Kentucky.* Lexington: University Press of Kentucky, 1995.

Boucher, John Newton, and John W. Jordan. *History of Westmoreland County, Pennsylvania.* Vol. I. New York: Lewis Publishing, 1906.

Boucher, John. ""Old and New Westmoreland"" University of Pittsburgh Digital Research Library. 1999. Accessed September 24, 2008. http://digital.library.pitt.edu/cgi-bin/t/text/text-idx?c=pitttext;page=browse;key=author;cc=pitttext;value=b. Volumes 1 & 3. Originally published in 1918.

Brown, Janice. "Susannah Caroline (Acton) Mitchell, April 8, 1826 - September 8, 1878." Ohio County, Kentucky History. June 5, 2013. Accessed June 30, 2014. http://ohiocountykentuckyhistory.blogspot.com/2013/06/susannah-caroline-acton-mitchell.html.

Bruce, Violet Laverne. *John Bruce of the Shenandoah*. Decorah, IA: Anundsen Pub., 1987.

Bruce, William. "Memoirs of the Bruce Family." *The Indiana Magazine of History* 23, no. 1 (1927): 63-72. January 4, 2016. http://scholarworks.iu.edu/journals/index.php/imh/article/view/6407/6535.

Busch, Charles M. *Record of Pennsylvania Marriages Prior to 1810*. Vol. 8. Second. Philadelphia: State Printer of Pennsylvania, 1895. Accessed April 22, 2009. http://www.usgwarchives.net/pa/1pa/paarchivesseries/series2/vol8/pass84.html. Marriage Record of Christ Church Philadelphia, 1709-1806.

Caldwell, Howard W. *A Source History of the United States, from Discovery (1492) to End of Reconstruction (1877) for Use in High Schools, Normal Schools, and Colleges*. Chicago: Ainsworth and Company, 1909.

Cary, Sydney. "Index to the Wills of the Diocese of Kildare." *Journal of the County Kildare Archeological Society,* 4 (1905): 473.

"Census Online - Pennsylvania - 1790 Census Records." Heritage Quest. Accessed April 18, 2011. S.v. William Albon, Westmoreland County, Rostraver Township.

No Author. "Certificate Book of the Virginia Land Commission 1779-1780". *The Register of the Kentucky Historical Society* 21 (1923).

Chalkley, Lyman. *Chronicles of the Scotch-Irish Settlement in Virginia: Extracted from the Original Court Records of Augusta County 1745-1800.* Vol. I. Rosslyn, VA: Commonwealth Printing, 1912.

Clark, Murtie June. *Colonial Soldiers of the South, 1732-1774.* Baltimore, MD: Genealogical Pub., 1983.

Clift, G. Glenn. *"Second Census" of Kentucky, 1800; a Privately Compiled and Published Enumeration of Tax Payers Appearing in the 79 Manuscript Volumes Extant of Tax Lists of the 42 Counties of Kentucky in Existence in 1800.* Baltimore: Genealogical Pub., 1966.

Cook, Michael L. *Jefferson County, Kentucky Records.* Vol. 5. Evansville, IN: Cook Publications, 1987.

Corbly, Don. *Letters, Journals, & Diaries of Ye Colonial America.* Self Published, 2009. Accessed May 27, 2013. https://books.google.com/books?id=BIaVAgAAQBAJ&pg=PP1&lpg=PP1&dq=Letters, Journals, & Diaries of ye Colonial America&source=bl&ots=yFCvV5k1si&sig=un4_huFvMFi8Y MNB_JrDbsu3JII&hl=en&sa=X&ved=0ahUKEwjDgtfqt avOAhXoz4MKHUcVC3YQ6AEIJDAB#v=onepage&q =Letters, Journals, & Diaries of ye Colonial America&f=false.

Craik, George L., and Charles MacFarlane. *The Pictorial History of England, Being a History of the People, as Well as a*

History of the Kingdom. Vol. I. New York: Harper & Bros., 1846.

Crumrine, Boyd. *History of Washington County, Pennsylvania: With Biographical Sketches of Many of Its Pioneers and Prominent Men.* Philadelphia: Everts & Co., 1882.

Dalton, Charles. *English Army Lists and Commission Registers, 1661-1714.* Vol. 6. London: Eyre & Spottiswoode, 1904.

Davis, W. W. H. *History of Bucks County, Pennsylvania: From the Discovery of the Delaware to the Present Time.* Vol. III. New York: Lewis Pub., 1905.

"Death Certificates in Ohio County." Ancestry.com.

No Author. "Deed Book Abstract, Book 6, 459." Roots Web, Ancestry. Accessed September 10, 2015. http://archiver.rootsweb.ancestry.com/th/read/MDSTMA RY/2008-04/1208032721. Nelson County, Kentucky 1803-1818.

No Author. *Deed Book Abstracts Books 8,9,10,11 Nelson County, KY 1803-1818,.* Bardstown: Nelson County Genealogical Roundtable, 200? Accessed May 27, 2013. http://archiver.rootsweb.ancestry.com/th/read/KYNELSO N/2009-03/1236282639.

"Deed Books, Grantee (Buyer) Index. H, 1688-1820." Archives & Record Services | Chester County, PA - Official Website. February 2014. Accessed February 11, 2014. http://pachestercounty.civicplus.com/DocumentCenter/Vi ew/3896.

Des Cognet, Louis. *English Duplicates of Lost Virginia Land Records.* Baltimore: Genealogical Publishing, 1958.

Dippel, John Van Houten. *Race to the Frontier: White Flight and Westward Expansion.* New York: Algora Pub., 2005.

No Author. *Early Kentucky Tax Records: From The Register of the Kentucky Historical Society.* Baltimore: Genealogical Pub., 1987.

Eckenrode, H. J., comp. *List of the Colonial Soldiers of Virginia. Special Report of the Department of Archives and History for 1913.* Richmond: Public Printing Office, 1917.

"Edward Hunter Family Document Collection." Edward Hunter Family Document Collection. Accessed April 17, 2013. http://www.georgeqcannon.com/edward_hunter_docs.htm.Documents, Section 12, Pedigree Chart of John Hunter.

Egle, William Henry. *Pennsylvania Archives: Third Series.* Vol. XXIII. Harrisburg: William Ray, 1897.

Ellis, Franklin. *History of Fayette County, Pennsylvania: With Biographical Sketches of Many of Its Pioneers and Prominent Men.* Philadelphia: L.H. Everts &, 1882.

"England, Derbyshire, Church of England Parish Registers 1538-1910." Family Search. Accessed August 6, 2015, https://familysearch.org/pal:/MM9.1.1/KBDB-DMV: citing Burial, South Wingfield, Derbyshire, England, Record Office, Matlock; FHL microfilm 1041630, image 13.

Egle, William H. *Return of Taxables for the Counties of Bedford (1773-1784), Huntington (1788), Westmoreland (1783,1786), Fayette (1785-1786), Allegheny (1791), Washington (1786), And Census of Bedford (1784) and Westmoreland (1783).* Harrisburg, PA: William S. Ray, 1898.

Freeman, Thomas Walter. *Pre-famine Ireland; a Study in Historical Geography.* Manchester, Eng.: Manchester University Press, 1957.

"From Oxcart to Atom Bomb." *Beaver Dam Kentucky Messenger*, December 2, 1977. Copy in author's possession.

No Author. *General Highway Map, Nelson County Kentucky.* Kentucky Department of Highways, 1999. Accessed May 24, 2014. http://ukcc.uky.edu/maps/ghm1999/nelson.gif.

Glenn, Thomas Allen. *Some Colonial Mansions and Those Who Lived in Them with Genealogies of the Various Families Mentioned.* Vol. 2. Philadelphia: H.T. Coates, 1900.

Glover, Stephen. *The History of the County of Derby, Pt II.* Derbyshire, England: Mozely and Son, 1829.

Godfrey, Carlos E. *The Commander-in-Chief's Guard: Revolutionary War.* Washington: D.C.: Clearfield Publishing, 1904.

Green, Karen Mauer. *The Kentucky Gazette, 1787-1800: Genealogical and Historical Abstracts.* Vol. X. Baltimore: Gateway Press, 1983.

Guthrie, Blaine. "Captain Richard Chenowith, A Founding Father of Louisville." *The Filson Club History Quarterly* 46, no. 2 (April 2, 1972): No Page given. Accessed May 16, 2014. http://www.chenowethsite.com/chfilson.htm.

Hassler, Edgar W. *Old Westmoreland: A History of Western Pennsylvania during the Revolution.* Pittsburg: J.R. Weldin &, Co., 1900.

"Heads of Families at the First Census of the United States Taken in the Year 1790: United States. Bureau of the Census: Free Download & Streaming: Internet Archive." Accessed April 30, 2014. http://www2.census.gov/prod2/decennial/documents/179 0g-02.pdf.

No Author. "Hearth Money Rolls for the Barony of Orior." *Journal of the County of Louth Archaeological Society* 7, no. 3 (December 1931): 421. Accessed April 11, 2014. https://www.jstor.org/stable/27728342?seq=1#page_scan _tab_contents.

Heinegg, Paul. *Free African Americans of North Carolina, Virginia, and South Carolina from the Colonial Period to about 1820.* Vol. I. Baltimore, MD: Genealogical Publishing, 2005.

Heinemann, Charles. *First Census of Kentucky, 1790.* Baltimore: Genealogical Pub., 1965.

Hofstra, Warren R. *The Planting of New Virginia: Settlement and Landscape in the Shenandoah Valley.* Baltimore: Johns Hopkins University Press, 2006.

"Home - The National Archives." UK National Archives/West Yorkshire Archive Service, Bradford. Accessed April 06, 2013. http://www.nationalarchives.gov.uk/a2a/records.aspx?cat =202-spst_1&cid=4-11-127-2#4-11-127-2.

Hunter, Wilmot J. *A Brief History of the Hunter Family.* Vineland, Ontario: Glenaden Press, 2002.

"Index to Irish Wills." Ancestry®. Accessed August 05, 2013. http://www.ancestry.com/. Volume I, A Calendar of Wills in the Diocese of Kildare.

Jenson, Andrew. *Latter-Day Saints Biographical Encyclopedia; a Compilation of Biographical Sketches of Prominent Men and Women in the Church of Jesus Christ of Latter-Day Saints.* Salt Lake City: A. Jenson History, 1901.

Joyner, Peggy S. *Abstracts of Virginia's Northern Neck Warrants & Surveys.* Vol. 2. Portsmouth, VA: P.S. Joyner, 1985.

Kellogg, Louise Phelps. *Frontier Advance on the Upper Ohio.* Madison: Wisconsin History Society, 1916.

"Kentucky, County Marriages, 1797-1954." Free Family History and Genealogy Records - FamilySearch.org. Accessed March 17, 2015. https://familysearch.org/ark:/61903/3:1:939K-Y63H-W2?mode=g&i=59&wc=S9CM-YWG:148165601?cc=1804888&cc=1804888. See Albin and Piety Bruce, 01 Jan 1802.

Kercheval, Samuel. *A History of the Valley of Virginia.* Winchester, VA: Samuel Davis Publishing, 1833.

Kerns, Wilmer L. *Historical Records of Old Frederick and Hampshire Counties, Virginia.* Bowie, MD: Heritage Books, 1992.

Kleber, John E. *The Kentucky Encyclopedia.* Lexington, KY: University Press of Kentucky, 1992.

Kleber, John E. *The Encyclopedia of Louisville.* Lexington: University Press of Kentucky, 2001.

No Author. "Land Office Patents and Grants/Northern Neck Grants and Surveys, Virginia." Library of Virginia. Accessed November 1, 2015. http://lva1.hosted.exlibrisgroup.com/F/6GU12171GVM MTRJU2SXPJP7YDG9P3CTSI97YM2IJY78P3U2ANV -61136?func=find-b&request=william albi-on&find_code=WRD&adjacent=N&x=36&y=6. s.v. William Albion 1764.

Leckey, Howard L. *The Tenmile Country and Its Pioneer Families: A Genealogical History of the Upper Monongahela Valley, with Surname Index.* Apollo, PA: Closson Press, 1993.

Lewis, Charles. *Journal of Captain Charles Lewis of the Virginia Regiment*. Edited by R. A. Brock. Richmond: Collections of the Virginia Historical Society, 1892.

Long, Jerry. *Early Settlers of Ohio County, Kentucky, 1799-1840: A Comparative Study of Census and Tax Records of Ohio County*. Owensboro, KY: McDowell Publications, 1983.

Luckman, Gene, and Miller, Ann Brush. *Frederick County Road Orders 1743-1772*. Richmond, VA: Virginia Transportation Research Council, 2005. Accessed March 20, 2014. http://www.virginiadot.org/vtrc/main/online_reports/pdf/05-r32.pdf.

No Author. "Marriages, Record of Joshua Corman, 1792-1793." Usgwarchives. Accessed December 11, 2013. Joshua Carmen.

Marshall, J. J., comp. *Cases at Law and Equity Argued and Decided in the Court of Appeals of the Commonwealth of Kentucky*. Vol. VI. Frankfort: State of Kentucky, 1833. "Sprigg's Heirs vs Albin's Heirs".

Martin, Asa Earl. *The Anti-slavery Movement in Kentucky Prior to 1850*. Louisville: Standard Printing, 1918.

McDonnell, Michael. *The Politics of War: Race, Class, and Conflict in Revolutionary Virginia*. Chapel Hill: UNC Press Books, 2012.

McIlwaine, H. R., ed. *Journals of the House of Burgesses of Virginia, 1742-1747, 1748-1749*. Vol. 7. Richmond, VA: Colonial Press, E. Waddey, 1909.

No Author. *Men of West Virginia*. Vol. II. Chicago: Biographical Pub., 1903. Accessed March 23, 2009. http://books.google.com/books?id=eqki8LI8mfUC&printsec=titlepage.

Midlam, Jim. *Nicolaus Heinrich Crist (1716 Germany - 1783 USA) & Ann Catherin Nowlin (1720-1783 USA)*. Ft. Mojave, AZ: Susan Peters Zmrzel, 1995. Accessed April 4, 2009. http://freepages.genealogy.rootsweb.ancestry.com/~ptson line/stories/cristaccountbook2.html.

Miller, Kerby A. *Irish Immigrants in the Land of Canaan: Letters and Memoirs from Colonial and Revolutionary America, 1675-1815*. Oxford: Oxford University Press, 2004.

Montgomery, Thomas Lynch, ed. *Pennsylvania Archives*. Vol. II. Harrisburg, PA: J. Severns, 1906.

Montgomery, Thomas Lynch. *Pennsylvania Archives Fifth Series Vols. I-VIII and Index Sixth Series, Vol. XV*. Vol. II. Harrisburg, PA: Harrisburg Pub., State Printer, 1906. Accessed April 11, 2014. http://books.google.com/books?id=ED4OAAAAIAAJ&p rintsec=frontcover&dq=joseph beckett westmoreland county pa#PPA290,M1.

Morton, Oren F. *The Story of Winchester in Virginia: The Oldest Town in the Shenandoah Valley*. Winchester, VA: Shenandoah Publishing House, 1925.

Nash, Gary B. *Freedom by Degrees: Emancipation in Pennsylvania and Its Aftermath*. New York: Oxford University Press, 1991.

Nash, Gary B. *The Urban Crucible: Social Change, Political Consciousness, and the Origins of the American Revolution*. Cambridge, MA: Harvard University Press, 1979.

O'Dell, Cecil. *Pioneers of Old Frederick County, Virginia*. Westminster: Heritage Books, 2007.

Parkman, Francis. *France and England in North America*. Vol. II. New York: Literary Classics of the United States, 1983.

Pender, Séamus. *A Census of Ireland, circa 1659, with Supplementary Material from the Poll Money Ordinances (1660-1661).* Dublin: Stationery Office, 1939.

Pennsylvania State Archives, Revolutionary War Military Abstract Card File,. Accessed April 11, 2014. http://www.digitalarchives.state.pa.us/archive.asp?view= AchiveItems&ArchiveID=13&FID=421275&LID=42137 4&FL=&Page=3. "William Albion".

"Pennsylvania, Probate Records, 1683-1994." Free Family History and Genealogy Records - FamilySearch.org. Accessed February 11, 2015. https://familysearch.org/pal:/MM9.3.1/TH-1971-28767- 13044-5?cc=1999196&wc=9PM6- 92D:268496301,268575301. Chester Decedents records 1741-1810 A, images 39 and 46.

Perrin, William. *Kentucky, a History of the State, Embracing a Concise Account of the Origin and Development of the Virginia Colony.* Louisville: E. A. Battey, 1888.

Phillimore, W. P. W. *Calendars of Wills & Administrations in the Consistory Court of the Bishop of Lichfield 1516 to 1652. Also Those in the "Peculiars" Now Deposited in the Probate Registries at Lichfield, Birmingham and Derby, 1529-1652: 1675-1790: 1753-1790.* London: British Record Society, 1892.

Pirtle, Alfred. *James Chenoweth, the Story of One of the Earliest Boys of Louisville, and Where Louisville Started.* Louisville, KY: Standard Printing, 1921.

Price, Edward T. *Dividing the Land: Early American Beginnings of Our Private Property Mosaic.* Chicago: University of Chicago Press, 1995.

No Author. "Quick Notes on Early Central KY Families"." Kentucky Gen Web. Accessed May 25, 2014. http://www.rootsweb.ancestry.com/~kybullit/bcqna.htm. Surnames beginning with "A".

Ramsey, Robert Wayne. *Carolina Cradle: Settlement of the Northwest Carolina Frontier, 1747-1762*. Chapel Hill: University of North Carolina Press, 1964.

Rennick, Robert M. *Kentucky Place Names*. Lexington, KY: University Press of Kentucky, 1984.

"Report of Adjutant General State of Kentucky, Union Kentucky Volunteers, Volume 2, Schedule C Militia Regiments and Components, "Roll of the Cromwell Home Guards of Ohio County." Ancestry.com.

Rone, Wendell. *A History of the Daviess-McLean Baptist Association in Kentucky, 1844-1943*. Owensboro, KY: Messenger Job Printing, 1944.

Rothert, Otto Arthur. *A History of Muhlenberg County*. Louisville, KY: J.P. Morton, 1913.

Sandifer, John. *Tracking TJ,*. Online Publishing: Xlibris, 2010.

Sellers, Edwin Jaquett. *English Ancestry of the Wayne Family of Pennsylvania*. Philadelphia: Press of Allen, Lane & Scott, 1927.

Simington, Robert C. *The Civil Survey AD 1654-1656 County of Meath*. Vol. 5. Dublin: Stationery Office, 1940.

Sosin, Jack M. *The Revolutionary Frontier, 1763-1783*. New York: Holt, Rinehart and Winston, 1967.

Spencer, John H. *A History of Kentucky Baptists. From 1769 to 1885, including More than 800 Biographical Sketches*. Vol. I & II. Cincinnati: J.R. Baumes, 1886.

Tallant, Harold D. *Evil Necessity: Slavery and Political Culture in Antebellum Kentucky.* Lexington: University Press of Kentucky, 2003.

"Tax Indexes, 18th Century Tax Records 1747-1764, A-B." Archives & Record Services | Chester County, PA - Official Website. Accessed February 28, 2014. http://www.chesco.org/DocumentCenter/View/5405. s.v. "John Alban".

No Author. "TAXLIST: Nelson County Tithes 1785-1791, Nelson Co., KY." USGenWeb Project. Accessed May 27, 2014. http://files.usgwarchives.net/ky/nelson/taxlists/taxes/nelson2.txt.

"The Agricultural Census for Kentucky 1850, 1860 & 1880, Ohio County." Microform.

"The Down Survey of Ireland Project." Accessed January 24, 2014. http://downsurvey.tcd.ie/down-survey-maps.php.

No Author. "The Hunter Family of Chester and Delaware Counties," *The Literary Era* 4, no. 8 (August 1897): 276. Accessed February 10, 2014. https://books.google.com/books?id=v-s5AQAAMAAJ&pg=PA275&lpg=PA275&dq=The Hunter Family of Chester and Delaware Counties&source=bl&ots=eeGdezYOkQ&sig=-P7000WUF_kIGgl9fAZbUo5jerE&hl=en&sa=X&ved=0ahUKEwj_n5nl8qzOAhURy2MKHY4bAlAQ6AEILzAE#v=onepage&q=The Hunter Family of Chester and Delaware Counties&f=false.

Tincey, John. *The British Army, 1660-1704.* London: Osprey, 1994.

Tracey, Grace L., and John P. Dern. *Pioneers of Old Monocacy: The Early Settlement of Frederick County, Maryland.* Baltimore, MD: Genealogical Pub., 1987.

"U.S. and International Marriage Records, 1560-1900." Accessed August 08, 2016. http://search.ancestry.com/search/db.aspx?dbid=7836. Sv. William Albin/spouse Liney.

"U.S. IRS Tax Assessment Lists, 1862-1918." Ancestry.com. Accessed July 11, 2010. S.v. B. T. Albin.

"United States World War I Draft Registration Cards, 1917-1918." Family Search. Accessed February 13, 2016. https://familysearch.org/ark:/61903/1:1:K78N-J9Y.

Vale, George Walker. *Genealogy of the Vale, Walker, Littler, and Other Related Families.* Winter Park, FL: Printed by Cowart's Rollins Press, 1973.

Van Voorhis, John. *The Old and New Monongahela.* Pittsburgh: Nicholson, 1893.

Vivian, Cassandra. *Monessen: A Typical Steel Country Town.* Charleston, SC: Arcadia Pub., 2002.

Ward, Matthew. *Breaking the Back Country, The Seven Years War in Virginia and Pennsylvania, 1754-1765.* Pittsburgh: U. of Pittsburgh Press, 2004.

Washington, George. *The Writings of George Washington.* Edited by John Fitzpatrick. Vol. I. Washington, DC: U.S. Government Printing Office, 1931.

Wayland, John Walter. *Hopewell Friends History, 1734-1934, Frederick County, Virginia; Records of Hopewell Monthly Meetings and Meetings Reporting to Hopewell; Two Hundred Years of History and Genealogy.* Vol. 1. Westminster, MD: Heritage Books, 2007.

250

"Whiskey Rebellion Resources in Southwestern Pennsylvania
MPS." National Register of Historic Places. Accessed
April 24, 2014.
http://www.phmc.state.pa.us/Portal/Communities/BHP/M
PDFs/Whiskey_Rebellion_Resources_in_Southwestern_
PA.pdf.

Willcox, Walter Temple. *The Historical Records of the Fifth
(Royal Irish) Lancers from Their Foundation as Wynne's
Dragoons, in 1689, to the Present Day.* London: A. Dou-
bleday, 1908.

Young, William R. *Fighters of Derry, Their Deeds and Descendants: Being a Chronicle of Events in Ireland during the
Revolutionary Period, 1688-1691.* Londonderry: Eyre
and Spottiswoode, 1932.

Chicago/Turabian formatting by BibMe.org.

ABOUT THE AUTHOR

Ray Albin has previously published two articles in California history journals and a non-fiction book, *Wealth, Land, and Slaveholding in Mississippi - A Planter Family's Life of Privilege 1818-1913.* He is currently researching the true story from 1855 of two black teenage inmates kidnapped from San Quentin Prison under the direction of the warden, transported to New Orleans, and then sold into slavery.

www.ingramcontent.com/pod-product-compliance
Lightning Source LLC
Chambersburg PA
CBHW050705280326
41926CB00088B/2559